Java Spring Framework

From Basics to Expert Proficiency

Contents

Introduction

The Java Spring Framework stands as one of the most significant frameworks in the modern Java ecosystem. Designed to simplify Java enterprise application development, Spring has grown exponentially since its inception and has become an essential toolkit for developers working on various Java applications.

Spring addresses a wide range of functionality, visibly improving development efficiency. It provides comprehensive infrastructure support for developing Java applications. By enabling loose coupling through dependency injection and inversion of control, Spring provides the ability to manage application components effectively.

Introduced by Rod Johnson in 2003, Spring was initially purposed to simplify the complex Enterprise JavaBeans (EJB) model. Over time, its ecosystem has expanded to include various projects such as Spring Boot, Spring Data, Spring Security, and Spring Cloud. Each of these projects builds upon the core principles of Spring, offering solutions to specific challenges in application development.

Among the plethora of benefits Spring offers, the most notable include improved testability, separation of concerns, and a modular approach to development. The framework allows developers to configure beans and manage transactions, all while improving flexibility and decreasing the dependence on boilerplate code.

Spring encapsulates a variety of modules, each focused on solving particular problems. The core container provides foundational functionalities like dependency injection and aspect-oriented programming. The data access module simplifies interactions with databases, while the web module offers robust tools for web applications, including the Spring MVC framework. Meanwhile, Spring Boot and Spring Cloud radically streamline the creation and deployment of microservice architectures.

When compared to other frameworks, Spring's ability to be non-intrusive and adaptable stands out. Developers can integrate Spring with other frameworks and libraries with minimal disruption. Furthermore, Spring's extensive documentation and the active community ensure that support and resources are readily available for anyone venturing into its landscape.

Throughout the years, the Spring ecosystem has aligned itself closely with industry developments, offering tools that integrate seamlessly with new technologies and methodologies. As a result, learning Spring not only enriches a developer's skill set but also ensures alignment with industry standards and practices.

To succeed in mastering the Java Spring Framework, one must adopt a methodical approach to understand its core principles, components, and best practices. This book is structured to provide a comprehensive path from the basics to advanced topics, ensuring that by the end, readers possess a robust understanding of Spring and its ecosystem.

In this book, we will begin with foundational concepts and setup practices. We will then progress through core functionalities such as dependency injection, data access, and web frameworks. Advanced topics such as security, testing, and microservices architecture will also be explored in detail.

As we embark on this exploration into the Spring Framework, it is essential to approach each section with the intent to both learn and apply. This hands-on perspective will provide actionable insights that are directly applicable to real-world software development challenges. Herein lies the essence of this book—offering a bridge between theory and practical application of the Java Spring Framework.

Chapter 1

Introduction to the Java Spring Framework

The Java Spring Framework is a comprehensive and modular framework designed to simplify enterprise Java application development. It offers core features such as dependency injection, aspect-oriented programming, and transaction management, all of which contribute to improved modularity, testability, and overall development efficiency. Originating as a response to the complexity of the Enterprise JavaBeans (EJB) model, Spring has evolved into a full-fledged ecosystem with various projects like Spring Boot, Spring Data, and Spring Security, each addressing specific development needs. This chapter provides an overview of Spring's history, core benefits, and its role in the modern Java development landscape.

1.1 What is the Java Spring Framework?

The Java Spring Framework is a comprehensive framework for enterprise Java development, offering a variety of tools and techniques designed to simplify the process of creating robust, scalable, and secure applications. Spring has established itself as a prominent player in the Java ecosystem, primarily due to its modular architecture and extensive range of features.

At its core, the Spring Framework addresses common problems encountered in enterprise applications, such as dependency management, transaction handling, and modular application design. The framework's objective is to make enterprise Java development easier and more consistent, reducing boilerplate code, and promoting best practices through its design principles.

One of the fundamental components of the Spring Framework is the concept of **dependency injection** (DI). DI is a design pattern that allows developers to build loosely coupled applications. Instead of creating dependencies manually within the application classes, the Spring container manages and injects these dependencies. This leads to greater flexibility and easier testing, as the dependencies can be changed without modifying the class behavior.

```
import org.springframework.beans.factory.annotation.Autowired;
import org.springframework.stereotype.Component;

@Component
public class ExampleService {
    private final DependencyComponent dependencyComponent;

    @Autowired
    public ExampleService(DependencyComponent dependencyComponent) {
        this.dependencyComponent = dependencyComponent;
    }

    public void performAction() {
        // Business logic utilizing dependencyComponent
        dependencyComponent.execute();
    }
}
```

In the code snippet above, the ExampleService class depends on DependencyComponent. The dependency is injected via the constructor, and the Spring container handles the lifecycle and injection of DependencyComponent.

Another critical aspect of Spring is **Aspect-Oriented Programming** (AOP). AOP helps separate cross-cutting concerns from the business logic, such as security, logging, and transaction management. By employing AOP, developers can encapsulate these concerns in a centralized manner and apply them declaratively across multiple points in the application.

```
import org.aspectj.lang.annotation.Aspect;
import org.aspectj.lang.annotation.Before;
import org.springframework.stereotype.Component;

@Aspect
@Component
public class LoggingAspect {
```

```
    @Before("execution(* com.example.service.*.*(..))")
    public void logBeforeMethod() {
        System.out.println("Logging before method execution");
    }
}
```

In this example, the LoggingAspect uses the @Before annotation to execute logging logic before any method in the com.example.service package is invoked. This effectively decouples the logging concern from the business logic.

Spring also simplifies **transaction management**. It provides a consistent programming model and abstraction over different transaction APIs, removing the need for intricate and error-prone manual transaction handling. With declarative transaction management support through annotations or XML configuration, developers can focus on business logic without worrying about transaction boundary demarcation.

```
import org.springframework.stereotype.Service;
import org.springframework.transaction.annotation.Transactional;

@Service
public class TransactionalService {

    @Transactional
    public void performTransactionalOperation() {
        // Business logic involving multiple database operations
        // Spring ensures atomicity and consistency of these operations
    }
}
```

In the snippet above, the @Transactional annotation enables transaction management for the performTransactionalOperation method. Spring ensures that all operations within this method are executed within a transaction context, providing atomicity and consistency.

Spring's modular architecture allows developers to pick and choose only those components that are necessary for their application. Modules such as Spring Core, Spring MVC, Spring Data, Spring Security, and Spring Integration address specific areas of application development, ensuring a tailored approach.

Moreover, Spring integrates seamlessly with various technologies and frameworks, making it versatile for different application contexts. Its support for Java Persistence API (JPA), Hibernate, Java Messaging Service (JMS), and others ensures that Spring remains agnostic and flexible.

To facilitate the rapid development of modern applications, Spring provides **Spring Boot**. Spring Boot layers atop the traditional Spring Framework, which simplifies configuration and dependency management. With pre-configured templates and embedded server support, developers achieve quicker startup times and reduced configuration efforts.

```
import org.springframework.boot.SpringApplication;
import org.springframework.boot.autoconfigure.SpringBootApplication;
import org.springframework.web.bind.annotation.GetMapping;
import org.springframework.web.bind.annotation.RestController;

@SpringBootApplication
public class ExampleApplication {

    public static void main(String[] args) {
        SpringApplication.run(ExampleApplication.class, args);
    }
}

@RestController
class HelloController {

    @GetMapping("/hello")
    public String sayHello() {
        return "Hello, Spring Boot!";
    }
}
```

The above example initializes a simple Spring Boot application with an embedded web server, exposing a REST endpoint at /hello. This highlights Spring Boot's ability to streamline application setup while maintaining the full power of the traditional Spring ecosystem.

Through these features and many others, the Java Spring Framework provides an extensive toolkit for developers, supporting the construction of enterprise-grade applications with reduced complexity and enhanced maintainability.

1.2 History and Evolution of Spring

The Java Spring Framework was conceived to address the complexities and limitations of the Enterprise JavaBeans (EJB) specification, and its evolution has been remarkable. The framework's roots can be traced back to the early 2000s, catalyzed by Rod Johnson's experiences and critiques of existing Java enterprise solutions.

A pivotal moment in the history of Spring was the publication of Rod Johnson's book, *Expert One-on-One J2EE Design and Development* in 2002. This work not only criticized EJB for its complexity but also proposed an alternative approach, laying the foundation for what would become the Spring Framework. Johnson's book introduced the basic idea of using lightweight containers to manage application components, which greatly influenced the design principles of Spring.

In March 2004, Spring version 1.0 was officially released. This initial release incorporated key concepts such as Dependency Injection (DI) and Inversion of Control (IoC), which were relatively new at the time. DI and IoC made it considerably easier to develop and test Java applications by decoupling component dependency management from the application logic.

Spring 1.x series aimed to simplify the development of Java applications, focusing on common tasks such as configuration management, transaction management, and AOP (Aspect-Oriented Programming). The framework's non-invasive nature and flexibility in replacing or integrating with existing J2EE components quickly gained traction among developers, leading to widespread adoption.

The subsequent versions brought robust enhancements and additional functionalities. Spring 2.0, released in 2006, marked a significant milestone by introducing XML namespaces and AspectJ integration, which facilitated easier configuration and more advanced AOP capabilities. Below is an XML configuration snippet illustrating the typical bean definition:

```
<beans xmlns="http://www.springframework.org/schema/beans"
      xmlns:xsi="http://www.w3.org/2001/XMLSchema-instance"
      xsi:schemaLocation="
      http://www.springframework.org/schema/beans
      http://www.springframework.org/schema/beans/spring-beans.xsd">

   <bean id="dataSource" class="org.apache.commons.dbcp.BasicDataSource">
      <property name="driverClassName" value="com.mysql.jdbc.Driver"/>
      <property name="url" value="jdbc:mysql://localhost:3306/mydb"/>
      <property name="username" value="user"/>
      <property name="password" value="password"/>
   </bean>

</beans>
```

With the release of Spring 3.0 in 2009, the framework embraced key developments in the Java ecosystem, such as the Java 5+ language features. Annotated-based configuration was introduced, reducing the reliance on XML configuration. This was a pivotal development, as it streamlined the configuration process and brought a modern flavor to the framework. Consider the typical use of annotations for defining beans:

```
@Configuration
public class AppConfig {

    @Bean
    public DataSource dataSource() {
        BasicDataSource dataSource = new BasicDataSource();
        dataSource.setDriverClassName("com.mysql.jdbc.Driver");
        dataSource.setUrl("jdbc:mysql://localhost:3306/mydb");
        dataSource.setUsername("user");
        dataSource.setPassword("password");
        return dataSource;
    }
}
```

Spring 4.x series, starting from 2013, brought compatibility with Java 8 and introduced many functional programming features, emphasizing lambda expressions and the 'Optional' class. This series also included the new '@RestController' annotation, simplifying the creation of RESTful web services:

```
@RestController
@RequestMapping("/api")
public class MyRestController {

    @GetMapping("/greeting")
    public String greeting() {
        return "Hello, World!";
    }
}
```

In 2014, Spring Boot was introduced as a part of the Spring framework ecosystem. Designed to simplify the process of creating standalone, production-grade Spring applications, Spring Boot provided a convention-over-configuration approach and embedded HTTP servers, significantly streamlining development. Below is an example of a main application class using Spring Boot:

```
@SpringBootApplication
public class Application {

    public static void main(String[] args) {
        SpringApplication.run(Application.class, args);
    }
}
```

The Spring 5.x series, released starting in 2017, fully embraced Reactive Programming, providing support for reactive streams and non-blocking execution. This was a response to the growing demand for scalable and resilient web applications capable of handling large amounts of asynchronous data streams. The '@EnableWebFlux' annotation enabled the configuration of Spring WebFlux, the reactive-stack web framework:

```
@Configuration
@EnableWebFlux
public class WebFluxConfig implements WebFluxConfigurer {

    // Configuration methods...
}
```

The evolution of Spring has been characterized by its adaptive nature and commitment to simplifying enterprise Java development. As technology paradigms shifted, Spring consistently incorporated relevant advancements, such as reactive programming and microservices architecture, ensuring its relevance and utility in contemporary software development. The framework's community-driven development model and extensive ecosystem, including projects like Spring Boot, Spring Data, and Spring Security, have cemented its position at the forefront of Java enterprise solutions.

1.3 Core Features and Benefits

The Java Spring Framework provides a robust set of features designed to simplify enterprise Java application development. By addressing the complexities inherent in the Enterprise JavaBeans (EJB) model, Spring has become a pivotal tool for modern Java enterprise applications. Key features such as dependency injection, aspect-oriented programming, and transaction management significantly enhance modularity, testability, and maintainability. This section delves into these core features and enumerates their associated benefits in detail.

Dependency Injection (DI)

Dependency Injection, a form of Inversion of Control (IoC), allows Spring to manage object creation and their dependencies. Rather than objects themselves creating or managing their dependencies, these are injected by the framework, reducing coupling and increasing flexibility. DI can be conducted through constructor injection, setter injection, and field injection, each with specific use cases and advantages.

Consider the following example where a service class ('MyService') depends on a repository class ('MyRepository'):

```
public class MyService {
    private final MyRepository repository;

    // Constructor Injection
```

```
    @Autowired
    public MyService(MyRepository repository) {
        this.repository = repository;
    }

    // Business logic
    public void performService() {
        repository.save();
    }
}
```

```
@Service
public class MyService {
    private final MyRepository repository;

    @Autowired
    public MyService(MyRepository repository) {
        this.repository = repository;
    }

    public void performService() {
        repository.save();
    }
}
```

Aspect-Oriented Programming (AOP)

AOP separates cross-cutting concerns (aspects) from primary business logic, making the code cleaner and more modular. Common aspects include logging, transaction management, and security. Spring AOP can be employed through annotations or configuration.

Consider an example where a logging aspect is applied to a service method:

```
@Aspect
@Component
public class LoggingAspect {

    @Before("execution(* com.example.service.*.*(..))")
    public void logBefore(JoinPoint joinPoint) {
        System.out.println("Executing method: " + joinPoint.getSignature().getName())
            ;
    }
}
```


```
@Aspect
@Component
public class LoggingAspect {

    @Before("execution(* com.example.service.*.*(..))")
    public void logBefore(JoinPoint joinPoint) {
        System.out.println("Executing method: " + joinPoint.getSignature().getName())
            ;
    }
}
```

Transaction Management

Spring's transaction management framework aims to provide a consistent programming model across different transaction APIs such as JTA, JDBC, Hibernate, and more. It supports both programmatic and declarative transaction management. Declarative transaction management can be achieved using annotations, making it less intrusive and enhancing readability.

An example of declarative transaction management using annotations:

```
@Service
public class TransactionalService {

    @Transactional
    public void executeTransaction() {
        // transactional code here
    }
}
```


```
@Service
public class TransactionalService {

    @Transactional
    public void executeTransaction() {
        // transactional code here
    }
}
```


Data Access and Persistence

Spring simplifies data access by integrating seamlessly with various persistence mechanisms like JDBC, JPA, and ORM frameworks such as Hibernate. It offers templates and APIs to handle the boilerplate code involved in data access, reducing complexity and potential errors.

For example, Spring's 'JdbcTemplate' can be used to execute SQL queries with minimal code:

```
@Autowired
private JdbcTemplate jdbcTemplate;

public void insertData() {
    String sql = "INSERT INTO customers (name, age) VALUES (?, ?)";
    jdbcTemplate.update(sql, "John Doe", 30);
}
```


```
@Autowired
private JdbcTemplate jdbcTemplate;

public void insertData() {
    String sql = "INSERT INTO customers (name, age) VALUES (?, ?)";
    jdbcTemplate.update(sql, "John Doe", 30);
}
```

Spring MVC Framework

The Spring MVC (Model-View-Controller) framework is designed to simplify web application development. By providing a clear separation of concerns, it enhances the ability to manage and maintain large applications. The framework supports RESTful APIs, conventional web applications, and response formats like JSON and XML.

An example of a simple Spring MVC controller:

```
@Controller
public class HomeController {

    @GetMapping("/home")
    public String home(Model model) {
        model.addAttribute("message", "Welcome to Spring MVC!");
        return "home";
    }
}
```


```
@Controller
public class HomeController {

    @GetMapping("/home")
    public String home(Model model) {
        model.addAttribute("message", "Welcome to Spring MVC!");
        return "home";
    }
}
```


Security

Spring Security is a powerful and customizable authentication and access control framework. It provides comprehensive security services for Java applications, including secure login, logout, URL restriction, role-based access control, and protection against common vulnerabilities like cross-site scripting (XSS) and cross-site request forgery (CSRF).

An example of a Spring Security configuration:

```
@EnableWebSecurity
public class WebSecurityConfig extends WebSecurityConfigurerAdapter {

    @Override
    protected void configure(HttpSecurity http) throws Exception {
        http
            .authorizeRequests()
                .antMatchers("/", "/home").permitAll()
                .anyRequest().authenticated()
                .and()
            .formLogin()
                .loginPage("/login")
                .permitAll()
                .and()
            .logout()
```

```
                .permitAll();
    }
}
```

```
@EnableWebSecurity
public class WebSecurityConfig extends WebSecurityConfigurerAdapter {

    @Override
    protected void configure(HttpSecurity http) throws Exception {
        http
            .authorizeRequests()
                .antMatchers("/", "/home").permitAll()
                .anyRequest().authenticated()
                .and()
            .formLogin()
                .loginPage("/login")
                .permitAll()
                .and()
            .logout()
                .permitAll();
    }
}
```

Benefits of Using Spring

Spring's features offer a multitude of benefits, enhancing enterprise applications in the following ways:

- **Modularity**: By decoupling application components through DI and AOP, Spring promotes high modularity.
- **Testability**: Dependency injection facilitates easier unit testing by allowing the injection of mock dependencies.
- **Performance**: Aspect-Oriented Programming (AOP) enables efficient handling of cross-cutting concerns, improving overall performance.
- **Flexibility**: Spring provides multiple ways (XML, annotations, JavaConfig) to configure beans and manage dependencies.
- **Transaction Management**: Simplifies transaction demarcation and ensures transactional integrity.
- **Scalability**: Supports large-scale solutions across various deployment environments.
- **Security**: Offers a wide range of customizable security options ensuring secure application development.
- **Community Support**: Active and large community contributing to the continuous improvement and support of the framework.

1.4 Spring Modules Overview

The Spring Framework is designed around a set of components or modules, each specializing in different aspects of enterprise application development. These modules are tightly integrated to provide a seamless development experience while allowing developers the flexibility to pick and choose the functionalities they need. This modular approach helps in addressing a wide range of development requirements while maintaining high cohesion and low coupling.

Core Container: The core container is the foundation of the Spring Framework. It includes the *spring-core*, *spring-beans*, *spring-context*, and *spring-expression* (Spring Expression Language, SpEL) modules. The responsibilities of these modules are outlined as follows:

- *spring-core* and *spring-beans*: These modules provide the fundamental parts of the framework, including the *IoC* (Inversion of Control) and Dependency Injection features. The *BeanFactory* is the heart of any Spring-based application. It represents the IoC container and is responsible for instantiating, configuring, and managing beans.

- *spring-context*: The context module builds on the solid base provided by the core and beans modules. It provides a way to access objects in a framework-style manner, resembling a JNDI registry. The ApplicationContext interface is a central interface used in the Spring context for configuring application models at runtime.

- *spring-expression* (SpEL): This module provides a powerful expression language for querying and manipulating an object graph at runtime. The expression language supports querying, calling, and accessing properties, methods, and arrays.

Data Access/Integration: This layer handles interacting with data and its subsequent processing. The following modules are particularly significant in this respect:

- *spring-jdbc*: This module provides comprehensive support for JDBC, enabling you to keep the boilerplate code to a minimum. It offers facilities for managing database resources and handling exceptions efficiently.

- *spring-tx*: Transaction management is a pivotal feature in enterprise applications. The spring-tx module provides both declarative and programmatic transaction management to control transactional behavior consistently across various transactional APIs, such as JDBC and JPA.
- *spring-orm*: This module facilitates integration with popular ORM frameworks like Hibernate, JPA, and JDO, providing both the full suite of ORM features and further integrations with Spring's simpler data access abstractions.
- *spring-oxm*: This module provides an abstraction layer for Object/XML mapping implementations, allowing seamless transformation between XML documents and Java objects.
- *spring-jms*: The spring-jms module simplifies working with the JMS API by providing facilities for sending and receiving messages.

Web and Reactive: The web layer makes the framework apt for web-based applications. It includes the following modules:

- *spring-web*: This is the core module that addresses web-oriented concerns by allowing for sets of tools and features. These include the standard HTTP and servlets API integration and much more.
- *spring-webmvc*: Often referred to as the Web-Servlet module, it provides the Model-View-Controller (MVC) and RESTful web services; it builds on servlet API and offers high-level configuration for typical modern web applications.
- *spring-webflux*: This module builds on reactive programming principles, providing support for reactive web applications. It offers an alternative to the standard servlet-based approach by using event-loop processing style akin to Node.js.

Other AOD, Messaging, Testing and Instrumentation: This cluster includes various other services, spanning areas such as aspect-oriented programming, messaging, testing, and even instrumentation for better manageability.

- *spring-aop*: This module provides aspect-oriented programming capabilities, enabling the separation of cross-cutting concerns such as logging or transaction management.

- *spring-messaging*: Facilitates various messaging scenarios and simplifies integration with messaging APIs from JMS to WebSockets.
- *spring-test*: The spring-test module supports unit testing and integration testing; it includes comprehensive support for testing Spring components with JUnit or TestNG integration.
- *spring-aspects*: This module integrates Spring with AspectJ, a powerful and mature AOP framework.
- *spring-instrumentation*: Provides support classes for JVM-level instrumentation, enabling runtime monitoring and management.

The discussed modules cooperate to build robust, maintainable, and scalable enterprise applications. Through their prudent combination, developers can devise solutions that are both efficient and aligned with modern technological needs. The modularity also implies that you can start small, integrating only the necessary components and gradually expanding as the application evolves in complexity and scope.

1.5 Spring vs Other Frameworks

Comparing the Java Spring Framework with other frameworks is essential for comprehending its unique advantages and situational suitability. This section exclusively examines how Spring stands apart from several prominent frameworks, including Java Enterprise Edition (Java EE), Apache Struts, Play Framework, and Google Guice. Each comparison highlights specific aspects such as design philosophy, ease of use, scalability, and extensibility.

Spring vs Java EE

Java EE, now Jakarta EE, historically served as a comprehensive suite for developing large-scale, multi-tiered, scalable enterprise applications. Spring emerged as a lightweight alternative to Java EE, offering simplicity and poise.

- **Design Philosophy:** Java EE emphasizes convention-based development with a focus on standardization and robustness. Components like Enterprise JavaBeans (EJB) are heavyweight. Spring advocates for lightweight components, non-invasive development, and full dependency injection (DI).

- **Configuration:** Java EE has moved towards annotations and CDI (Contexts and Dependency Injection) for configuration, but still relies on XML. Spring offers multiple configuration modes: XML, annotations, and JavaConfig, with a focus on reducing boilerplate code.

- **Modularity:** Spring's modular design allows inclusion of only necessary components. Java EE's inclusive specification tends to load various services, impacting performance.

- **Ecosystem Integration:** Spring's ecosystem complements external tools and libraries effortlessly. Java EE integration is often tightly coupled with its specification.

The following code snippet demonstrates Spring's dependency injection using annotations, showcasing simplicity and clarity:

```
@Configuration
public class AppConfig {

    @Bean
    public MyService myService() {
        return new MyServiceImpl();
    }
}

@Service
public class MyServiceImpl implements MyService {
    // service-related methods
}
```

Spring vs Apache Struts

Struts, an open-source web application framework, has been a staple for building web projects using the Model-View-Controller (MVC) pattern.

- **MVC Framework:** Both frameworks implement the MVC design pattern. Struts provides a traditional action-based MVC design, while Spring MVC offers a more flexible, annotation-based approach.

- **Extensibility:** Spring's modularity allows facile integration and replacement of components. Struts is more monolithic, making extension and integration of third-party libraries less straightforward.

- **Configuration:** Struts configurations are typically XML-based.

Spring uses a mix of annotations and XML, favoring annotation-based configuration for conciseness.

- **Community Support:** While Struts has a significant user base, Spring's active community and extensive documentation provide more robust support and resource availability.

An example illustrating Spring MVC's ease of configuration:

```
@Controller
public class MyController {

    @GetMapping("/welcome")
    public String welcome(Model model) {
        model.addAttribute("message", "Welcome to Spring MVC");
        return "welcome";
    }
}
```

Spring vs Play Framework

Play Framework, developed by Lightbend, is designed for building web applications with an emphasis on developer productivity and reactive principles.

- **Reactive Programming:** Play is inherently reactive and adopts non-blocking IO, making it optimal for applications demanding high concurrency. Spring integrates Project Reactor for reactive programming but is not inherently reactive.
- **Scalability:** Both frameworks are designed for high scalability. However, Play's architecture is built from the ground up to handle large-scale applications seamlessly.
- **Ease of Use:** Play employs a convention-over-configuration approach, reducing boilerplate code. Spring provides more configuration options, which can lead to a steeper learning curve.
- **Integration:** Spring's extensive ecosystem and integration capabilities with databases, security frameworks, etc., surpass those of Play.

Sample reactive endpoint in Spring using WebFlux:

```
@RestController
public class ReactiveController {

    @GetMapping("/flux")
    public Flux<String> flux() {
```

```
        return Flux.just("Spring", "WebFlux");
    }
}
```

Spring vs Google Guice

Google Guice is a lightweight dependency injection framework primarily aimed at simplifying development and providing loose coupling.

- **Dependency Injection:** Both frameworks provide robust DI capabilities. Guice is lightweight and focuses solely on DI, while Spring DI is part of its broad ecosystem.
- **Configuration:** Guice uses Java annotations and code for configuration, similar to Spring's JavaConfig approach.
- **Flexibility:** Spring provides a more extensive set of features including AOP, transaction management, and integration with numerous frameworks. Guice remains focused on DI with fewer integrated features.
- **Learning Curve:** Guice is simpler due to its focused nature, making it easier to learn. Spring's broader context and more extensive capabilities require a deeper understanding.

Illustrating Guice's simplicity in configuring dependency injection:

```
public class AppModule extends AbstractModule {
    @Override
    protected void configure() {
        bind(MyService.class).to(MyServiceImpl.class);
    }
}
```

Overall, Spring's strengths lie in its comprehensive ecosystem, flexibility, and robust community support, distinguishing it as a favored choice for a wide array of enterprise applications. Each framework compared offers unique advantages and may be preferred based on specific application requirements and developer expertise.

1.6 Spring Ecosystem and Community

The Spring ecosystem is a vast and diverse collection of projects, each designed to address specific practices and challenges in modern Java development. The core of the ecosystem revolves around the Spring

Framework, but many auxiliary projects enhance its capabilities, extending its versatility and applicability to a wide array of use cases. These projects are well-maintained and actively developed, benefiting from a robust, engaged community of developers and contributors.

Spring Boot is arguably one of the most significant projects in the Spring ecosystem. It simplifies application development by providing default configurations and a streamlined setup process. With Spring Boot, developers can quickly create stand-alone, production-ready Spring applications with embedded servers like Tomcat or Jetty. The framework abstracts away much of the boilerplate configuration, emphasizing convention over configuration. To illustrate, consider the following SpringBootApplication:

```
import org.springframework.boot.SpringApplication;
import org.springframework.boot.autoconfigure.SpringBootApplication;

@SpringBootApplication
public class Application {
    public static void main(String[] args) {
        SpringApplication.run(Application.class, args);
    }
}
```

Execution of this minimal setup initiates a Spring application with an embedded server.

Spring Data simplifies data access by providing a consistent and flexible approach to managing relational and non-relational data stores. It builds on the repository design pattern, reducing the boilerplate code associated with data access layers. Here is an example of a typical Spring Data repository interface:

```
import org.springframework.data.repository.CrudRepository;

public interface UserRepository extends CrudRepository<User, Long> {
    List<User> findByLastName(String lastName);
}
```

Executing a code block to populate and retrieve data:

```
@Autowired
private UserRepository userRepository;

public void addAndFetchUser() {
    User user = new User("John", "Doe");
    userRepository.save(user);
    List<User> users = userRepository.findByLastName("Doe");
    users.forEach(System.out::println);
}
```

The above example illustrates the simplicity and power of Spring Data repositories.

Spring Security is a powerful and highly customizable authentication and access-control framework. It provides protection against common exploits and integrates seamlessly with the core Spring Framework. Below is a basic security configuration using Spring Security:

```
import org.springframework.context.annotation.Configuration;
import org.springframework.security.config.annotation.authentication.builders.
    AuthenticationManagerBuilder;
import org.springframework.security.config.annotation.web.builders.HttpSecurity;
import org.springframework.security.config.annotation.web.configuration.
    WebSecurityConfigurerAdapter;

@Configuration
public class SecurityConfig extends WebSecurityConfigurerAdapter {
    @Override
    protected void configure(HttpSecurity http) throws Exception {
        http.authorizeRequests()
                .antMatchers("/public/**").permitAll()
                .anyRequest().authenticated()
                .and()
                .formLogin().loginPage("/login").permitAll()
                .and()
                .logout().permitAll();
    }

    @Override
    protected void configure(AuthenticationManagerBuilder auth) throws Exception {
        auth.inMemoryAuthentication()
                .withUser("user").password("{noop}password").roles("USER");
    }
}
```

This configuration allows unrestricted access to public URLs while restricting access to other URLs, requiring users to log in.

Spring Cloud provides tools for developers to quickly build some of the common patterns in distributed systems, such as configuration management, service discovery, and circuit breakers. It is particularly useful in the development of microservices. Here is a Spring Cloud configuration applying a Netflix Eureka service discovery setup:

```
@SpringBootApplication
@EnableEurekaServer
public class EurekaServerApplication {
    public static void main(String[] args) {
        SpringApplication.run(EurekaServerApplication.class, args);
    }
}
```

Configuration file:

```
# application.properties
spring.application.name=eureka-server
server.port=8761
eureka.client.register-with-eureka=false
eureka.client.fetch-registry=false
```

Running the EurekaServerApplication will start a Eureka service discovery server on port 8761.

Spring Batch is designed for batch processing, supporting both the transaction management and the scheduling of jobs. A Spring Batch job consists of several steps, each representing a phase in the execution. Here's an example of a simple batch configuration:

```
import org.springframework.batch.core.Job;
import org.springframework.batch.core.JobExecution;
import org.springframework.batch.core.JobParameters;
import org.springframework.batch.core.configuration.annotation.EnableBatchProcessing;

import org.springframework.batch.core.launch.JobLauncher;
import org.springframework.batch.core.repository.JobRepository;
import org.springframework.batch.core.step.builder.StepBuilderFactory;
import org.springframework.batch.core.step.tasklet.Tasklet;
import org.springframework.batch.repeat.RepeatStatus;
import org.springframework.context.annotation.Bean;
import org.springframework.context.annotation.Configuration;

@Configuration
@EnableBatchProcessing
public class BatchConfiguration {

    @Bean
    public Tasklet tasklet() {
        return (contribution, chunkContext) -> {
            System.out.println("Tasklet executed");
            return RepeatStatus.FINISHED;
        };
    }

    @Bean
    public Job job(JobRepository jobRepository, StepBuilderFactory
            stepBuilderFactory, Tasklet tasklet) {
        return jobRepository.createJobBuilder("job")
                .start(stepBuilderFactory.get("step1").tasklet(tasklet).build())
                .build();
    }
}
```

Executing this job results in:

```
Tasklet executed
```

The success and growth of the Spring ecosystem are attributable to its vibrant and engaged community. The community contributes to maintaining, enhancing, and expanding the projects through various channels, including GitHub repositories, forums, and conferences. The biannual SpringOne conference is a notable event driving innovation and collaboration within the developer base. Various forums such as Stack Overflow and Gitter also play significant roles in assisting developers, ensuring continuous collective growth and knowledge sharing within the Spring ecosystem.

1.7 Tools and Resources for Learning Spring

Effective mastery of the Java Spring Framework requires access to a robust set of tools and resources. This section delves into the essential utilities, documentation, and community-driven materials that facilitate the learning process.

Integrated Development Environments (IDEs)

Choosing the right Integrated Development Environment (IDE) is a critical first step for any developer looking to work with the Spring Framework. IDEs provide code templating, debugging, and integration features for building, testing, and deploying Spring applications.

- **IntelliJ IDEA**: IntelliJ IDEA from JetBrains is highly recommended for Spring development due to its in-built Spring support. The IDE provides comprehensive tools for Spring Boot initialization, autocomplete features for annotations and properties, and seamless integration with version control systems such as Git. A noteworthy feature is its Spring Assistant which helps manage Spring dependencies and configurations smoothly.
- **Eclipse**: Eclipse, particularly when combined with the Spring Tools Suite (STS) plugin, offers a robust environment for Spring development. STS provides extensive support for Spring projects, including wizards for Spring Boot, graphical editors for Spring configuration files, and built-in support for dependency management through Maven and Gradle.
- **Spring Tool Suite (STS)**: A specialized development environment tailored for Spring, STS builds on Eclipse and adds bespoke functionalities for Spring applications. It offers a direct way to initialize new Spring projects, perform refactoring tasks, and manage Spring-specific configurations effectively.

Build Tools

Spring heavily relies on build tools to manage dependencies, build artifacts, and scripts for various development tasks. Key build tools include:

- **Maven**: Apache Maven is a widely-used build automation tool that uses an XML file to manage project dependencies, build configuration, and plugins necessary for development. It allows for consistent project configuration and lifecycle management, which are crucial for larger Spring projects.
- **Gradle**: Gradle provides a more flexible and faster build system using Groovy or Kotlin DSLs. It offers enhanced performance through incremental builds and supports dependency management with clear syntax. Gradle's compatibility with both Java and Groovy languages makes it a popular choice for Spring projects.

Learning Resources

Various official and community-based resources are available to help developers enhance their understanding of the Spring Framework:

- **Official Documentation**: The official Spring documentation (https://spring.io/docs) is comprehensive and regularly updated. It includes detailed guides, API references, and best practices. The Spring Guides section offers samples and practical examples to help developers get started quickly with specific parts of the framework.
- **Books**: Several authoritative texts provide in-depth knowledge of Spring. Notable examples include:
  - Spring in Action: Authored by Craig Walls, this book offers a hands-on approach, covering the latest features and providing plenty of practical examples.
  - Pro Spring 5: Written by Iuliana Cosmina et al., this text dives deeply into advanced features and best practices, blending theoretical knowledge with practical insights.
- **Online Courses**: Multiple platforms such as Udemy, Coursera, and Pluralsight offer courses tailored to different skill levels. Courses range from introductory topics to advanced use-cases, often including assignments and projects to practice newly acquired skills.

- **Community Forums and Q&A Sites**: Online forums (e.g., Stack Overflow, Reddit) and the official Spring community (https://spring.io/community) are valuable for troubleshooting and exchanging knowledge. Participating in these forums allows developers to learn from the experiences of others and receive feedback on specific issues they encounter.

- **GitHub Repositories**: Exploring open-source projects on GitHub (https://github.com/spring-projects) can provide real-world code examples and foster collaborative learning. The official Spring GitHub repositories contain numerous sample applications, configurations, and plugins that developers can study and emulate.

Additional Tooling and Plugins

To further enhance the development process, several plugins and tools are tailored specifically for Spring Framework development:

- **Lombok**: Project Lombok (https://projectlombok.org/) is a Java library that helps to reduce boilerplate code. It can be particularly beneficial when used with Spring, simplifying the creation of boilerplate-intensive constructs like getters, setters, and constructors.

- **JRebel**: JRebel (https://www.jrebel.com/) is a Java development tool that allows developers to instantly see code changes without restarting their applications. This can significantly enhance productivity during intense development phases.

- **Spring Boot DevTools**: Part of the Spring ecosystem, Spring Boot DevTools facilitates a more rapid development cycle by providing features like automatic restarts, live reload, and configurations for improved productivity.

Configuration Management

Effective management of application configurations is essential for developing robust Spring applications. Tools aiding configuration management include:

- **Spring Cloud Config**: This tool centralizes configuration management by providing server-side and client-side support for externalized configuration in distributed systems.

- **Consul, Vault**: Integration with HashiCorp's Consul for service discovery and Vault for secure secret management enhances the security and reliability of Spring applications in production environments.

Accessing these tools and leveraging the rich set of available resources forms the foundation for effective learning and practical application of the Spring Framework. This investment in tooling and resources will pay dividends as developers advance from basic implementations to more complex, enterprise-level projects.

Chapter 2

Setting Up Your Development Environment

This chapter details the steps necessary to establish an effective development environment for Java Spring applications. It begins with installing the Java Development Kit (JDK) and setting up an Integrated Development Environment (IDE) such as IntelliJ IDEA or Eclipse. The chapter also introduces essential build tools like Maven and Gradle, guiding you through the creation of your first Spring project using Spring Initializr. Additionally, it covers project configuration, dependency management, and the process of running and debugging Spring applications. Finally, it touches on integrating version control systems like Git and GitHub to streamline development workflows.

2.1 Introduction to Development Environments

A robust development environment forms the cornerstone for efficient and streamlined application development. It serves as the interface through which developers interact with their codebase, manage dependencies, and ensure consistent builds. The primary components of a development environment typically include an operating system, a text or code editor, build tools, debuggers, and version control systems. In the context of Java Spring applications, this environment also necessitates specific tools like the Java Development Kit (JDK) and an Integrated Development Environment (IDE) such as IntelliJ IDEA or Eclipse. The development environment is not merely a set of tools but a well-configured ecosystem that enhances productivity and reduces the likelihood of errors.

At the core of any Java development environment lies the Java Development Kit (JDK). The JDK is an essential tool that provides the Java Runtime Environment (JRE) along with compilers and various tools (e.g., JavaDoc, Java Debugger) necessary for developing Java applications. The choice of JDK version can greatly impact application compatibility and performance. It is advisable to use a Long-Term Support (LTS) version of the JDK, which ensures stability and extended support from Oracle or other JDK distributors. Proper installation and configuration of the JDK pave the way for a seamless development experience.

Complementing the JDK is the choice of an Integrated Development Environment (IDE). An IDE integrates various development tools into a single user interface, offering features like code editors, syntax highlighting, code completion, version control integration, and debugging capabilities. Popular IDEs for Java development include IntelliJ IDEA, Eclipse, and NetBeans. Of these, IntelliJ IDEA is often preferred for its intuitive interface, advanced refactoring tools, and support for various Java frameworks, including Spring. Eclipse, on the other hand, offers robust plugin support and is highly customizable, making it a favorite among developers who prefer a tailored development experience.

The role of build tools in a development environment cannot be overstated. Build tools automate the process of compiling source code, managing dependencies, and packaging executables. Maven and Gradle are the most prevalent build tools in the Java ecosystem. Maven uses a declarative approach, where the project structure and dependencies are described in an XML file (pom.xml). Gradle, in contrast, employs a Groovy-based DSL for its build scripts, offering more flexibility and advanced features like incremental builds.

Dependency management is a critical aspect of any development environment. It ensures that all necessary libraries and frameworks are available and correctly versioned. Maven and Gradle both provide robust dependency management capabilities. They handle the retrieval, versioning, and inclusion of libraries into the project, resolving conflicts and maintaining a consistent development environment. This process involves accessing repositories (centralized locations for storing libraries) and automatically downloading the required dependencies.

Project configuration involves setting up project-specific settings such as source code directory structures, library paths, and environment variables. Proper configuration ensures that the project can be built, run, and debugged without repeated adjustments to the environment. Spring Initializr simplifies this process by automatically generating a pre-configured Spring project, which can then be imported into the IDE and customized as needed.

Version control systems (VCS) are indispensable in modern software development. Git, a distributed version control system, and GitHub, a cloud-based Git repository hosting service, facilitate collaborative development, version tracking, and code review. Integrating Git and GitHub into the development environment allows for efficient branch management, code merging, and conflict resolution. IDEs like IntelliJ IDEA and Eclipse offer built-in support for Git, making version control operations seamless.

```
# Clone a repository
git clone https://github.com/username/repository.git

# Create a new branch
git branch new-feature

# Switch to the new branch
git checkout new-feature

# Add changes to staging
git add .

# Commit changes
git commit -m "Implement new feature"

# Push changes to remote
git push origin new-feature
```

Finally, running and debugging applications is a crucial part of development. The IDEs provide integrated tools for running Spring applications directly within the development environment. Debugging tools offer breakpoint management, variable inspection, and step-wise execution, enabling developers to diagnose and resolve issues efficiently. Proper setup of these tools ensures quick feedback and rapid iteration during development.

Establishing an effective development environment involves meticulous configuration and continuous refinement. Each component, from the JDK and IDE to build tools and version control systems, plays a vital role in creating a cohesive, productive setup for Java Spring application development.

2.2 Installing Java Development Kit (JDK)

The Java Development Kit (JDK) is a crucial component for developing Java Spring applications. The JDK provides the necessary tools to compile, run, and debug Java applications. It includes the Java Runtime Environment (JRE), an interpreter/loader (Java), a compiler (javac), an archiver (jar), and various other tools for Java development.

To install the JDK, follow these detailed steps:

- **Downloading the JDK**

  First, you need to download the JDK from the official Oracle website or an OpenJDK provider, such as AdoptOpenJDK, depending on your preference for open-source options.

  Navigate to the following URL: https://www.oracle.com/java/technologies/javase-downloads.html. Choose the appropriate JDK version. It is advisable to select the Long-Term Support (LTS) version for stability unless your project requires features from newer versions.

- **Selecting the Operating System**

  Select the correct installer for your operating system. The Oracle site provides installers for Windows, macOS, and Linux. For example, if you are using a Windows machine, you will typically download a .exe file, whereas macOS and Linux users will download .dmg or .tar.gz files, respectively.

- **Installing on Windows**

  Run the downloaded .exe file, and follow the installation wizard steps:

  1. Double-click the downloaded executable file to start the installation wizard.
  2. Click Next to continue.
  3. Choose the destination folder where you want the JDK to be installed. The default directory is usually C:\Program Files\Java\jdk-X.

4. Click Next.
5. The installation will begin. Once it completes, click Close to finish the installation process.

- **Installing on macOS**

  For macOS, double-click the downloaded .dmg file to open it, and then double-click the .pkg file inside:

  1. Follow the installation instructions provided by the installer.
  2. Accept the license agreement.
  3. Select the installation location or use the default location.
  4. After the installation completes, verify the installation by opening the Terminal and typing java -version.

- **Installing on Linux**

  For Linux users, the installation process will vary based on the distribution. Below is an example for Ubuntu:

```
# Update the package index
sudo apt update

# Install OpenJDK
sudo apt install openjdk-11-jdk -y

# Verify the installation
java -version
```

- **Setting the JAVA_HOME Environment Variable**

  After installing the JDK, it is essential to configure the JAVA_HOME environment variable. This variable tells the system where the JDK is located.

  - **For Windows:**

    1. Open the Start menu and search for Environment Variables.
    2. In the System Properties window, click Environment Variables.
    3. Under System variables, click New.
    4. Set JAVA_HOME as the variable name and the path to your JDK directory as the variable value (e.g., C:\Program Files\Java\jdk-X).
    5. Click OK to close each dialog box.

- **For macOS/Linux:**

  Add the following lines to your shell configuration file (e.g., ~/.bashrc, ~/.bash_profile, or ~/.zshrc):

  ```
  export JAVA_HOME=/path/to/your/jdk
  export PATH=$JAVA_HOME/bin:$PATH
  ```

  After editing the file, apply the changes by sourcing it:

  ```
  source ~/.bashrc # or the appropriate file
  ```

- **Verifying the Installation**

  To verify that the JDK is correctly installed and configured, open a command line interface (Terminal on macOS/Linux or Command Prompt on Windows) and enter:

  ```
  java -version
  javac -version
  ```

  You should see output indicating the installed JDK version, such as:

  ```
  java version "11.0.2" 2019-01-15 LTS
  Java(TM) SE Runtime Environment 18.9 (build 11.0.2+9-LTS)
  Java HotSpot(TM) 64-Bit Server VM 18.9 (build 11.0.2+9-LTS, mixed mode)
  ```

  This ensures that the JDK is correctly installed and accessible from your command line.

By following the above steps meticulously, the JDK installation process should be smooth, providing a robust foundation for developing Java-based applications using the Spring Framework. Ensuring that the correct version of JDK is installed and configured properly is critical for the seamless execution of all Java-based programs and scripts in subsequent steps of setting up your development environment.

2.3 Setting Up Integrated Development Environment (IDE)

An Integrated Development Environment (IDE) is essential for efficiently building, running, and debugging Java Spring applications. This section will cover setting up two popular IDEs: IntelliJ IDEA and Eclipse. Each IDE is robust and provides various features to streamline the development process.

IntelliJ IDEA Installation and Setup

To install IntelliJ IDEA:

- Visit the official JetBrains website.
- Download the Community Edition, which is free and sufficient for most Java Spring projects.
- Run the installer and follow the on-screen instructions to complete the installation.

Once IntelliJ IDEA is installed, open the application. The welcome screen provides options to create a new project, open an existing project, or check out a project from version control. For our purposes, select New Project. In the new project wizard:

- Choose Spring Initializr as the project type.
- Configure the project's metadata, such as Group and Artifact.
- Select Java as the language and set the appropriate Spring Boot version.
- Add necessary dependencies, such as Spring Web, Spring Data JPA, and Thymeleaf.

Click Finish to create the project. IntelliJ will download the required dependencies and set up the project structure.

```
// Example structure of a simple Spring Boot application in IntelliJ IDEA
src/main/java
    com.example.demo
        DemoApplication.java
src/main/resources
    application.properties
```

Eclipse Installation and Setup

To set up Eclipse IDE:

- Navigate to the Eclipse official website.
- Download the installer for Eclipse IDE for Java Developers.
- Follow the installation instructions provided by the Eclipse installer.

Launch Eclipse after installation. The welcome screen will have options to create a new project or import an existing one. Select File → New → Spring Starter Project. The Spring Starter Project wizard will prompt you to:

- Enter the project name and choose the location.
- Configure the Group, Artifact, and dependencies similarly to IntelliJ IDEA.

Completing this wizard sets up the Spring Boot project in Eclipse. Ensure that the project structure correctly includes the necessary Spring Boot files.

```
// Example structure of a simple Spring Boot application in Eclipse
src/main/java
    com.example.demo
        DemoApplication.java
src/main/resources
    application.properties
```

Common Configuration for IntelliJ IDEA and Eclipse

Both IntelliJ IDEA and Eclipse require a few common configurations to improve development efficiency.

JDK Configuration: Ensure that the installed JDK is correctly configured in the IDE.

In IntelliJ IDEA, navigate to File → Project Structure → SDKs. Click the + button and add the path to your JDK installation.

In Eclipse, navigate to Window → Preferences → Java → Installed JREs. Click Add to include the JDK path.

Maven/Gradle Configuration: Configure build tools for dependency management.

In IntelliJ IDEA, go to Preferences → Build, Execution, Deployment → Build Tools. Select Maven or Gradle and set the correct home directory and service directory.

In Eclipse, go to Window → Preferences → Maven/Gradle to configure the settings.

Run your project by navigating to the main application class (DemoApplication.java) and clicking the Run button in both IDEs. You will see the application start-up logs in the console, verifying that everything is set up correctly.

```
  .   ____          _            __ _ _
 /\\ / ___'_ __ _ _(_)_ __  __ _ \ \ \ \
( ( )\___ | '_ | '_| | '_ \/ _` | \ \ \ \
 \\/  ___)| |_)| | | | | || (_| |  ) ) ) )
  '  |____| .__|_| |_|_| |_\__, | / / / /
 =========|_|==============|___/=/_/_/_/
 :: Spring Boot ::        (v2.5.4)

...
```

Git Integration in the IDEs enhances version control capabilities. In IntelliJ IDEA, navigate to VCS → Enable Version Control Integration. Choose Git and initialize the repository. For Eclipse, right-click on the project, navigate to Team → Share Project, and select Git.

Lastly, ensure that both IDEs support essential plugins for enhanced development. Install the Spring Boot plugin in IntelliJ IDEA (File → Settings → Plugins). In Eclipse, navigate to Help → Eclipse Marketplace and install the Spring Tools Suite (STS) plugin.

Properly setting up the IDE streamlines the development workflow, providing a solid foundation for building robust Java Spring applications.

2.4 Introduction to Build Tools: Maven and Gradle

Efficient build tools form an integral part of modern software development, providing capabilities to manage project dependencies, automate compilation, and streamline various phases of the software development life cycle. In Java Spring development, Maven and Gradle have emerged as the build tools of choice. This section delves into the essential aspects of Maven and Gradle, offering a detailed comparison and guidance on their utilization within Spring projects.

Maven is a project management and comprehension tool that provides developers with a unified method for managing a project's build, reporting, and documentation from a central piece of information. The core functionalities of Maven include project structure standardization, dependency management, build lifecycle management, and plugin-driven deployment. The standardization aspect ensures that Maven projects adhere to a uniform directory structure, facilitating better maintenance and understanding of the project layout across different teams. Dependency management is tackled through a declarative approach using a pom.xml (Project Object Model) file which lists all project dependencies, plugins, and essential configuration details.

```
<project xmlns="http://maven.apache.org/POM/4.0.0"
        xmlns:xsi="http://www.w3.org/2001/XMLSchema-instance"
        xsi:schemaLocation="http://maven.apache.org/POM/4.0.0
                            http://maven.apache.org/xsd/maven-4.0.0.xsd">
    <modelVersion>4.0.0</modelVersion>

    <groupId>com.example</groupId>
    <artifactId>demo-app</artifactId>
    <version>1.0-SNAPSHOT</version>

    <dependencies>
        <dependency>
            <groupId>org.springframework.boot</groupId>
            <artifactId>spring-boot-starter-web</artifactId>
            <version>2.7.0</version>
        </dependency>
    </dependencies>
</project>
```

The structure of the pom.xml file is both hierarchical and extensible, enabling fine-grained control over project configurations. Maven supports a standardized build lifecycle, comprising phases such as validate, compile, test, package, verify, install, and deploy, each performing a specific task within the build process.

On the other hand, **Gradle** introduces a more flexible and powerful approach to build automation. It combines the best elements of Apache Ant and Apache Maven, including deep extensibility, a rich domain model, and a Groovy-based DSL (Domain-Specific Language) for configuration. Gradle build scripts, written in Groovy or Kotlin, allow for programmatic manipulation of the build process, providing more agility and allowing custom tasks creation with ease.

```
plugins {
    id 'org.springframework.boot' version '2.7.0'
    id 'io.spring.dependency-management' version '1.0.11.RELEASE'
    id 'java'
}

group = 'com.example'
version = '1.0-SNAPSHOT'
sourceCompatibility = '11'

repositories {
    mavenCentral()
}

dependencies {
    implementation 'org.springframework.boot:spring-boot-starter-web'
    testImplementation 'org.springframework.boot:spring-boot-starter-test'
}

test {
    useJUnitPlatform()
}
```

The flexibility inherent in Gradle scripts allows developers to define build logic that closely matches their project requirements and organizational standards. Gradle's incremental build capability ensures that tasks are executed only when inputs or outputs change, significantly speeding up the build process. The tool also enables parallel execution of tasks to optimize performance further.

Both Maven and Gradle support extensive community ecosystems with numerous plugins available for tasks such as code quality checks, testing, deployment, and documentation. Integrating these tools with Continuous Integration (CI) systems like Jenkins, GitLab CI, and others is seamless, ensuring that builds are automated and consistent across different environments.

Selecting between Maven and Gradle generally hinges on factors such as team familiarity, project requirements, and preferred build script verbosity and complexity. Maven's convention-over-configuration approach and XML-based configuration may appeal to teams favoring standardization and minimal custom scripting. Conversely, Gradle's build scripts offer high configurability and scripting capabilities that may be leveraged for more complex or dynamic build processes.

The subsequent sections will present step-by-step guides for incorporating Maven and Gradle into your Spring projects, ensuring that you can harness the full potential of these build tools efficiently.

2.5 Creating Your First Spring Project with Spring Initializr

To start developing applications with the Spring Framework, the Spring Initializr offers a streamlined and efficient method to generate a fully structured Spring project. This tool allows you to customize your project settings, select dependencies, and download a pre-configured template, thus enabling you to dive straight into coding with minimal setup.

Step 1: Accessing Spring Initializr

Spring Initializr can be accessed through its web interface at https://start.spring.io. The interface presents a straightforward form allowing developers to fill in the details required for their new project.

Step 2: Project Metadata

Begin by specifying the foundational project metadata:

- **Project**: Choose between **Maven** and **Gradle** for project build management. Maven is widely popular and recommended for developers who prefer declarative dependency management using XML. Gradle offers a more flexible and powerful approach using Groovy or Kotlin DSL.

- **Language**: Select **Java** as the programming language.

- **Spring Boot**: Choose an appropriate Spring Boot version. It is advisable to select the latest stable release to leverage the latest features and improvements.

- **Project Metadata**: Fill in the following fields:

  - **Group**: This usually corresponds to the organization or domain of the project, such as com.example.
  - **Artifact**: The name of the project, such as demo.
  - **Name**: This field will default to the Artifact name but can be adjusted if necessary.
  - **Description**: Provide a brief description of the application.
  - **Package name**: This field will deduce from the Group and Artifact fields but can be modified.
  - **Packaging**: Choose between jar or war. A JAR file is suitable for standalone applications, while a WAR file is typical for web deployments on an application server.
  - **Java**: Select the version of Java to use, ensuring compatibility with your development environment.

Step 3: Dependency Selection

Next, add the necessary dependencies that your project will use. Spring Initializr categorizes dependencies to make this process efficient:

- **Core**: Essential libraries like **Spring Boot DevTools** for development utilities.

- **Web**: Frameworks such as **Spring Web** and **Spring WebFlux** for building web applications and reactive systems.

- **Template Engines**: Include libraries like **Thymeleaf** for server-side rendering of HTML.

- **SQL**: Integrate with databases using **Spring Data JPA** and **MySQL Driver** or **H2 Database** for in-memory databases.
- **NoSQL**: Add support for NoSQL databases like **MongoDB**.
- **Cloud**: Dependencies for cloud-based applications, such as **Spring Cloud**.

Step 4: Generating and Downloading the Project

With the dependencies selected, click the "Generate" button. This action compiles all the provided information and produces a compressed ZIP file containing the project structure and code. Download and extract this ZIP file to your desired directory on your local machine.

Step 5: Exploring the Project Structure

The generated project incorporates a standard Maven or Gradle project structure. Navigate through the following directories and files to understand their purpose:

- **src/main/java**: Contains application source code.

```
com/
  example/
    demo/
      DemoApplication.java
```

- **src/main/resources**: Directory for configuration files and resources like application.properties.
- **src/test/java**: Holds test source code.

```
com/
  example/
    demo/
      DemoApplicationTests.java
```

- **pom.xml** (for Maven projects) or **build.gradle** (for Gradle projects): These files define project dependencies and build configurations.

Step 6: Importing the Project into an IDE

Open your chosen Integrated Development Environment (IDE) and follow these general steps to import the project:

- For **IntelliJ IDEA**:

- Navigate to File > New > Project from Existing Sources.
- Select the extracted project directory.
- IntelliJ will auto-detect the Maven or Gradle configuration and import the project accordingly.

- For **Eclipse**:
  - Navigate to File > Import.
  - Choose Maven > Existing Maven Projects or Gradle > Existing Gradle Project.
  - Select the project directory and follow the prompts to complete the import.

Finally, locate the DemoApplication.java file and run it as a Java application. Your Spring Boot application should start, and you will see the following output in the console:

```
  .   ____          _            __ _ _
 /\\ / ___'_ __ _ _(_)_ __  __ _ \ \ \ \
( ( )\___ | '_ | '_| | '_ \/ _` | \ \ \ \
 \\/  ___)| |_)| | | | | || (_| |  ) ) ) )
  '  |____| .__|_| |_|_| |_\__, | / / / /
 =========|_|==============|___/=/_/_/_/
 :: Spring Boot ::                (v2.5.4)

2023-10-10 10:00:00.000  INFO 123456 --- [           main] c.e.demo.DemoApplication            : Starting DemoApplication using Java 11
2023-10-10 10:00:00.500  INFO 123456 --- [           main] c.e.demo.DemoApplication            : Started DemoApplication in 1.5 seconds
```

This verifies a successful setup. The application is now ready for further development.

2.6 Importing and Configuring a Project in Your IDE

Once you have created your initial Spring project configuration using Spring Initializr, the next step is to import this project into your Integrated Development Environment (IDE). Properly configuring your IDE will facilitate a streamlined and efficient development workflow. In this section, we will go through the process of importing your Spring project into popular IDEs such as IntelliJ IDEA and Eclipse, and cover essential configurations step-by-step.

To begin, let's discuss the general process applicable to most IDEs:

- Open your IDE.
- Navigate to the option to import a project (this is often found under File > Import).

- Select the type of project you are importing (Maven, Gradle, etc.).
- Locate the project directory and complete the import wizard.

IntelliJ IDEA:

For IntelliJ IDEA, follow these detailed steps to import and configure your Spring project:

1. Open IntelliJ IDEA.
2. On the welcome screen, click on Import Project.
3. In the file chooser dialog, navigate to the directory where you have your Spring project (e.g., the directory created by Spring Initializr) and click OK.
4. In the next dialog, select Import project from external model and choose either Maven or Gradle, depending on your build tool.
5. Follow the prompts to complete the import process. Ensure that auto-import is enabled to automatically sync dependencies when you update your pom.xml or build.gradle file.

To configure your project in IntelliJ IDEA, you may need to adjust some settings to match your development requirements:

- Navigate to File > Project Structure and configure the SDK to use the correct JDK version.
- Under the Modules section, ensure your project dependencies are correctly set up.
- Open Run > Edit Configurations and create a new Spring Boot configuration for your main application class. Provide the necessary parameters such as application arguments, VM options, and working directory, to ensure your application runs with the correct settings.

Eclipse:

For Eclipse, use the following steps to import and configure your Spring project:

1. Open Eclipse.

2. Select File > Import.
3. In the import dialog, expand Maven or Gradle and select Existing Maven Projects or Existing Gradle Project respectively. Click Next.
4. Click Browse and navigate to the directory where your Spring project resides. Click Finish to complete the import process.

To configure the project within Eclipse:

- Right-click on your project in the Project Explorer and select Properties.
- Go to Java Build Path and ensure that the JDK configured matches the version required by your project.
- Under Run > Run Configurations, create a new Spring Boot configuration. Set the main class, application arguments, and VM arguments as required for your Spring application.

Configuring Build Tools:

Regardless of the IDE, you will need to configure your build tool for dependency management and project builds.

- For Maven, ensure your pom.xml file includes the necessary dependencies for your Spring Boot application. IntelliJ IDEA and Eclipse typically auto-import these configurations.
- For Gradle, verify that your build.gradle file has the correct plugin and dependency declarations. You may also customize the gradle.properties file for project-specific settings.
- It is good practice to periodically refresh or reimport the project to ensure that all dependencies and configurations are up to date.

Running and Debugging:

Both IntelliJ IDEA and Eclipse provide robust tools for running and debugging Spring applications:

- In IntelliJ IDEA, you can run your application by selecting the Spring Boot configuration and clicking the Run button. Debugging can be initiated similarly using the Debug button.

- In Eclipse, right-click on your main application class or configuration and select Run As > Spring Boot App or Debug As > Spring Boot App.

Example of running the application from the command line when applicable:

```
./mvnw spring-boot:run
```

This command will invoke the Spring Boot plugin in Maven to run your application. If using Gradle, the equivalent command would be:

```
./gradlew bootRun
```

Ensuring your IDE is properly configured simplifies the process of developing, running, and debugging your Spring applications. Human errors are reduced, and software development lifecycles are optimized through consistent and effective project configuration settings.

2.7 Managing Dependencies with Maven and Gradle

Managing dependencies is a critical aspect of Java development, especially when working with the Spring Framework. Dependencies are external libraries that your project requires to compile and run. Using dependency management tools like Maven and Gradle simplifies the process of handling these libraries. Let us delve into the specifics of managing dependencies with Maven and Gradle.

Maven and Gradle serve as build automation tools, but their role extends beyond merely compiling and packaging code. They are proficient in managing project dependencies, ensuring that all requisite libraries are available in the correct versions. This section elaborates on how to utilize these tools effectively.

1. Apache Maven

Apache Maven is a popular tool for project management and comprehension. Its primary function is to allow developers to manage a project's build, reporting, and documentation from a central piece of information. Here's a breakdown of how to manage dependencies in Maven.

pom.xml: The *Project Object Model* or pom.xml file is the heart of a Maven project. It contains project details including dependencies. To add a dependency, you include it in the <dependencies> section of pom.xml.

```
<project xmlns="http://maven.apache.org/POM/4.0.0"
    xmlns:xsi="http://www.w3.org/2001/XMLSchema-instance"
    xsi:schemaLocation="http://maven.apache.org/POM/4.0.0
                        http://maven.apache.org/maven-v4_0_0.xsd">
  <modelVersion>4.0.0</modelVersion>
  <groupId>com.example</groupId>
  <artifactId>my-spring-app</artifactId>
  <version>1.0-SNAPSHOT</version>
  <dependencies>
    <dependency>
      <groupId>org.springframework.boot</groupId>
      <artifactId>spring-boot-starter-web</artifactId>
      <version>2.5.4</version>
    </dependency>
    <!-- Other dependencies -->
  </dependencies>
</project>
```

The example above adds the spring-boot-starter-web dependency to your project. Maven will automatically download this dependency and any transitive dependencies it requires (those libraries that the spring-boot-starter-web depends on).

Maven's dependency resolution mechanism ensures that the correct versions of libraries are used and avoids conflicts by managing both direct and transitive dependencies. Furthermore, Maven repositories, such as Maven Central, host a vast array of libraries. If a dependency's version is omitted, Maven uses the version defined in the parent POM or defaults to the latest available version.

Dependency Scope: Maven provides several dependency scopes to control how dependencies are used and included:

- compile – Default scope, available in all classpaths.
- provided – Available only during compilation, not included in the final artifact.
- runtime – Not available during compilation, but included in runtime and test classpaths.
- test – Available only during testing.
- system – Similar to provided, but the JAR is explicitly included.
- import – Used with dependency management within a larger build.

compile is the default scope if none is specified.

2. Gradle

Gradle is another powerful build automation tool that offers a flexible build script written in Groovy or Kotlin. Like Maven, Gradle excels in simplifying dependency management.

build.gradle: Dependencies in Gradle are managed within the build.gradle script. The dependencies are declared inside the dependencies block.

```
plugins {
    id 'org.springframework.boot' version '2.5.4'
    id 'io.spring.dependency-management' version '1.0.11.RELEASE'
    id 'java'
}

group = 'com.example'
version = '1.0-SNAPSHOT'
sourceCompatibility = '11'

repositories {
    mavenCentral()
}

dependencies {
    implementation 'org.springframework.boot:spring-boot-starter-web'
    testImplementation 'org.springframework.boot:spring-boot-starter-test'
}

test {
    useJUnitPlatform()
}
```

In this example, the implementation configuration is used for the spring-boot-starter-web dependency, ensuring it is included in both compile and runtime classpaths. The testImplementation configuration is used for dependencies only required during testing.

Gradle Dependency Configurations:

- implementation – Dependency is added to both compile and runtime.
- compileOnly – Available during compilation, not included in runtime.
- runtimeOnly – Not available during compilation, included during runtime.
- testImplementation – Only included during testing phase.
- testCompileOnly – Available during test compilation only.

- testRuntimeOnly – Available during test runtime only.

Gradle's flexibility with its domain-specific language (DSL) allows for a more declarative way of managing dependencies. As with Maven, dependencies can be retrieved from repositories like Maven Central by declaring them in the repositories block.

Verifying and troubleshooting dependencies in Gradle is facilitated by tasks like dependencies for viewing the dependency tree and resolving conflicts.

Comparison between Maven and Gradle reveals that both provide robust dependency management capabilities, with Gradle often praised for its flexibility and performance due to its use of a dynamic DSL over Maven's XML configuration.

Effective dependency management ensures that your Spring application runs smoothly with all required libraries, resolving potential conflicts and maintaining compatibility across varying environments.

2.8 Running and Debugging Spring Applications

To effectively run and debug Spring applications, a comprehensive understanding of Spring Boot's execution mechanisms and the debugging tools provided by Integrated Development Environments (IDEs) is essential.

Spring Boot applications are typically packaged as JAR files and executed using an embedded server, such as Tomcat. This setup simplifies deployment by bundling all necessary dependencies and configurations into a single archive. To run a Spring Boot application, ensure that the Maven or Gradle build is up-to-date. Execute the build process with the following Maven command:

```
mvn clean install
```

Or for Gradle:

```
./gradlew build
```

Upon successfully building the project, execute the JAR file created in the target (for Maven) or build/libs (for Gradle) directory:

```
java -jar target/spring-boot-application.jar
```

Or in the case of Gradle:

```
java -jar build/libs/spring-boot-application.jar
```

Executing the command launches the embedded server, making the Spring application accessible at the defined port (default is 8080). Verify the application is running by accessing the root URL, for example, http://localhost:8080, using a web browser or a tool like cURL:

```
curl http://localhost:8080
```

Debugging Spring Boot applications involves understanding breakpoints, stepping through code, and inspecting variable states during execution. The two commonly used IDEs for debugging are IntelliJ IDEA and Eclipse. In IntelliJ IDEA, follow these steps:

- **Set Breakpoints**: Navigate to the desired line and click in the left margin or press Ctrl + F8.
- **Run in Debug Mode**: Click the bug icon in the toolbar or press Shift + F9 to start the application in debug mode.
- **Inspect Variables**: When execution pauses at the breakpoint, hover over variables to inspect their current state.
- **Step Through Code**: Use F8 to step over, F7 to step into functions, and Shift + F8 to step out.

In Eclipse, the procedure is similar:

- **Set Breakpoints**: Click on the left margin at the desired line or press Ctrl + Shift + B.
- **Launch Debug Configuration**: Right-click the project, select Debug As, followed by Spring Boot App.
- **Inspect and Modify Variables**: Use the Variables view to inspect values during a paused execution.
- **Control Execution Flow**: Utilize buttons in the debug toolbar for stepping over (F6), into (F5), and out (F7) of functions.

Effective debugging often involves analyzing the application's logs. Spring Boot uses SLF4J and Logback as the default logging framework allowing log levels configuration via the application.properties file:

```
logging.level.root=INFO
logging.level.com.example=DEBUG
logging.file.name=logs/myapp.log
```

These settings ensure log messages of interest are captured and persisted.

For remote debugging, configure the Spring Boot application to listen for debug connections by adding the following JVM options:

```
java -agentlib:jdwp=transport=dt_socket,server=y,suspend=n,address=*:5005 -jar
    target/spring-boot-application.jar
```

This configures the JVM to open a socket at port 5005 for remote debugging. Connect to it from the IDE's remote debug configuration, specifying the appropriate host and port.

Handling exceptions and utilizing unit tests is integral to debugging. Employing @ExceptionHandler annotations in Spring Controllers can manage exceptions:

```
@RestController
public class MyController {
    @GetMapping("/example")
    public String example() {
        // some code that may throw an exception
    }

    @ExceptionHandler(MyException.class)
    public ResponseEntity<String> handleMyException(MyException ex) {
        return ResponseEntity.status(HttpStatus.BAD_REQUEST).body(ex.getMessage
            ());
    }
}
```

Finally, unit testing with frameworks like JUnit and Mockito is pivotal. Annotate test classes with @ExtendWith(SpringExtension.class) and use @SpringBootTest for integration tests:

```
@SpringBootTest
public class MyServiceTests {

    @Autowired
    private MyService myService;

    @Test
    public void testServiceMethod() {
        // Arrange
        MyEntity entity = new MyEntity();
        // Act
        String result = myService.serviceMethod(entity);
        // Assert
        assertEquals("expectedResult", result);
    }
}
```

Effective application of running and debugging techniques enhances the development workflow, ensuring robust and well-tested Spring applications.

2.9 Version Control Systems: Git and GitHub Integration

Version control systems are integral to modern software development practices, enabling developers to track changes, collaborate on codebases, and maintain a history of project evolution. Git, an open-source distributed version control system, is among the most popular and widely used tools. GitHub, a hosting service for Git repositories, enhances Git's capabilities by providing a user-friendly web interface, collaboration features, and integration with various development tools.

To begin integrating Git into your development environment, initiate by installing Git. Visit the official Git website and download the appropriate installer for your operating system. After installation, verify your setup by opening a command line interface and executing the following commands:

```
git --version
```

Configuring Git with your user information is crucial to ensure that commits are correctly attributed. Substitute "Your Name" and "your.email@example.com" with your actual name and email address:

```
git config --global user.name "Your Name"
git config --global user.email "your.email@example.com"
```

With Git properly configured, you can now create a new repository. Navigate to your project's root directory and execute:

```
git init
```

This command initializes a new Git repository, creating a .git directory that contains all necessary metadata and version history. To track files, add them to the staging area and commit them to the repository:

```
git add .
git commit -m "Initial commit"
```

To leverage GitHub for remote repository hosting, create an account on their platform. Once logged in, create a new repository using the GitHub web interface. Provide a repository name, description, and select visibility (public or private).

After creating the repository, link it with your local repository. Copy the provided remote URL from GitHub and execute:

```
git remote add origin https://github.com/yourusername/your-repository.git
git push -u origin master
```

This command associates your local repository with the remote GitHub repository and pushes the initial commit. The -u option sets the remote repository (origin) and branch (master) as the default for subsequent pushes and pulls.

Collaboration often necessitates pulling changes from the remote repository. Use:

```
git pull origin master
```

This ensures your local repository is synchronized with the latest changes from the remote repository.

Branches provide an isolated environment for feature development. Create and switch to a new branch with:

```
git checkout -b feature-branch
```

After implementing and testing the feature, commit the changes and push the branch to GitHub:

```
git add .
git commit -m "Implement feature"
git push origin feature-branch
```

Using the GitHub web interface, initiate a pull request to merge the feature branch into the master branch. This process involves code review, automated testing, and approval steps to ensure code quality.

Conflicts may arise when multiple developers modify the same file. Git marks conflicting sections, allowing manual resolution. To address conflicts, edit the file to incorporate all necessary changes, then stage and commit the resolved file:

```
git add .
git commit -m "Resolve merge conflict"
```

Finally, integrate Git and GitHub into your IDE, such as IntelliJ IDEA or Eclipse, to streamline version control operations. Both IDEs offer robust Git integration, allowing you to perform version control tasks within the development environment's graphical interface.

IntelliJ IDEA users can use the VCS (Version Control Systems) menu to initialize, clone, and manage Git repositories. Eclipse users can install the Egit plugin for similar functionality. Both tools support viewing the version history, creating branches, managing stashes, and resolving conflicts.

[Successful Git operations provide clear indications of changes]

Chapter 3

Spring Core Concepts

This chapter explores the foundational architecture and essential components of the Spring Framework. It begins with an overview of Spring's architecture, followed by in-depth discussions on beans, their lifecycle, and scopes. The chapter explains the crucial concepts of application context and dependency injection, illustrating various configurations through XML and Java annotations. Topics such as Spring Profiles for environment-specific configurations, Spring Expression Language (SpEL), event handling, internationalization, and Aspect-Oriented Programming (AOP) are also covered, providing a comprehensive understanding of Spring's core functionalities.

3.1 Overview of Spring Architecture

The Spring Framework operates on a layered architecture composed of several well-defined modules, enabling developers to choose the components that best fit their needs. Spring's architecture is particularly designed to be non-invasive, providing the ability to build loosely coupled applications. A comprehensive understanding of Spring's architecture involves exploring its key modules, the core container, and the fundamental principles of Dependency Injection (DI) and Aspect-Oriented Programming (AOP).

The primary layers of Spring architecture are:

- **Core Container**
- **AOP Modules**
- **Data Access/Integration**
- **Web**
- **Other Modules**

The **Core Container** consists of the spring-core, spring-beans, spring-context, spring-context-support, and spring-expression modules. These modules form the foundation of the Spring Framework.

spring-core and spring-beans provide the fundamental parts of the framework, including the IoC (Inversion of Control) container. The IoC container is pivotal to Spring, facilitating Dependency Injection. The BeanFactory interface is a central component of the core container. It is responsible for instantiating, configuring, and assembling the objects, or "beans," in a Spring application. Here is an example in a simplified format demonstrating Bean instantiation:

```
ApplicationContext context = new ClassPathXmlApplicationContext("Beans.xml");
MyBean obj = (MyBean) context.getBean("myBean");
```

The spring-context module is built on top of the core and beans modules and is most commonly used by developers. It provides a framework for defining and accessing the various aspects of an application. It builds on the solid base provided by the core and beans modules and supports internationalization (I18N), event propagation, resource loading, and transparent creation of contexts by, for example, JavaServer Pages (JSP).

spring-context-support provides support for integrating common third-party libraries into the Spring context. Examples include caching support (EhCache, JCache), mail (JavaMail), and scheduling (Quartz, Timer).

spring-expression enables powerful querying and manipulation of an object graph at runtime, which is what the Spring Expression Language (SpEL) is built upon.

Aspect-Oriented Programming (AOP) is modularized via AspectJ in Spring. Contributions from the **AOP modules** provide sophisticated program partitioning, enabling the segregation of cross-cutting concerns from business logic. This modularization facilitates maintaining a clean, readable codebase. A typical example of AOP usage in Spring might comprise defining an aspect to log method execution times:

```
@Aspect
public class LoggingAspect {
    @Around("execution(* com.example.service.*.*(..))")
    public Object logExecutionTime(ProceedingJoinPoint joinPoint) throws Throwable
        {
        long start = System.currentTimeMillis();
        Object proceed = joinPoint.proceed();
        long executionTime = System.currentTimeMillis() - start;
        System.out.println(joinPoint.getSignature() + " executed in " + executionTime
             + "ms");
        return proceed;
    }
}
```

When exploring **Data Access/Integration**, Spring provides diverse capabilities via ORM (Object Relational Mapping), OXM (Object XML Mapping), JMS (Java Messaging Service), and Transaction Management modules. spring-jdbc and spring-tx packages stand pivotal in data access, providing integration with JDBC and managing transactions declaratively.

The **Web** layer of Spring architecture includes Spring MVC (Model-View-Controller), which hosts modules such as spring-webmvc, enabling web application development with robust model-binding and expansive view resolution capabilities. Furthermore, the spring-websocket module facilitates WebSocket-based, full-duplex communication between the client and server.

Additionally, Spring encompasses a multitude of **Other Modules** such as Spring Batch, Spring Security, Spring Integration, and Spring Cloud. These modules extend Spring's capabilities to batch processing, application security management, and cloud-native application development.

Spring's overarching architecture, built on POJOs (Plain Old Java Objects), fosters modularization by handling cross-cutting concerns through AOP and promoting robust application configurations with Dependency Injection. Utilizing XML and Java annotations, this architecture empowers developers to create scalable, maintainable applications efficiently, equipped with a comprehensive set of tools for data access, transaction management, and web framework integration.

3.2 Understanding Beans in Spring

In the Spring Framework, a bean is a key concept that represents an object whose lifecycle and dependencies are managed by the Spring IoC (Inversion of Control) container. Beans are the backbone of a Spring-based application and are defined in the Spring context configuration files or annotated within the source code. Understanding beans is essential for leveraging the full capabilities of Spring, as they encapsulate the application's data and business logic.

Defining Beans

Beans can be defined in multiple ways in Spring, including XML configuration, Java-based configuration, and component-scanning using annotations.

XML Configuration

In XML-based configuration, beans are declared within the <beans> element in an XML configuration file. Below is an example of defining a bean in XML:

```
<bean id="exampleBean" class="com.example.ExampleBean">
    <property name="property1" value="value1" />
    <property name="property2" value="value2" />
</bean>
```

In this example, the <bean> element defines a bean with an ID of exampleBean and a class of com.example.ExampleBean. The <property> elements set the properties of the bean.

Java-based Configuration

Alternatively, beans can be defined using Java-based configuration with the @Configuration and @Bean annotations. Here is an example:

```
@Configuration
public class AppConfig {

    @Bean
    public ExampleBean exampleBean() {
        ExampleBean exampleBean = new ExampleBean();
        exampleBean.setProperty1("value1");
        exampleBean.setProperty2("value2");
        return exampleBean;
    }
}
```

In this configuration style, a Java class annotated with @Configuration acts as a source of bean definitions. The @Bean annotated methods return an instance of the bean.

Component-Scanning and Annotations

Spring also supports component-scanning to automatically detect and register beans via annotations such as @Component, @Service, @Repository, and @Controller:

```
@Component
public class ExampleBean {
    private String property1;
    private String property2;

    // Getters and Setters for properties
}
```

For component-scanning to work, the configuration must include the @ComponentScan annotation:

```
@Configuration
@ComponentScan(basePackages = "com.example")
public class AppConfig {
    // Configuration details
}
```

This instructs Spring to scan the specified package and its sub-packages for classes annotated with stereotypes like @Component, @Service, etc., which then are registered as beans.

Bean Properties

Beans have properties that can be set either via XML configuration or Java-based configuration. These properties define the data the bean holds or references to other beans it depends on. Properties can be set using setter methods or through constructor arguments.

Setter-based configuration in XML:

```
<bean id="exampleBean" class="com.example.ExampleBean">
    <property name="property1" value="value1" />
    <property name="property2" value="value2" />
</bean>
```

Constructor-arg-based configuration in XML:

```
<bean id="exampleBean" class="com.example.ExampleBean">
    <constructor-arg value="value1" />
    <constructor-arg value="value2" />
</bean>
```

Using Java-based configuration, setter-based configuration is implemented inside the @Bean method:

```
@Bean
```

```
public ExampleBean exampleBean() {
    ExampleBean exampleBean = new ExampleBean();
    exampleBean.setProperty1("value1");
    exampleBean.setProperty2("value2");
    return exampleBean;
}
```

Constructor-based configuration:

```
@Bean
public ExampleBean exampleBean() {
    return new ExampleBean("value1", "value2");
}
```

Bean Scope

The scope of a bean defines the lifecycle and visibility of that bean within the container. Spring supports several bean scopes:

- **Singleton** (default): A single instance of the bean is created, shared across the entire context.
- **Prototype**: A new instance of the bean is created every time it is requested.
- **Request**: A single instance of the bean is created and available during a single HTTP request.
- **Session**: A single instance of the bean is created and available during an HTTP session.
- **Global Session**: A single instance of the bean is created for a global HTTP session; typically applicable in portlet applications.
- **Application**: A bean instance is available for the lifecycle of a web application, similar to singleton but specific to web applications.

Bean scope can be set in XML configuration:

```
<bean id="exampleBean" class="com.example.ExampleBean" scope="prototype">
    <!-- Bean details -->
</bean>
```

Or using annotations with Java-based configuration:

```
@Bean
@Scope(value = ConfigurableBeanFactory.SCOPE_PROTOTYPE)
public ExampleBean exampleBean() {
    return new ExampleBean();
}
```

Bean Lifecycle

The lifecycle of a Spring bean consists of several phases, managed by the container. These phases include instantiation, property population, initialization, and destruction. Beans can implement lifecycle interfaces or use annotations to perform actions during these phases.

To perform actions upon initialization and destruction, beans can implement the InitializingBean and DisposableBean interfaces:

```
public class ExampleBean implements InitializingBean, DisposableBean {

    @Override
    public void afterPropertiesSet() throws Exception {
        // Code to execute after properties are set
    }

    @Override
    public void destroy() throws Exception {
        // Code to execute before bean destruction
    }
}
```

Alternatively, Java-based configuration can use annotations @PostConstruct and @PreDestroy:

```
public class ExampleBean {

    @PostConstruct
    public void init() {
        // Initialization code
    }

    @PreDestroy
    public void cleanup() {
        // Cleanup code
    }
}
```

XML-based configuration for initializing and destruction methods:

```
<bean id="exampleBean" class="com.example.ExampleBean"
      init-method="init" destroy-method="cleanup">
    <!-- Bean details -->
</bean>
```

In these configurations, init and cleanup are methods defined in the ExampleBean class.

Understanding these fundamental elements of Spring beans and their configurations will enable you to effectively utilize the Spring IoC container for building robust and maintainable applications.

3.3 Bean Lifecycle and Scopes

Understanding the lifecycle and scopes of beans in the Spring Framework is crucial for effectively managing lifecycle management and broadening the ability to implement sophisticated application functionality.

In the Spring Framework, a bean's lifecycle starts when the container is instantiated and ends when the container is destroyed. The lifecycle is controlled by the Spring IoC container and can be altered using various callback methods. The lifecycle comprises multiple phases: instantiation, dependency injection, initialization, and destruction.

Instantiation: This phase begins with the IoC container creating an instance of the bean. During this phase, the container analyzes the bean's configuration metadata to determine how to instantiate the bean. Beans can be instantiated through a no-argument constructor, a static factory method, or an instance factory method as defined in the bean definitions.

```
// No-argument Constructor Instantiation
public class MyBean {
    public MyBean() {
        // constructor code
    }
}

// Static Factory Method Instantiation
public class MyFactory {
    public static MyBean createBean() {
        return new MyBean();
    }
}

// Instance Factory Method Instantiation
public class MyFactory {
    public MyBean createBean() {
        return new MyBean();
    }
}
```

Dependency Injection: Once the bean is instantiated, the container proceeds to populate all necessary properties as specified in the bean definition. Dependency Injection (DI) can be performed via setter injection, constructor injection, or field injection (using annotations).

```
// Setter Injection
public class MyBean {
    private DependencyBean dependency;

    public void setDependency(DependencyBean dependency) {
        this.dependency = dependency;
```

```
    }
}

// Constructor Injection
public class MyBean {
    private final DependencyBean dependency;

    public MyBean(DependencyBean dependency) {
        this.dependency = dependency;
    }
}

// Field Injection (using @Autowired annotation)
public class MyBean {
    @Autowired
    private DependencyBean dependency;
}
```

Initialization: After dependency injection, the Spring container calls the bean's initialization callbacks. These can be custom initialization methods defined by the developer or initializations provided by interfaces such as InitializingBean and @PostConstruct annotations.

```
// Using InitializingBean Interface
public class MyBean implements InitializingBean {

    @Override
    public void afterPropertiesSet() throws Exception {
        // custom initialization code
    }
}

// Using @PostConstruct Annotation
public class MyBean {
    @PostConstruct
    public void init() {
        // custom initialization code
    }
}
```

The method afterPropertiesSet from InitializingBean and methods annotated with @PostConstruct are invoked after the bean properties have been set, allowing the bean to perform any necessary initialization work.

Destruction: The Spring container is responsible for destroying all beans when the application is shut down. This involves calling custom destroy methods defined by the developer or those provided by interfaces such as DisposableBean and @PreDestroy annotations.

```
// Using DisposableBean Interface
public class MyBean implements DisposableBean {

    @Override
    public void destroy() throws Exception {
        // custom cleanup code
    }
}
```

```
// Using @PreDestroy Annotation
public class MyBean {
    @PreDestroy
    public void cleanup() {
        // custom cleanup code
    }
}
```

The method destroy from DisposableBean and methods annotated with @PreDestroy are invoked during the bean's destruction phase, enabling the bean to perform any necessary cleanup tasks.

Scopes of Beans: Bean scopes define the lifecycle and visibility range of the bean instances. The Spring Framework supports several scopes, of which the most commonly used are singleton and prototype.

Singleton: The singleton scope ensures that there is a single instance of the bean per Spring IoC container. This is the default scope in Spring. Consequently, all requests for the bean will return the same instance.

```
// XML Configuration for Singleton Scope
<bean id="myBean" class="com.example.MyBean" scope="singleton" />
```

```
// Java Configuration for Singleton Scope
@Bean
@Scope("singleton")
public MyBean myBean() {
    return new MyBean();
}
```

Prototype: The prototype scope creates a new instance of the bean every time a request is made. Beans with prototype scope do not undergo destruction phase callbacks by the container, as the container does not manage their complete lifecycle.

```
// XML Configuration for Prototype Scope
<bean id="myBean" class="com.example.MyBean" scope="prototype" />
```

```
// Java Configuration for Prototype Scope
@Bean
@Scope("prototype")
public MyBean myBean() {
    return new MyBean();
}
```

Besides these, there are additional scopes such as request, session, and application, primarily utilized in web-aware Spring Application contexts. These scopes handle beans differently based on the lifecycle of web-based applications or sessions.

Understanding and correctly implementing the lifecycle and scope of

Spring beans lays the foundation for efficient resource management and effective design of scalable applications.

3.4 Application Context and Dependency Injection

The **Application Context** in Spring Framework is a central interface to provide configuration information to the application. It initializes various beans configured in the Spring container and manages their entire lifecycle. Think of it as a more robust extension of the **BeanFactory** interface, further enhanced with several enterprise-specific features such as event propagation, declarative mechanisms to create beans, and specific scopes. The ApplicationContext allows for a generic way to load configuration metadata, either as XML, Java annotations, or Java code.

A fundamental aspect of the Spring Framework is dependency injection (DI). DI is a design pattern that allows object dependencies to be injected at runtime, rather than at compile time. This leads to a more flexible and maintainable code architecture.

Application Context

To understand the ApplicationContext better, consider the following constructor-based dependency injection example:

```
public class TextEditor {
    private SpellChecker spellChecker;

    public TextEditor(SpellChecker spellChecker) {
        this.spellChecker = spellChecker;
    }

    public void spellCheck() {
        spellChecker.checkSpelling();
    }
}
```

Here, TextEditor depends on SpellChecker. Using Spring, we can describe these bean definitions and their dependencies in an XML configuration file:

```
<beans xmlns="http://www.springframework.org/schema/beans"
       xmlns:xsi="http://www.w3.org/2001/XMLSchema-instance"
       xsi:schemaLocation="http://www.springframework.org/schema/beans
       http://www.springframework.org/schema/beans/spring-beans.xsd">

    <bean id="spellChecker" class="com.example.SpellChecker">
```

```
    </bean>

    <bean id="textEditor" class="com.example.TextEditor">
        <constructor-arg ref="spellChecker"/>
    </bean>
</beans>
```

To load this configuration file into the Spring container and retrieve the configured beans, one would employ the ClassPathXmlApplicationContext:

```
ApplicationContext context = new ClassPathXmlApplicationContext("Beans.xml");
TextEditor te = (TextEditor) context.getBean("textEditor");
te.spellCheck();
```

Dependency Injection

Constructor-Based Injection is the showcased form in the above example. Another common pattern is **Setter-Based Injection**, where dependencies are provided through setter methods rather than constructors. Here's how TextEditor can be refactored for setter-based injection:

```
public class TextEditor {
    private SpellChecker spellChecker;

    // a setter method to inject the dependency.
    public void setSpellChecker(SpellChecker spellChecker) {
        this.spellChecker = spellChecker;
    }

    public void spellCheck() {
        spellChecker.checkSpelling();
    }
}
```

In the XML configuration file, the bean definition would be updated accordingly:

```
<bean id="textEditor" class="com.example.TextEditor">
    <property name="spellChecker" ref="spellChecker"/>
</bean>
```

For **Field-Based Injection**, Spring provides a more concise mechanism using Java annotations. Leveraging the @Autowired annotation:

```
public class TextEditor {

    @Autowired
    private SpellChecker spellChecker;

    public void spellCheck() {
        spellChecker.checkSpelling();
    }
}
```

Enable annotation in the Spring configuration file by including <context:annotation-config/>:

```
<beans xmlns="http://www.springframework.org/schema/beans"
      xmlns:xsi="http://www.w3.org/2001/XMLSchema-instance"
      xmlns:context="http://www.springframework.org/schema/context"
      xsi:schemaLocation="http://www.springframework.org/schema/beans
      http://www.springframework.org/schema/beans/spring-beans.xsd
      http://www.springframework.org/schema/context
      http://www.springframework.org/schema/context/spring-context.xsd">

   <context:annotation-config/>

   <bean id="spellChecker" class="com.example.SpellChecker"/>
   <bean id="textEditor" class="com.example.TextEditor"/>
</beans>
```

Regardless of the form, the Application Context manages bean dependencies by injecting required fields, methods, or constructors seamlessly as part of the bean initialization process.

Annotations

In modern Spring applications, annotations offer a more straightforward configuration approach compared to XML. For example, the @Component annotation can designate a class as a Spring component:

```
@Component
public class SpellChecker {
   public void checkSpelling() {
      System.out.println("Checking spelling...");
   }
}
```

The TextEditor class can be similarly annotated:

```
@Component
public class TextEditor {

   @Autowired
   private SpellChecker spellChecker;

   public void spellCheck() {
      spellChecker.checkSpelling();
   }
}
```

The XML configuration then only needs to include a component scan to detect these annotated classes:

```
<beans xmlns="http://www.springframework.org/schema/beans"
      xmlns:xsi="http://www.w3.org/2001/XMLSchema-instance"
      xmlns:context="http://www.springframework.org/schema/context"
      xsi:schemaLocation="http://www.springframework.org/schema/beans
```

```
        http://www.springframework.org/schema/beans/spring-beans.xsd
        http://www.springframework.org/schema/context
        http://www.springframework.org/schema/context/spring-context.xsd">

    <context:component-scan base-package="com.example"/>
</beans>
```

This approach enhances maintainability and reduces XML boilerplate, allowing more elegant and concise configuration. The advantages of leveraging ApplicationContext along with various forms of dependency injection cannot be overstated in the facet of constructing a decoupled, modular, and testable application architecture.

3.5 Spring Configuration: XML vs Java Annotations

Spring configuration can be achieved primarily through two approaches: XML-based configuration and Java-based annotations. Both have their distinct advantages and use cases, and understanding their differences and applications is crucial for effectively leveraging the Spring Framework for enterprise-level development.

XML configuration is the traditional method of defining the Spring beans and their dependencies. This approach entails writing detailed XML files where beans, their properties, and their lifecycle methods are explicitly defined. XML-based configuration is well-suited for large projects where configuration might need to be separated and managed independently from the source code. An example XML configuration file, applicationContext.xml, is illustrated below:

```
<beans xmlns="http://www.springframework.org/schema/beans"
       xmlns:xsi="http://www.w3.org/2001/XMLSchema-instance"
       xsi:schemaLocation="http://www.springframework.org/schema/beans
           http://www.springframework.org/schema/beans/spring-beans.xsd">

    <bean id="exampleBean" class="com.example.ExampleBean">
        <property name="propertyName" value="propertyValue"/>
    </bean>

</beans>
```

In this file, the beans element is the root element which contains all bean definitions. Each bean element specifies a bean id, its fully qualified class name, and any properties that need to be set upon bean initialization.

Java-based annotations, introduced in Spring 2.5, provide a more concise and type-safe method of configuration by using Java's annotation mechanism. This method integrates configuration directly into the source code, making the application more cohesive and easier to navigate. To use annotations, you typically enable component scanning in your configuration class as shown below:

```
@Configuration
@ComponentScan(basePackages = "com.example")
public class AppConfig {
    @Bean
    public ExampleBean exampleBean() {
        return new ExampleBean();
    }
}
```

Here, the @Configuration annotation marks the class as a source of bean definitions, and @ComponentScan directs Spring to look for other components, configurations, and services in the specified package. Additionally, @Bean annotated methods within @Configuration classes define bean instances.

One significant difference between XML and Java-based annotation is the rigor of type safety. Annotations benefit from Java's compile-time type checks, reducing the risk of errors compared to XML. For example:

```
@Autowired
private ExampleBean exampleBean;
```

In this code, the @Autowired annotation injects the ExampleBean dependency, leveraging Spring's dependency injection. This annotation-based injection is flexible, allowing for constructor, field, and setter injection, enhancing readability and maintainability.

XML configuration proves beneficial in cases where configurations need to be externalized away from application code, easily modified without recompiling the Java classes. This can be particularly useful in environments where system administrators who may not be well-versed in Java manage the deployment and configuration.

Annotation-based configuration, on the other hand, co-locates the configuration within the code, which can improve cohesiveness and readability. However, it can potentially lead to harder-to-maintain codebases as the configuration complexity increases.

Spring 3.0 introduced JavaConfig, a type-safe and powerful configuration mechanism using Java classes. This approach can be seen as a blend of the simplicity and conciseness of annotations with the flexibility of XML configuration. Below is an example of JavaConfig:

```
@Configuration
public class JavaConfig {
    @Bean
    public ExampleBean exampleBean() {
        return new ExampleBean("propertyValue");
    }
}
```

Here, JavaConfig allows the definition of beans in a more structured manner with all the benefits of type safety and ease of configuration. It also provides the flexibility of invoking Java methods and customizing configuration logic through Java's programming capabilities.

Spring's flexibility allows mixing both XML-based and annotation-based configuration. This hybrid approach can leverage the strengths of both methods while mitigating their individual weaknesses. For example, you can define core infrastructure components in XML and annotate domain-specific configurations within Java classes.

In practice, the choice between XML, annotations, or hybrid approaches often depends on project-specific requirements, team expertise, maintenance considerations, and deployment environments. Java-based annotation and JavaConfig are generally preferred for new projects due to their modern and more straightforward approach, while XML configuration is still relevant for legacy systems and projects requiring extensive, separate configuration files.

3.6 Spring Profiles for Environment-Specific Configurations

Spring Profiles provide a flexible mechanism to segregate parts of an application configuration and make it only available in certain environments. This capability is instrumental in managing different environments, such as development, testing, and production, where each environment might require different configurations.

Profile Annotation: The primary annotation to denote a Spring Profile is @Profile. By attaching this annotation to any component or configuration class, you can specify conditions under which that particular component or configuration should be active. For example:

```
@Configuration
@Profile("development")
public class DevelopmentConfig {
```

```
    // Development-specific beans go here
}
@Configuration
@Profile("production")
public class ProductionConfig {
    // Production-specific beans go here
}
```

In this code snippet, DevelopmentConfig and ProductionConfig are two configuration classes that will only be loaded if their respective profiles are active.

Activating Profiles: Profiles can be activated declaratively using property files or programmatically. To activate a profile using a properties file, you can set the spring.profiles.active property in your application.properties file:

```
spring.profiles.active=development
```

Or, if you're using YAML:

```
spring:
  profiles:
    active: development
```

Programmatic Activation: Profiles can also be activated programmatically before the application context is refreshed. This is typically done in the main method of a Spring Boot application:

```
public static void main(String[] args) {
    SpringApplication app = new SpringApplication(MySpringBootApplication.class);
    app.setAdditionalProfiles("development");
    app.run(args);
}
```

Profile-Specific Properties Files: Another way to manage environment-specific configurations is through profile-specific properties files. For example, you can create separate application-development.properties and application-production.properties files in the src/main/resources directory. Spring will load these files based on the active profile.

Bean Definitions: Profiles can also be used to conditionally register beans. This is particularly useful when you have beans that are only required under certain conditions:

```
@Bean
@Profile("development")
public DataSource h2DataSource() {
    return new EmbeddedDatabaseBuilder()
            .setType(EmbeddedDatabaseType.H2)
            .build();
```

```
}

@Bean
@Profile("production")
public DataSource productionDataSource() {
    return new DriverManagerDataSource("jdbc:mysql://prod_db_url");
}
```

In this example, h2DataSource is only available when the development profile is active, and productionDataSource is only available under the production profile.

@Profile with @Component: Besides configuration classes and beans, the Profile annotation can also be applied to @Component classes:

```
@Component
@Profile("development")
public class DevelopmentBean {
    // Development-specific implementation
}

@Component
@Profile("production")
public class ProductionBean {
    // Production-specific implementation
}
```

To ensure clarity and structure in a large application, always remember to group the profile-specific configurations together logically, both in terms of files and their logical functionality. Through these mechanisms, Spring Profiles provide a powerful way to manage different environments smoothly, ensuring that the right configurations and beans are available in each respective environment.

3.7 Spring Expression Language (SpEL)

The Spring Expression Language (SpEL) is a powerful expression language that supports querying and manipulating an object graph at runtime. It is an important feature of the Spring Framework, providing a rich syntax for querying properties, calling methods, and accessing collections in Spring-managed beans. SpEL is used extensively within Spring, primarily in configuration metadata to provide dynamic behavior.

SpEL expressions are typically embedded in the configuration and can be used with both XML and annotation-based configurations. The following section elucidates the syntax and usage of SpEL through various examples and details its integration with the Spring Framework.

Basic Syntax and Operators:

SpEL supports a wide range of operators and expressions. The syntax of SpEL is similar to many programming languages, making it intuitive for most developers. Basic operators include:

- **Arithmetic Operators**: +, -, *, /, %
- **Relational Operators**: ==, !=, <, <=, >, >=
- **Logical Operators**: &&, ||, !
- **Conditional Operators**: ? : (ternary operator)

Accessing Properties and Methods:

Properties and methods of Spring beans can be accessed easily using SpEL. Consider the following simple Java bean:

```
public class Person {
    private String name;
    private int age;

    public String getName() {
        return name;
    }

    public void setName(String name) {
        this.name = name;
    }

    public int getAge() {
        return age;
    }

    public void setAge(int age) {
        this.age = age;
    }
}
```

In an XML configuration, SpEL can be used to set properties dynamically:

```
<bean id="person" class="com.example.Person">
    <property name="name" value="John Doe"/>
    <property name="age" value="#{20 + 5}"/>
</bean>
```

In the above example, the age property is set using an arithmetic expression evaluated by SpEL.

Calling Methods:

SpEL also allows for calling methods on beans:

```
<bean id="person" class="com.example.Person">
    <property name="name" value="John Doe"/>
    <property name="age" value="#{T(java.lang.Math).random() * 100}"/>
</bean>
```

Here, the Math.random() static method is called to provide a random age value.

Working with Collections:

SpEL facilitates working with collections such as lists, maps, and sets. Consider a bean containing a list:

```
public class Classroom {
    private List<Person> students;

    public List<Person> getStudents() {
        return students;
    }

    public void setStudents(List<Person> students) {
        this.students = students;
    }
}
```

Using SpEL, you can access and manipulate collections:

```
<bean id="classroom" class="com.example.Classroom">
    <property name="students">
        <list>
            <value>#{new com.example.Person('John', 23)}</value>
            <value>#{new com.example.Person('Jane', 22)}</value>
        </list>
    </property>
</bean>
```

To filter a list, SpEL provides selection and projection features:

```
<bean id="selectedStudents" class="java.util.ArrayList">
    <constructor-arg>
        <list>
            <value>#{classroom.students.?[age > 22]}</value>
        </list>
    </constructor-arg>
</bean>
```

In this example, classroom.students....?[age > 22] uses SpEL to filter students over the age of 22.

String Manipulation:

SpEL offers various methods for string manipulation:

```
<bean id="person" class="com.example.Person">
    <property name="name" value="#{'John Doe'.toUpperCase()}"/>
</bean>
```

Here, 'John Doe'.toUpperCase() converts the string to uppercase.

Mathematical and Logical Operations:

Complex mathematical and logical operations can be performed using SpEL's extensive operator support:

```
public class MathBean {
    private double result;

    public double getResult() {
        return result;
    }

    public void setResult(double result) {
        this.result = result;
    }
}
```

```
<bean id="mathBean" class="com.example.MathBean">
    <property name="result" value="#{T(java.lang.Math).pow(2, 3)}"/>
</bean>
```

Here, T(java.lang.Math).pow(2, 3) calculates 2^3 (i.e., 8.0) and sets it as the result.

Integration with Spring Beans:

Spring's @Value annotation allows for seamless integration of SpEL expressions within Spring beans. Example:

```
@Component
public class AppConfig {
    @Value("#{systemProperties['java.version']}")
    private String javaVersion;

    // Getter and setter
    public String getJavaVersion() {
        return javaVersion;
    }

    public void setJavaVersion(String javaVersion) {
        this.javaVersion = javaVersion;
    }
}
```

This configuration injects the Java system property for the Java version into the javaVersion field.

Conditional Evaluation:

SpEL provides support for conditional expressions using the ternary operator:

```
<bean id="sampleBean" class="com.example.SampleBean">
    <property name="status" value="#{systemProperties['os.name'] == 'Linux' ? '
        Running on Linux' : 'Not Running on Linux'}"/>
```

```
</bean>
```

This expression evaluates the operating system name and sets the status property accordingly.

Each of these examples demonstrates the utility and versatility of SpEL within the Spring Framework. Proper comprehension and application of SpEL can significantly enhance the flexibility and functionality of Spring-based applications.

3.8 Event Handling in Spring

Event handling in Spring is a powerful mechanism that facilitates communication between beans, providing a means for decoupled components to interact by sending and receiving event notifications. This mechanism is particularly useful in large, complex applications where loose coupling is desirable to enhance modularity, reusability, and maintainability. Spring's event handling capabilities are built on the observer design pattern and enable asynchronous processing of events.

In Spring, there are three primary components involved in the event handling mechanism: **events**, **event publishers**, and **event listeners**. The following sections will cover each of these components in detail and provide practical examples.

A **Spring event** is a subclass of ApplicationEvent. An ApplicationEvent is a platform-specific event that extends from the java.util.EventObject class. Any custom event created by the developer should extend from ApplicationEvent.

Here is an example of a custom event:

```
public class CustomSpringEvent extends ApplicationEvent {

    private String message;

    public CustomSpringEvent(Object source, String message) {
        super(source);
        this.message = message;
    }

    public String getMessage() {
        return message;
    }
}
```

Event publishers are responsible for publishing events. The ApplicationEventPublisher interface provides a method to publish an event to all interested listeners. A typical class implementing event publication would look like this:

```
@Component
public class CustomSpringEventPublisher {

    @Autowired
    private ApplicationEventPublisher applicationEventPublisher;

    public void publishCustomEvent(String message) {
        CustomSpringEvent customSpringEvent = new CustomSpringEvent(this,
              message);
        applicationEventPublisher.publishEvent(customSpringEvent);
    }
}
```

In this example, CustomSpringEventPublisher is a Spring-managed component (denoted by @Component) that uses ApplicationEventPublisher to publish the CustomSpringEvent.

The final component of Spring's event handling is the **event listener**. An event listener is a method annotated with @EventListener that processes the event.

Here is an example of an event listener:

```
@Component
public class CustomSpringEventListener {

    @EventListener
    public void handleCustomSpringEvent(CustomSpringEvent event) {
        System.out.println("Received spring custom event - " + event.getMessage());
    }
}
```

In this example, the handleCustomSpringEvent method is annotated with @EventListener, indicating that it listens for CustomSpringEvent instances. When an event is published, Spring catches the event and invokes the appropriate listener methods.

- **Synchronous vs Asynchronous Event Listeners**

  By default, event listeners in Spring are invoked synchronously. This means that the thread that publishes the event is the same thread that handles the event. While this approach ensures that events are handled immediately, it can introduce delays and affect performance if the event handling logic is time-consuming.

  To make an event listener asynchronous, the event handler method needs to be annotated with @Async, and the application needs to enable asynchronous support by annotating a configuration class with @EnableAsync.

Here is an example of an asynchronous event listener:

```
@Async
@EventListener
public void handleCustomSpringEventAsync(CustomSpringEvent event) {
    System.out.println("Received spring custom event asynchronously - " +
          event.getMessage());
}
```

Additionally, ensure that asynchronous processing is enabled in the configuration as follows:

```
@Configuration
@EnableAsync
public class AsyncConfig {
}
```

By marking the event listener method with @Async, Spring will handle the event asynchronously, allowing the publisher thread to continue its execution without waiting for the event handling to complete.

- **Event Prioritization**

  In scenarios where multiple listeners are interested in the same event, it may be necessary to prioritize the order in which listeners are invoked. This is accomplished using the @Order annotation.

  Here is an example of prioritizing event listeners:

```
@Component
public class FirstEventListener {

    @Order(1)
    @EventListener
    public void handleFirstEvent(CustomSpringEvent event) {
        System.out.println("First listener received event - " + event.
              getMessage());
    }
}

@Component
public class SecondEventListener {

    @Order(2)
    @EventListener
    public void handleSecondEvent(CustomSpringEvent event) {
        System.out.println("Second listener received event - " + event.
              getMessage());
    }
}
```

  In this example, the FirstEventListener is assigned a higher priority (lower order value) than the SecondEventListener. As a result, the FirstEventListener will handle the event before the SecondEventListener.

Spring's event handling capabilities offer a robust and flexible approach for facilitating loosely coupled components within an application. Through synchronous and asynchronous processing, custom event types, and listener prioritization, developers can design sophisticated event-driven architectures tailored to their specific needs.

3.9 Internationalization in Spring

Internationalization (i18n) is the process of designing an application so that it can be adapted to various languages and regions without requiring engineering changes. Spring Framework offers robust support for internationalization, allowing developers to effortlessly expose their applications to a global audience. This section delves into the key elements of implementing internationalization in Spring, including message sources, locale resolution, and using resource bundles.

Message Sources

In Spring, message sources are used to resolve messages for different locales. A message source is essentially a repository of messages where each message is identified by a unique key. The most common implementation is the ResourceBundleMessageSource, which retrieves messages from properties files. Below is an example configuration for a ResourceBundleMessageSource in a Spring application context:

```
@Configuration
public class AppConfig {

    @Bean
    public ResourceBundleMessageSource messageSource() {
        ResourceBundleMessageSource messageSource = new
                ResourceBundleMessageSource();
        messageSource.setBasename("messages");
        messageSource.setDefaultEncoding("UTF-8");
        return messageSource;
    }
}
```

With the above configuration, the message source will look for property files named messages_en.properties, messages_fr.properties, etc., depending on the locale.

Locale-Specific Properties Files

Locales in Spring are typically defined using properties files. Each file corresponds to a specific language and region, identified using a combination of the language code and an optional country code. For instance, here are two sample properties files for English and French:

messages_en.properties:

```
greeting=Hello
farewell=Goodbye
```

messages_fr.properties:

```
greeting=Bonjour
farewell=Au revoir
```

When the application is running, Spring automatically selects the appropriate resource bundle based on the current locale.

Locale Resolution

Locale resolution is the process of determining which locale to use for a given request. Spring provides several strategies for locale resolution, encapsulated in the LocaleResolver interface. Common implementations include:

- AcceptHeaderLocaleResolver: Uses the Accept-Language header from the HTTP request.
- SessionLocaleResolver: Stores the locale in the user's session.
- CookieLocaleResolver: Stores the locale in a cookie.

An example of configuring the LocaleResolver in a Spring application context is shown below:

```
@Configuration
public class WebConfig implements WebMvcConfigurer {

    @Bean
    public LocaleResolver localeResolver() {
        CookieLocaleResolver cookieLocaleResolver = new CookieLocaleResolver();
        cookieLocaleResolver.setDefaultLocale(Locale.US);
        return cookieLocaleResolver;
    }

    @Bean
    public LocaleChangeInterceptor localeChangeInterceptor() {
        LocaleChangeInterceptor localeChangeInterceptor = new
                LocaleChangeInterceptor();
        localeChangeInterceptor.setParamName("lang");
        return localeChangeInterceptor;
    }

    @Override
    public void addInterceptors(InterceptorRegistry registry) {
```

```
        registry.addInterceptor(localeChangeInterceptor());
    }
}
```

In the above configuration, the CookieLocaleResolver is used to store the locale in a cookie, and a LocaleChangeInterceptor is added to intercept URL parameters to change the locale.

Using Messages in Application

Once the message source and locale resolver are configured, messages can be accessed in controllers, services, and views. The MessageSource interface provides methods to fetch the appropriate messages. Below is an example illustrating how to use MessageSource in a Spring controller:

```
@Controller
public class GreetingController {

    @Autowired
    private MessageSource messageSource;

    @GetMapping("/greeting")
    public String greeting(Locale locale, Model model) {
        String greetingMessage = messageSource.getMessage("greeting", null, locale);
        model.addAttribute("message", greetingMessage);
        return "greeting";
    }
}
```

In the example above, the MessageSource bean is injected into the controller, and the greeting message is resolved based on the current locale.

Testing Internationalization

Testing internationalization involves ensuring that the correct messages are displayed for different locales. This can be done by changing the locale dynamically and verifying the application's behavior. For instance, if the URL contains a parameter to switch locales, accessing different URLs should result in different message outputs:

Accessing http://localhost:8080/greeting?lang=en might produce:

```
Hello
```

While accessing http://localhost:8080/greeting?lang=fr would display:

```
Bonjour
```

By following these practices, developers can build Spring applications that are easily adaptable to various languages and regions, thereby extending their reach to a global audience.

3.10 Spring AOP (Aspect Oriented Programming)

Aspect-Oriented Programming (AOP) in Spring provides a robust mechanism to manage cross-cutting concerns, modularizing these aspects and minimizing their impact on business logic. Cross-cutting concerns, such as logging, security, and transaction management, often span multiple modules, making their management challenging using traditional object-oriented methodologies.

Spring AOP facilitates the implementation of these concerns in a declarative manner, enhancing code modularity and readability. The AOP framework allows developers to define aspects, join points, pointcuts, advice, and weaving, providing a clear separation of concerns without altering the underlying business logic.

An **aspect** is a module expressing a cross-cutting concern. This module encapsulates behaviors affecting multiple classes resided in a reusable unit. For example, logging or transaction management can be defined as separate aspects to be applied across different application layers.

A **join point** refers to a specific point in the execution of the program, such as method execution or exception handling, where an aspect can be applied. In Spring AOP, join points are always method executions.

A **pointcut** is an expression that matches join points. Spring AOP uses AspectJ pointcut expressions to specify the join points where aspects should be applied. Annotations like @Pointcut, combined with expressions, define precisely where advice should be executed.

An **advice** is an action taken by the aspect at a particular join point. Spring supports various types of advice:

- **Before Advice:** Executes before a matched method's execution.
- **After Returning Advice:** Executes after a matched method successfully returns.
- **After Throwing Advice:** Executes if a matched method exits by throwing an exception.

- **After Advice:** Executes after a matched method finishes executing, regardless of its outcome.
- **Around Advice:** Surrounds a join point, potentially controlling whether method execution occurs and performing operations before and after method execution.

Finally, **weaving** is the process of linking aspects with other application types or objects to create an advised object. Spring performs dynamic weaving at runtime.

To illustrate these concepts, we shall implement a simple logging aspect using Spring AOP. Assume we have a service class responsible for processing user information:

```
package com.example.service;

public class UserService {
    public void createUser(String username) {
        // Core business logic for user creation
        System.out.println("User " + username + " created.");
    }

    public void deleteUser(String username) {
        // Core business logic for user deletion
        System.out.println("User " + username + " deleted.");
    }
}
```

We'll define a logging aspect to log the execution of these methods.

```
package com.example.aspect;

import org.aspectj.lang.annotation.Aspect;
import org.aspectj.lang.annotation.Before;
import org.springframework.stereotype.Component;

@Aspect
@Component
public class LoggingAspect {
    @Before("execution(* com.example.service.UserService.*(..))")
    public void logBefore() {
        System.out.println("Method execution started...");
    }
}
```

In the example above, the @Aspect annotation denotes the class as an aspect. The @Before annotation declares a before advice to log a message before the execution of any method in the UserService class. The pointcut expression execution(* com.example.service.UserService.*(..)) specifies that the advice applies to any method within UserService.

Next, the Spring configuration is needed to enable the aspect support.

This can be achieved either through XML configuration or by using Java annotations.

XML Configuration:

```
<aop:aspectj-autoproxy />
<bean id="userService" class="com.example.service.UserService" />
<bean id="loggingAspect" class="com.example.aspect.LoggingAspect" />
```

Java Annotation-based Configuration:

```
package com.example.config;

import org.springframework.context.annotation.ComponentScan;
import org.springframework.context.annotation.Configuration;
import org.springframework.context.annotation.EnableAspectJAutoProxy;

@Configuration
@EnableAspectJAutoProxy
@ComponentScan(basePackages = "com.example")
public class AppConfig {
}
```

In this configuration, the @EnableAspectJAutoProxy annotation is crucial for enabling Spring AOP with AspectJ's annotation-based configuration.

To validate the aspect, the UserService methods can be invoked from the main application context:

```
package com.example;

import org.springframework.context.ApplicationContext;
import org.springframework.context.annotation.AnnotationConfigApplicationContext;
import com.example.service.UserService;

public class MainApp {
    public static void main(String[] args) {
        ApplicationContext context = new AnnotationConfigApplicationContext(com.
            example.config.AppConfig.class);
        UserService userService = context.getBean(UserService.class);

        userService.createUser("john_doe");
        userService.deleteUser("john_doe");
    }
}
```

Executing this main program yields:

```
Method execution started...
User john_doe created.
Method execution started...
User john_doe deleted.
```

This output demonstrates the cross-cutting logging functionality applied before the execution of each user service method, illustrating the power and flexibility that Spring AOP adds to the Spring application ecosystem in managing cross-cutting concerns.

Chapter 4

Dependency Injection and Inversion of Control

This chapter delves into the principles of Dependency Injection (DI) and Inversion of Control (IoC), which are central to the Spring Framework. It begins by explaining the concepts and benefits of DI and IoC, detailing the different types of dependency injection such as constructor, setter, and field injection. The chapter also covers the Spring IoC container, the various methods for defining and injecting beans using XML configuration, Java annotations, and Java-based configuration. Additionally, it highlights the use of annotations like @Autowired and @Qualifier and their application in Spring Boot, concluding with best practices for employing dependency injection effectively in Spring applications.

4.1 Introduction to Dependency Injection (DI)

Dependency Injection (DI) is a software design pattern that is fundamental to the Spring Framework. It enables the creation of loosely coupled applications by promoting a clear separation of concerns and enhancing modularity. In DI, objects are provided their dependencies at runtime, rather than being responsible for obtaining them, which leads to a higher degree of flexibility and testability in application design.

To understand DI, consider that a dependency is any object that another object requires to function correctly. For instance, in a Java application, if class A uses an instance of class B, then class B is a dependency of class A. Dependency Injection facilitates the provision of these dependencies from an external source, rather than having the class A instantiate or acquire the dependency B itself. This paradigm shift in how dependencies are managed and injected can be described with the following key concepts:

- **Inversion of Control (IoC)**: The overarching principle wherein control is transferred from the application to a framework, which manages the creation and lifecycle of objects.
- **Loose Coupling**: A design goal where objects are less dependent on each other, increasing the flexibility and ease of maintenance.
- **Service Locator Pattern**: An alternative to DI, where a central registry known as a service locator is responsible for providing dependencies to classes upon request.

In the Spring Framework, DI is achieved through the use of the Spring IoC container. The container manages the creation, configuration, and lifecycle of beans. A bean is an object that is instantiated, assembled, and managed by the Spring IoC container. Dependencies between beans are specified by populating bean properties via configuration metadata, which can take multiple forms such as XML configuration, annotations, or Java-based configuration.

Consider the following example of a class that requires a dependency:

```
public class TextEditor {
    private SpellChecker spellChecker;

    public TextEditor(SpellChecker spellChecker) {
        this.spellChecker = spellChecker;
    }

    public void performSpellCheck() {
        spellChecker.checkSpelling();
    }
}
```

In this scenario, TextEditor depends on SpellChecker to perform its functionality. By using DI, we shift the responsibility of providing an instance of SpellChecker to an external entity:

```
public class SpellChecker {
```

```
    public void checkSpelling() {
        System.out.println("Checking spelling...");
    }
}
```

Using an XML-based configuration, the dependencies can be defined in the Spring configuration file:

```
<beans xmlns="http://www.springframework.org/schema/beans"
       xmlns:xsi="http://www.w3.org/2001/XMLSchema-instance"
       xsi:schemaLocation="http://www.springframework.org/schema/beans
       http://www.springframework.org/schema/beans/spring-beans.xsd">

    <bean id="spellChecker" class="com.example.SpellChecker" />

    <bean id="textEditor" class="com.example.TextEditor">
        <constructor-arg ref="spellChecker" />
    </bean>
</beans>
```

In this configuration snippet, two beans are defined:

- A SpellChecker bean with the id="spellChecker".
- A TextEditor bean with the id="textEditor", which has a dependency on spellChecker injected via the <constructor-arg> element.

When the Spring IoC container is initialized, it constructs and wires the beans together according to the configuration metadata, thus injecting the SpellChecker dependency into the TextEditor bean. This injection allows the TextEditor to perform its function without being tightly coupled to the SpellChecker implementation.

Additionally, the use of Java annotations can simplify dependency injection. For instance, the @Autowired annotation can be used to automatically wire dependencies:

```
public class TextEditor {
    @Autowired
    private SpellChecker spellChecker;

    public void performSpellCheck() {
        spellChecker.checkSpelling();
    }
}
```

Here, the @Autowired annotation instructs the Spring container to inject an instance of SpellChecker into the spellChecker field, eliminating the need for explicit configuration.

Dependency Injection promotes cleaner, more maintainable code by decoupling the components and fostering a more modular design. This approach not only eases unit testing by allowing mock implementations of dependencies but also enhances application scalability and manageability.

```
Output example:
Checking spelling...
```

4.2 Benefits of Dependency Injection

- **Reduced Code Complexity:** Dependency Injection (DI) significantly reduces the complexity of code by decoupling the creation and binding of dependent objects. It enables the client code to focus on the core business logic rather than the initialization and management of dependencies. This separation of concerns leads to cleaner and more maintainable codebases.
- **Increased Testability:** One of the paramount benefits of DI is the improvement in testability. By injecting dependencies rather than hard-coding them, it becomes straightforward to substitute real implementations with mock or stub versions during unit testing. This allows for more comprehensive and isolated tests, leading to higher quality and more robust software.
- **Improved Code Reusability:** DI promotes reusability by encouraging the development of loosely coupled components. When classes are designed to receive their dependencies through injection, these classes can be easily reused in different contexts without modification. This modularity also aligns well with the principles of SOLID design, particularly the dependency inversion principle.
- **Simplified Configuration Management:** The Spring Framework uses DI to handle complex configuration needs, allowing developers to define and manage dependencies externally via configuration files or annotations. This approach centralizes configuration management and reduces the overhead associated with changes. For instance, modifying a dependency can often be achieved through a simple XML or Java-based configuration change rather than altering the application code itself.
- **Enhanced Maintainability:** Decoupling components through DI simplifies the process of updating and maintaining the application code. Changes in the requirements or updates to individual

components do not require extensive refactoring of dependent classes. Furthermore, the use of interface-based injection ensures that implementations can be swapped without affecting the client code, facilitating easier upgrades and maintenance.

- **Promotes Adherence to Design Patterns:** DI naturally leads to adherence to established design patterns such as Factory, Singleton, and Builder patterns. For example, the Singleton pattern can be seamlessly integrated with DI to ensure a single instance of a dependency throughout the application. Similarly, DI containers act as factories that instantiate and inject dependencies as required, streamlining object creation and dependency resolution processes.

- **Support for Aspect-Oriented Programming (AOP):** The Spring Framework's support for DI enhances its capability to integrate Aspect-Oriented Programming (AOP). With DI, aspects such as logging, transaction management, and security can be injected without changing the core business logic. This separation of cross-cutting concerns from the application logic aligns with the principles of AOP, resulting in cleaner and more maintainable code.

```
package com.example.service;

import org.springframework.beans.factory.annotation.Autowired;
import org.springframework.stereotype.Service;

@Service
public class UserService {
    private final UserRepository userRepository;

    @Autowired
    public UserService(UserRepository userRepository) {
        this.userRepository = userRepository;
    }

    public User findUserById(Long id) {
        return userRepository.findById(id).orElse(null);
    }
}
```

```
Unit Test Output:
-----------------
[INFO] Running com.example.service.UserServiceTest
[INFO] Tests run: 1, Failures: 0, Errors: 0, Skipped: 0, Time elapsed: 0.095 sec
```

The above code snippet demonstrates the use of constructor-based injection in Spring. By annotating the constructor with @Autowired, Spring automatically injects the UserRepository dependency. This approach makes the UserService class highly testable, as the UserRepository can be mocked or stubbed during unit tests.

- **Flexibility through Configuration:** DI provides flexibility by allowing the configuration of different implementations or settings without code changes. For example, an application can be easily reconfigured for different environments (development, production, testing) by using different configuration profiles. This flexibility extends to dependency versions, enabling smooth upgrades and downgrades without altering the application's core logic.

The aforementioned benefits collectively contribute to building scalable, maintainable, and robust applications using the Spring Framework. By leveraging the principles of DI, developers can achieve a significant reduction in code complexity, improved testability, and an overall enhancement in software quality.

4.3 Types of Dependency Injection: Constructor, Setter, and Field

Dependency Injection (DI) is a fundamental concept in the Spring Framework, which involves providing an external dependency to a class rather than allowing the class to create the dependency itself. This practice promotes loose coupling and enhances code maintainability. There are three primary methods for injecting dependencies in Spring: Constructor Injection, Setter Injection, and Field Injection. Each method has its specific use cases, advantages, and potential drawbacks.

Constructor Injection involves passing dependencies to a class via its constructor. This method is particularly useful for mandatory dependencies, ensuring that a class cannot be instantiated without its required dependencies. Constructor Injection is straightforward and takes advantage of Java's type checking mechanism at compile-time. The following example demonstrates Constructor Injection:

```
public class AccountService {
    private final AccountRepository accountRepository;

    public AccountService(AccountRepository accountRepository) {
        this.accountRepository = accountRepository;
    }
```

```
    public void manageAccount() {
        // Logic to manage account
    }
}
```

In XML configuration, Constructor Injection can be defined as follows:

```
<bean id="accountRepository" class="com.example.AccountRepository" />

<bean id="accountService" class="com.example.AccountService">
    <constructor-arg ref="accountRepository" />
</bean>
```

Using Java-based configuration, the equivalent would be:

```
@Configuration
public class AppConfig {

    @Bean
    public AccountRepository accountRepository() {
        return new AccountRepository();
    }

    @Bean
    public AccountService accountService(AccountRepository accountRepository) {
        return new AccountService(accountRepository);
    }
}
```

Setter Injection allows dependencies to be injected via public setter methods. This method provides flexibility in that dependencies can be modified after the object's creation. Setter Injection is a good choice for optional dependencies or when constructing objects that may benefit from more granularity in their configuration. Here's an example of Setter Injection:

```
public class PaymentService {
    private PaymentProcessor paymentProcessor;

    public void setPaymentProcessor(PaymentProcessor paymentProcessor) {
        this.paymentProcessor = paymentProcessor;
    }

    public void processPayment() {
        // Logic to process payment
    }
}
```

In XML configuration, Setter Injection would be specified as follows:

```
<bean id="paymentProcessor" class="com.example.PaymentProcessor" />

<bean id="paymentService" class="com.example.PaymentService">
    <property name="paymentProcessor" ref="paymentProcessor" />
</bean>
```

With Java-based configuration, the equivalent Setter Injection would be:

```
@Configuration
public class AppConfig {

    @Bean
    public PaymentProcessor paymentProcessor() {
        return new PaymentProcessor();
    }

    @Bean
    public PaymentService paymentService() {
        PaymentService paymentService = new PaymentService();
        paymentService.setPaymentProcessor(paymentProcessor());
        return paymentService;
    }
}
```

Field Injection directly injects dependencies into fields using annotations, such as @Autowired. This method requires less boilerplate code compared to Constructor or Setter Injection. However, Field Injection has drawbacks, such as making the code less decoupled from the DI container and potential issues with immutability. Example of Field Injection:

```
@Service
public class NotificationService {

    @Autowired
    private EmailService emailService;

    public void notifyUser() {
        // Logic to notify user
    }
}
```

For Java-based configuration, the injection remains the same, but the @Autowired annotation eliminates the need for explicit wiring:

```
@Configuration
public class AppConfig {

    @Bean
    public EmailService emailService() {
        return new EmailService();
    }

    @Bean
    public NotificationService notificationService() {
        return new NotificationService();
    }
}
```

While Constructor Injection is generally preferred for its clarity, especially for required dependencies, Setter Injection provides greater flexibility, and Field Injection offers succinct code. By understanding the contexts where each type excels, developers can make informed decisions to enhance their Spring application's architecture.

4.4 Understanding Inversion of Control (IoC)

Inversion of Control (IoC) is a fundamental principle central to the Spring Framework and many other frameworks in the world of software development. IoC refers to the design principle in which the control of objects or portions of a program is transferred to a container or framework. This principle is pivotal in enabling loose coupling and promoting code reuse and flexibility.

To grasp the essence of IoC, one needs to contrast it with the traditional control flow. In conventional programming, the application dictates the flow of control by creating instances of classes and invoking their methods. This leads to tight coupling, making the system rigid and hard to maintain or extend. IoC, on the other hand, reverses this control, hence permitting the framework to impose the flow and lifecycle of objects. When a framework takes up the responsibility for instantiating and managing objects, it effectively "inverts" the control from the application to the framework.

In the Spring Framework, IoC is primarily realized through the BeanFactory or ApplicationContext containers, which manage the lifecycle of beans and the relationships between them. The beans are created, wired together, configured, and managed by the container. The developer defines how the beans should be instantiated and assembled within the container, either through configuration metadata or annotations, leaving the wiring and injection of dependencies to the IoC container.

A practical illustration of IoC can be found in the way services and repositories interact within a typical layered Spring application. Consider a scenario where a service layer requires a repository layer to fetch data. Without IoC, the service layer would instantiate the repository directly, as shown:

```
public class UserService {

    private UserRepository userRepository;

    public UserService() {
        this.userRepository = new UserRepository();
    }
```

```
    public User getUserById(Long id) {
        return userRepository.findById(id);
    }
}
```

In this typical tightly-coupled code, the UserService class takes responsibility for creating an instance of UserRepository. Any change in UserRepository (like changes in constructor arguments) would necessitate alterations in UserService, resulting in a fragile codebase.

Leveraging IoC, the responsibility of instantiating UserRepository and injecting it into UserService is transferred to the Spring IoC container. The UserService class is refactored to accept a UserRepository instance during construction rather than creating it itself:

```
public class UserService {

    private UserRepository userRepository;

    public UserService(UserRepository userRepository) {
        this.userRepository = userRepository;
    }

    public User getUserById(Long id) {
        return userRepository.findById(id);
    }
}
```

In this arrangement, UserRepository is supplied to UserService by the Spring IoC container. IoC manages the wiring between these classes, ensuring dependencies are provided rather than created within the class. This significantly decouples the service layer from the repository layer.

The process of defining and managing such dependencies is achieved through configuration metadata in XML files, Java-based configuration, or via annotations. Below is an example of Java-based configuration utilizing the @Configuration and @Bean annotations to wire our UserService and UserRepository:

```
@Configuration
public class AppConfig {

    @Bean
    public UserRepository userRepository() {
        return new UserRepository();
    }

    @Bean
    public UserService userService() {
        return new UserService(userRepository());
    }
```

```
}
```

While utilizing annotations, one can use the @Autowired annotation to inject the UserRepository into UserService:

```
@Service
public class UserService {

    @Autowired
    private UserRepository userRepository;

    public User getUserById(Long id) {
        return userRepository.findById(id);
    }
}
```

Here, the @Service and @Autowired annotations inform the Spring IoC container to manage the lifecycle of these beans and inject dependencies where needed.

IoC brings several advantages:

- **Decoupling:** By inverting control, classes focus on specific tasks rather than managing dependencies.
- **Testability:** Loosely coupled code is easier to test. Mocking dependencies becomes straightforward.
- **Maintainability:** Enhancements and refactoring become simpler since the object creation logic is centralized.
- **Scalability:** Applications can be scaled effortlessly by injecting enhanced or alternative implementations without changing existing code structures.

By embracing IoC, developers can create modular, maintainable, and extendable applications. The flexibility achieved through IoC is fundamental to the robustness that the Spring Framework provides, facilitating the seamless integration and management of complex systems.

4.5 Spring IoC Container

The Spring Inversion of Control (IoC) container is the core component of the Spring Framework. It facilitates the management of bean creation, wiring, lifecycle, and configuration. The IoC container relies on configurations provided either through XML, annotations, or Java-based setup. Once configured, it manages the complete lifecycle of the Spring beans.

At its core, the IoC container provides two primary packages: org.springframework.beans and org.springframework.context. The former offers fundamental interfaces like BeanFactory and related classes for managing and instantiating beans, whereas the latter builds upon BeanFactory to provide more enterprise-specific functionalities required in a contemporary application.

The central interface, ApplicationContext, represents the IoC container and is extended by several implementations, including ClassPathXmlApplicationContext, FileSystemXmlApplicationContext, and AnnotationConfigApplicationContext.

To create a simple Spring application using the IoC container, consider the following XML-based configuration approach. Here, we will define a few beans and demonstrate their instantiation and injection by the IoC container:

```
<beans xmlns="http://www.springframework.org/schema/beans"
      xmlns:xsi="http://www.w3.org/2001/XMLSchema-instance"
      xsi:schemaLocation="http://www.springframework.org/schema/beans
      http://www.springframework.org/schema/beans/spring-beans.xsd">

   <bean id="employeeService" class="com.example.EmployeeService">
      <property name="employeeRepository" ref="employeeRepository"/>
   </bean>

   <bean id="employeeRepository" class="com.example.EmployeeRepository"/>
</beans>
```

In the above beans.xml file, two beans are defined: EmployeeService and EmployeeRepository. The EmployeeService bean has a dependency on EmployeeRepository, which is injected by referencing the id of the EmployeeRepository bean.

To load and use this configuration in a Java application, the ClassPathXmlApplicationContext can be used as follows:

```
import org.springframework.context.ApplicationContext;
import org.springframework.context.support.ClassPathXmlApplicationContext;
import com.example.EmployeeService;

public class Main {
    public static void main(String[] args) {
        ApplicationContext context = new ClassPathXmlApplicationContext("beans.
            xml");

        EmployeeService employeeService = context.getBean(EmployeeService.class);
        employeeService.performOperations();
    }
```

```
}
```

In this Java code, the application context is initialized using the XML configuration file named beans.xml. The bean EmployeeService is retrieved from the context and used in the application.

The IoC container also supports annotations to define bean configurations. Here, we provide a similar configuration using annotations:

```
import org.springframework.beans.factory.annotation.Autowired;
import org.springframework.stereotype.Service;

@Service
public class EmployeeService {
    private EmployeeRepository employeeRepository;

    @Autowired
    public void setEmployeeRepository(EmployeeRepository employeeRepository) {
        this.employeeRepository = employeeRepository;
    }

    public void performOperations() {
        // Business logic
    }
}
```

```
import org.springframework.stereotype.Repository;

@Repository
public class EmployeeRepository {
    // Implementation details
}
```

Here, annotations such as @Service and @Repository are used to define the beans. The @Autowired annotation is employed to inject the EmployeeRepository bean into the EmployeeService bean.

To load and utilize this annotation-based configuration, we use AnnotationConfigApplicationContext:

```
import org.springframework.context.ApplicationContext;
import org.springframework.context.annotation.AnnotationConfigApplicationContext;
import com.example.EmployeeService;

public class Main {
    public static void main(String[] args) {
        ApplicationContext context = new AnnotationConfigApplicationContext(
                AppConfig.class);

        EmployeeService employeeService = context.getBean(EmployeeService.class);
        employeeService.performOperations();
    }
}
```

```
import org.springframework.context.annotation.ComponentScan;
import org.springframework.context.annotation.Configuration;
```

```
@Configuration
@ComponentScan(basePackages = "com.example")
public class AppConfig {
    // Additional configuration if necessary
}
```

Here, the AppConfig class is crucial as it is annotated with @Configuration to signify that it contains Spring configuration. The @ComponentScan annotation instructs the IoC container to scan the com.example package for components, services, and repositories.

This section extends understanding by highlighting how the IoC container facilitates the management and wiring of beans in a Spring application, whether using XML configuration or annotations. It underscores the seamless and flexible nature of Spring's IoC container, which simplifies the overall application development process.

4.6 Defining Beans for Dependency Injection

In the Spring Framework, a bean is an object that is instantiated, assembled, and managed by the Spring IoC container. Beans form the backbone of any Spring application. When working with dependency injection (DI), it is crucial to understand how to define beans, as this directly affects how dependencies are injected into the application components. The Spring Framework provides multiple ways to define beans, including XML configuration, Java annotations, and Java-based configuration.

The traditional and one of the most flexible methods to define beans is through XML configuration. This method involves using Spring's XML schema for configuration and provides a clear and comprehensive way to specify bean definitions.

```
<beans xmlns="http://www.springframework.org/schema/beans"
       xmlns:xsi="http://www.w3.org/2001/XMLSchema-instance"
       xsi:schemaLocation="http://www.springframework.org/schema/beans
       http://www.springframework.org/schema/beans/spring-beans.xsd">

    <bean id="exampleBean" class="com.example.ExampleBean">
        <property name="propertyOne" value="ValueOne"/>
        <property name="propertyTwo" ref="anotherBean"/>
    </bean>

    <bean id="anotherBean" class="com.example.AnotherBean"/>
</beans>
```

In the above XML configuration, two beans are defined: exampleBean and anotherBean. The exampleBean has two properties: propertyOne, which is assigned a literal value of "ValueOne", and propertyTwo, which is a reference to another bean defined in the context, anotherBean.

Java annotations provide another powerful method for bean definition, which promotes a more concise and readable configuration by leveraging Java's annotation capabilities. By annotating classes with @Component, @Service, @Repository, or @Controller, Spring automatically detects and registers these classes as beans.

```
package com.example;

import org.springframework.stereotype.Component;

@Component
public class ExampleBean {
    private AnotherBean anotherBean;

    public ExampleBean(AnotherBean anotherBean) {
        this.anotherBean = anotherBean;
    }
}
```

Here, the @Component annotation marks the ExampleBean class as a Spring-managed bean. Dependency injection is managed by Spring, which resolves the dependency on AnotherBean, assuming that AnotherBean is also annotated and registered as a bean.

Java-based configuration, introduced in Spring 3.0, is another modern and type-safe method to define beans. It involves using Java classes along with the @Configuration and @Bean annotations.

```
package com.example;

import org.springframework.context.annotation.Bean;
import org.springframework.context.annotation.Configuration;

@Configuration
public class AppConfig {

    @Bean
    public ExampleBean exampleBean() {
        return new ExampleBean(anotherBean());
    }

    @Bean
    public AnotherBean anotherBean() {
        return new AnotherBean();
    }
}
```

In this case, the @Configuration annotation indicates that the class contains one or more @Bean definitions. Each @Bean annotated method returns an object that Spring registers as a bean within the application context. The exampleBean method creates and returns an instance of ExampleBean, which depends on AnotherBean. The anotherBean method provides the required instance of AnotherBean.

It is essential to note that Java-based configuration provides several advantages, including the use of full Java capabilities, such as invoking methods conditionally. Moreover, it ensures stronger type checking and greater flexibility during development.

By understanding these approaches to defining beans, developers can effectively manage object creation and dependency injection within their Spring applications. Each method has its benefits and can be chosen based on the specific needs and context of the project being developed.

4.7 Injecting Dependencies with XML Configuration

The Spring Framework provides multiple methods for configuring and managing dependencies, with XML configuration being one of the classic approaches. In this method, beans and their dependencies are defined in an XML file, which is subsequently parsed by the Spring IoC container to assemble the application components. This section explores the details of creating, managing, and injecting dependencies using XML configuration, enabling a deeper understanding of its capabilities and nuances.

To begin with, let us consider a simple example where a Car class depends on an Engine class. These classes may appear as follows:

```
public class Car {
    private Engine engine;

    // Constructor-based dependency injection
    public Car(Engine engine) {
        this.engine = engine;
    }

    // Getter method for engine
    public Engine getEngine() {
        return engine;
    }

    // Setter method for engine
    public void setEngine(Engine engine) {
        this.engine = engine;
    }
```

```
}
```

```
public class Engine {
    private String type;

    // Constructor
    public Engine(String type) {
        this.type = type;
    }

    // Getter method for type
    public String getType() {
        return type;
    }

    // Setter method for type
    public void setType(String type) {
        this.type = type;
    }
}
```

The Car class depends on an instance of the Engine class. Next, we define the beans for these classes in an XML configuration file, typically named applicationContext.xml:

```
<beans xmlns="http://www.springframework.org/schema/beans"
    xmlns:xsi="http://www.w3.org/2001/XMLSchema-instance"
    xsi:schemaLocation="
        http://www.springframework.org/schema/beans
        http://www.springframework.org/schema/beans/spring-beans.xsd">

    <!-- Definition of the Engine bean -->
    <bean id="engine" class="com.example.Engine">
        <constructor-arg value="V8"/>
    </bean>

    <!-- Definition of the Car bean -->
    <bean id="car" class="com.example.Car">
        <constructor-arg ref="engine"/>
    </bean>

</beans>
```

In the XML configuration file, we define the Engine bean with an ID of "engine" and a constructor argument specifying the type of engine. Similarly, we define the Car bean and specify a reference to the engine bean using the ref attribute within the constructor-arg element.

To create the Spring IoC container and retrieve the Car bean, we use the following code:

```
import org.springframework.context.ApplicationContext;
import org.springframework.context.support.ClassPathXmlApplicationContext;

public class Main {
    public static void main(String[] args) {
        ApplicationContext context =
```

```
            new ClassPathXmlApplicationContext("applicationContext.xml");

        Car car = (Car) context.getBean("car");
        System.out.println("Car engine type: " + car.getEngine().getType());
    }
}
```

When this code is executed, the output would be:

```
Car engine type: V8
```

This demonstrates the constructor-based dependency injection using XML configuration. Similarly, setter-based dependency injection can be employed by defining `property` elements instead of `constructor-arg` elements in the XML file:

```
<beans xmlns="http://www.springframework.org/schema/beans"
    xmlns:xsi="http://www.w3.org/2001/XMLSchema-instance"
    xsi:schemaLocation="
        http://www.springframework.org/schema/beans
        http://www.springframework.org/schema/beans/spring-beans.xsd">

    <!-- Definition of the Engine bean -->
    <bean id="engine" class="com.example.Engine">
        <property name="type" value="V8"/>
    </bean>

    <!-- Definition of the Car bean -->
    <bean id="car" class="com.example.Car">
        <property name="engine" ref="engine"/>
    </bean>

</beans>
```

The corresponding `Car` class can be updated to use the setter method for dependency injection:

```
public class Car {
    private Engine engine;

    // Default constructor
    public Car() {}

    // Getter method for engine
    public Engine getEngine() {
        return engine;
    }

    // Setter method for engine
    public void setEngine(Engine engine) {
        this.engine = engine;
    }
}
```

Upon execution, the result remains consistent:

```
Car engine type: V8
```

By using the XML configuration method, Spring offers a flexible and highly readable approach to managing bean definitions and their dependencies. This method allows for clear separation of configuration and business logic, ensuring that components remain loosely coupled and easy to manage.

4.8 Injecting Dependencies with Java Annotations

Java annotations provide a powerful and concise way to manage dependency injection in the Spring Framework. Annotations reduce the verbosity of XML-based configurations and make the code easier to read and maintain. This section explores how to inject dependencies using Java annotations, illustrating the process with relevant examples and best practices.

Spring supports various annotations for dependency injection, primarily @Autowired and @Qualifier, among others. These annotations facilitate the injection of beans directly within the code, reducing the need for external configuration files.

The @Autowired annotation marks a constructor, field, setter method, or config method as to be autowired by Spring's dependency injection facilities. Let's look at examples to understand how this is applied in different contexts.

First, consider the case of constructor-based injection. This type of dependency injection is implemented through a class constructor, making sure dependencies are immutable and available as soon as the class is instantiated.

```
import org.springframework.beans.factory.annotation.Autowired;
import org.springframework.stereotype.Component;

@Component
public class CustomerService {

    private final CustomerRepository customerRepository;

    @Autowired
    public CustomerService(CustomerRepository customerRepository) {
        this.customerRepository = customerRepository;
    }

    public void performSomeService() {
        // business logic that uses customerRepository
    }
}
```

Next, we examine setter-based injection, where dependencies are set through setter methods. This allows for more flexibility since a class can change its dependencies at runtime.

```
import org.springframework.beans.factory.annotation.Autowired;
import org.springframework.stereotype.Component;

@Component
public class OrderService {

    private OrderRepository orderRepository;

    // Setter method
    @Autowired
    public void setOrderRepository(OrderRepository orderRepository) {
        this.orderRepository = orderRepository;
    }

    public void processOrder() {
        // business logic that uses orderRepository
    }
}
```

Lastly, consider field-based injection, where dependencies are injected directly into the field. This approach is more concise but less flexible than the previous methods, as it does not support mutable or optional dependencies well.

```
import org.springframework.beans.factory.annotation.Autowired;
import org.springframework.stereotype.Component;

@Component
public class ProductService {

    @Autowired
    private ProductRepository productRepository;

    public void manageProduct() {
        // business logic that uses productRepository
    }
}
```

In cases where multiple beans of the same type exist, the @Qualifier annotation helps to differentiate which specific bean should be injected. This annotation uses a value, which corresponds to the bean name, to resolve ambiguities.

```
import org.springframework.beans.factory.annotation.Autowired;
import org.springframework.beans.factory.annotation.Qualifier;
import org.springframework.stereotype.Component;

@Component
public class PaymentService {
```

```
    private final PaymentProcessor paymentProcessor;

    @Autowired
    public PaymentService(@Qualifier("paypalProcessor") PaymentProcessor
            paymentProcessor) {
        this.paymentProcessor = paymentProcessor;
    }

    public void processPayment() {
        // Use the specified paymentProcessor bean
    }
}
```

In scenarios requiring optional dependencies, the @Autowired annotation can be configured with the required attribute set to false, enabling the injection to proceed even if the dependency is not present.

```
import org.springframework.beans.factory.annotation.Autowired;
import org.springframework.stereotype.Component;
import java.util.Optional;

@Component
public class NotificationService {

    private final Optional<NotificationProvider> notificationProvider;

    @Autowired(required = false)
    public NotificationService(Optional<NotificationProvider> notificationProvider) {
        this.notificationProvider = notificationProvider;
    }

    public void sendNotification() {
        notificationProvider.ifPresent(provider -> provider.send());
    }
}
```

Annotations such as @Primary can be employed to designate a primary candidate when multiple beans of the same type coexist. This directive steers Spring toward using the annotated bean over others in non-qualifying scenarios.

Incorporating Java annotations streamlines Spring application configurations and fosters a more intuitive and modular approach to dependency management. The @Autowired and @Qualifier annotations substantively enhance code readability and promote a cleaner, annotation-driven dependency injection paradigm.

4.9 Injecting Dependencies with Java-based Configuration

In the Spring Framework, Java-based configuration provides a robust and type-safe approach to define beans and wire dependencies. This method leverages Java code to configure the Spring container instead of XML or annotations. This section explains how to use Java-based configuration to inject dependencies, and discusses the benefits and application of this approach.

Java-based configuration is typically achieved using @Configuration and @Bean annotations. A class annotated with @Configuration indicates that it contains one or more @Bean methods which can be processed by the Spring container to generate bean definitions and service requests for those beans during runtime.

Example of Java-based Configuration

Firstly, consider a simple example where we define and configure two classes: ServiceA and ServiceB. ServiceA requires ServiceB as a dependency.

Define the two service classes as follows:

```
public class ServiceA {
    private final ServiceB serviceB;

    public ServiceA(ServiceB serviceB) {
        this.serviceB = serviceB;
    }

    public void performService() {
        serviceB.assist();
    }
}

public class ServiceB {
    public void assist() {
        System.out.println("ServiceB assisting ServiceA");
    }
}
```

Next, create a Java configuration class to define these beans and their relationships:

```
import org.springframework.context.annotation.Bean;
import org.springframework.context.annotation.Configuration;

@Configuration
public class AppConfig {

    @Bean
```

```
    public ServiceB serviceB() {
        return new ServiceB();
    }

    @Bean
    public ServiceA serviceA(ServiceB serviceB) {
        return new ServiceA(serviceB);
    }
}
```

In this configuration class, the serviceB method is responsible for creating an instance of ServiceB, and the serviceA method creates an instance of ServiceA, taking ServiceB as a constructor parameter. The Spring container ensures that the appropriate ServiceB instance is injected into ServiceA.

Using the Java-based Configuration

To bootstrap the Spring application context with this configuration, use the following code:

```
import org.springframework.context.ApplicationContext;
import org.springframework.context.annotation.AnnotationConfigApplicationContext;

public class MainApp {
    public static void main(String[] args) {
        ApplicationContext context = new AnnotationConfigApplicationContext(
                AppConfig.class);
        ServiceA serviceA = context.getBean(ServiceA.class);
        serviceA.performService();
    }
}
```

Executing the MainApp class will produce the following output:

```
ServiceB assisting ServiceA
```

Understanding the Benefits

Java-based configuration offers several benefits over other methods of bean definition:

- **Type Safety**: Since the configuration is in Java, the compiler provides type-checking, reducing the risk of errors compared to string-based XML configuration.
- **Refactor-Friendly**: IDEs offer better refactoring tools for Java code.
- **Readability and Maintainability**: Java-based configuration can be more readable and easier to debug than XML. Developers can make full use of Java's strengths, including scopes, IDE supports, and other language features.

Advanced Configuration Techniques

Java-based configuration also supports advanced techniques such as profile-based configuration, conditional beans, and lazy initialization:

```
import org.springframework.context.annotation.Bean;
import org.springframework.context.annotation.Configuration;
import org.springframework.context.annotation.Lazy;
import org.springframework.context.annotation.Profile;

@Configuration
public class AdvancedAppConfig {

    @Bean
    @Profile("dev")
    public ServiceB devServiceB() {
        return new DevServiceB();
    }

    @Bean
    @Profile("prod")
    public ServiceB prodServiceB() {
        return new ProdServiceB();
    }

    @Bean
    @Lazy
    public ServiceA serviceA(ServiceB serviceB) {
        return new ServiceA(serviceB);
    }
}
```

In this example:

- The @Profile annotation is used to define beans that are only available under specific profiles (e.g., dev or prod).

- The @Lazy annotation defers the bean initialization until it's first needed.

Using profiles and conditions enhances the flexibility and customization of the Spring application context.

Java-based configuration empowers developers to leverage Java's capabilities while managing dependencies in a type-safe and manageable manner. This approach is integral to creating maintainable and agile applications using the Spring Framework.

4.10 Using @Autowired and @Qualifier Annotations

The @Autowired and @Qualifier annotations in the Spring Framework are essential tools for achieving fine-grained control over dependency injection. These annotations facilitate the automatic resolution of dependencies and provide a mechanism to specify which bean should be injected when multiple candidates are present.

The @Autowired annotation is used to mark a constructor, field, or setter method for dependency injection. Spring's IoC container automatically injects the appropriate bean into the marked variable. By default, @Autowired resolves dependencies by type.

```
import org.springframework.beans.factory.annotation.Autowired;
import org.springframework.stereotype.Service;

@Service
public class OrderService {

    @Autowired
    private PaymentService paymentService;

    public void processOrder() {
        paymentService.pay();
    }
}

@Service
public class PaymentService {
    public void pay() {
        System.out.println("Payment processed.");
    }
}
```

In the above example, the OrderService class depends on the PaymentService class. Using the @Autowired annotation on the paymentService field informs the Spring IoC container to inject an instance of PaymentService into OrderService automatically.

Additionally, @Autowired can be used on constructors, enabling the injection of dependencies when the object is instantiated. This approach is often preferred for mandatory dependencies and ensures that the object is always created in a valid state.

```
import org.springframework.beans.factory.annotation.Autowired;
import org.springframework.stereotype.Service;

@Service
public class OrderService {

    private final PaymentService paymentService;
```

```
    @Autowired
    public OrderService(PaymentService paymentService) {
        this.paymentService = paymentService;
    }

    public void processOrder() {
        paymentService.pay();
    }
}
```

Setter injection using @Autowired involves placing the annotation on the setter method, allowing the Spring IoC container to inject the dependency via the method.

```
import org.springframework.beans.factory.annotation.Autowired;
import org.springframework.stereotype.Service;

@Service
public class OrderService {

    private PaymentService paymentService;

    @Autowired
    public void setPaymentService(PaymentService paymentService) {
        this.paymentService = paymentService;
    }

    public void processOrder() {
        paymentService.pay();
    }
}
```

When multiple beans of the same type exist in the Spring IoC container, ambiguity arises during dependency injection. The @Qualifier annotation resolves this ambiguity by specifying the exact bean that should be injected.

Consider the following example with two implementations of the PaymentService interface:

```
import org.springframework.beans.factory.annotation.Qualifier;
import org.springframework.stereotype.Service;

public interface PaymentService {
    void pay();
}

@Service
@Qualifier("creditCardPaymentService")
public class CreditCardPaymentService implements PaymentService {
    public void pay() {
        System.out.println("Payment made with credit card.");
    }
}

@Service
@Qualifier("paypalPaymentService")
```

```
public class PaypalPaymentService implements PaymentService {
    public void pay() {
        System.out.println("Payment made with PayPal.");
    }
}
```

In this scenario, the OrderService class can specify which implementation of the PaymentService interface to inject by using the @Qualifier annotation in conjunction with the @Autowired annotation.

```
import org.springframework.beans.factory.annotation.Autowired;
import org.springframework.beans.factory.annotation.Qualifier;
import org.springframework.stereotype.Service;

@Service
public class OrderService {

    private final PaymentService paymentService;

    @Autowired
    public OrderService(@Qualifier("creditCardPaymentService") PaymentService
            paymentService) {
        this.paymentService = paymentService;
    }

    public void processOrder() {
        paymentService.pay();
    }
}
```

Using @Qualifier in this manner allows precise control over which beans are injected when multiple candidates are available.

The @Autowired annotation provides a required attribute (by default set to true). By setting required to false, the dependency becomes optional, and no exception is thrown if the bean cannot be found.

```
import org.springframework.beans.factory.annotation.Autowired;
import org.springframework.stereotype.Service;

@Service
public class OrderService {

    @Autowired(required = false)
    private DiscountService discountService;

    public void applyDiscount() {
        if (discountService != null) {
            discountService.apply();
        } else {
            System.out.println("No discount available.");
        }
    }
}
```

In the example above, the OrderService class depends on the DiscountService class optionally. If the DiscountService bean is present in the context, it will be injected; otherwise, the discountService field remains null.

Overall, the @Autowired and @Qualifier annotations provide flexible and powerful mechanisms for dependency injection in Spring applications, promoting maintainable and decoupled code. By leveraging these annotations, developers can fine-tune their applications' behavior and differentiate between multiple bean instances effectively.

4.11 Dependency Injection in Spring Boot

Spring Boot provides a comprehensive yet straightforward mechanism to manage dependencies and configure applications, leveraging the dependency injection models of the Spring Framework. It simplifies the dependency injection process through out-of-the-box features, auto-configuration, and intelligent defaults, allowing developers to rapidly develop robust applications. Understanding how to effectively use these features is vital for creating maintainable and scalable applications.

At the core of Spring Boot's dependency injection lies the @SpringBootApplication annotation, which encompasses three critical annotations: @Configuration, @EnableAutoConfiguration, and @ComponentScan. These annotations work together to bootstrap the application and enable automatic configuration and component scanning. Here is an example of a basic Spring Boot application:

```
package com.example.demo;

import org.springframework.boot.SpringApplication;
import org.springframework.boot.autoconfigure.SpringBootApplication;

@SpringBootApplication
public class DemoApplication {
    public static void main(String[] args) {
        SpringApplication.run(DemoApplication.class, args);
    }
}
```

The @SpringBootApplication annotation enables automatic scanning of Spring components within the same package and its sub-packages. It is essential to understand how the auto-configuration and component scanning work closely with dependency injection.

- **Component Scanning and Stereotype Annotations**

Spring Boot uses component scanning to automatically detect and register beans within the Spring application context. Stereotype annotations such as @Component, @Service, @Repository, and @Controller are pivotal in this process. These annotations indicate that a class is a candidate for auto-detection:

```
package com.example.demo.service;

import org.springframework.stereotype.Service;

@Service
public class UserService {
    // Service logic
}
```

In the example above, the @Service annotation indicates that UserService is a Spring bean, and it will be managed by the Spring IoC container.

- **Using @Autowired for Dependency Injection**

  The @Autowired annotation is used to inject bean dependencies into other beans managed by Spring. This can be done through constructor, setter, or field injection. Constructor injection is generally recommended due to its advantages related to immutability and better testability. Here is an example:

```
package com.example.demo.controller;

import org.springframework.beans.factory.annotation.Autowired;
import org.springframework.stereotype.Controller;
import org.springframework.web.bind.annotation.GetMapping;
import org.springframework.web.bind.annotation.ResponseBody;
import com.example.demo.service.UserService;

@Controller
public class UserController {

    private final UserService userService;

    @Autowired
    public UserController(UserService userService) {
        this.userService = userService;
    }

    @GetMapping("/user")
    @ResponseBody
    public String getUser() {
        return userService.getUserDetails();
    }
}
```

  In the example above, UserController is a Spring-managed bean, where UserService is injected via the constructor.

- **Qualifying Beans with** @Qualifier

  When multiple beans of the same type exist, Spring requires an additional qualifier to differentiate the correct bean for injection. The @Qualifier annotation achieves this by specifying the bean name explicitly:

```
package com.example.demo.service;

import org.springframework.beans.factory.annotation.Qualifier;
import org.springframework.stereotype.Service;

@Service
public class PremiumUserService implements UserService {
    // Service logic
}

@Service
@Qualifier("basicUserService")
public class BasicUserService implements UserService {
    // Service logic
}
```

  To inject a specific implementation, use the @Qualifier annotation within the constructor:

```
package com.example.demo.controller;

import org.springframework.beans.factory.annotation.Autowired;
import org.springframework.beans.factory.annotation.Qualifier;
import org.springframework.stereotype.Controller;

@Controller
public class UserController {

    private final UserService userService;

    @Autowired
    public UserController(@Qualifier("basicUserService") UserService userService
        ) {
        this.userService = userService;
    }

    // Rest of the controller
}
```

- **Profiles in Spring Boot**

  Spring profiles provide a way to segregate parts of your application configuration and make it available only in particular environments. These can be set up using annotations like @Profile:

```
package com.example.demo.config;

import org.springframework.context.annotation.Bean;
import org.springframework.context.annotation.Configuration;
import org.springframework.context.annotation.Profile;
import javax.sql.DataSource;
```

```
@Configuration
public class AppConfig {

    @Bean
    @Profile("development")
    public DataSource devDataSource() {
        // Development DataSource configuration
    }

    @Bean
    @Profile("production")
    public DataSource prodDataSource() {
        // Production DataSource configuration
    }
}
```

The profiles can be activated via application properties or command-line arguments. This feature allows for clean separation of configuration for different environments.

- **Application Properties**

  Spring Boot promotes the use of externalized configuration, where you can define properties in application.properties or application.yml files. These properties can be injected directly into beans using the @Value annotation:

```
package com.example.demo.config;

import org.springframework.beans.factory.annotation.Value;
import org.springframework.stereotype.Component;

@Component
public class AppProperties {

    @Value("${app.name}")
    private String appName;

    public String getAppName() {
        return appName;
    }
}
```

The application.properties file would contain the properties:

```
app.name=Spring Boot Application
```

Combining these elements allows for powerful and flexible configuration management, leading to more maintainable and scalable Spring Boot applications, achieving the principles of dependency injection and inversion of control.

4.12 Best Practices for Dependency Injection

Adhering to best practices in Dependency Injection (DI) ensures efficient, maintainable, and scalable Spring applications. Following these recommendations aids in harnessing the full potential of DI and promoting clean, modular code.

First, prefer constructor injection over setter injection for mandatory dependencies. Constructor injection makes it clear which dependencies are required, as they can be enforced via final fields and injected only during object construction. This approach aligns with immutability principles, preventing accidentally uninitialized dependencies. Consider the following example:

```
public class Service {
    private final Repository repository;

    public Service(Repository repository) {
        this.repository = repository;
    }

    // Business methods
}
```

Field injection, while concise, is generally discouraged except for specific use cases such as integration tests or framework-managed objects. It hinders the ability to implement immutability and makes unit testing without a DI container more cumbersome.

Secondly, avoid using the Spring context (ApplicationContext) directly within application code when injecting dependencies. Direct interaction with the container violates the DI principle by creating tight coupling to the framework. Instead, leverage annotations or explicit configuration.

Thirdly, utilize the @Autowired annotation judiciously. Overuse of @Autowired can obscure the wiring of dependencies, making the code less transparent. Prefer constructor injection to @Autowired fields. When @Autowired is necessary, ensure clarity by explicitly specifying the required attribute:

```
@Autowired(required = true)
private Service service;
```

Fourth, manage the scope of your beans appropriately. By default, Spring beans are singleton scoped, meaning the container creates only one instance of the bean per Spring IoC container. For stateless services, this is generally desirable. However, certain beans may require different scopes, such as prototype, request, session, application, or websocket. Choose the scope based on the specific use case to ensure optimal resource management and avoid unintended state sharing.

Next, using @Qualifier is best when multiple beans of the same type exist. @Qualifier provides a clear and explicit mechanism to specify which bean should be injected, thereby preventing ambiguity:

```
@Autowired
@Qualifier("primaryRepository")
private Repository repository;
```

Another critical practice involves leveraging Spring's Java-based configuration over XML wherever possible. Java-based configuration (using @Configuration and @Bean) benefits from type safety and refactoring support within IDEs, making it preferable for most use cases. For instance:

```
@Configuration
public class AppConfig {

    @Bean
    public Service service() {
        return new Service(repository());
    }

    @Bean
    public Repository repository() {
        return new RepositoryImpl();
    }
}
```

Furthermore, write unit tests that do not rely on the Spring container. Light-weight testing frameworks such as JUnit in combination with mocking frameworks like Mockito can effectively test the business logic without the need for Spring dependency injection. This approach ensures faster test execution and reduces complexity:

```
@RunWith(MockitoJUnitRunner.class)
public class ServiceTest {

    @Mock
    private Repository repository;

    @InjectMocks
    private Service service;

    @Test
    public void testBusinessMethod() {
        // Define repository behavior
        when(repository.getData()).thenReturn(mockData());

        // Assert the business logic
```

```
        assertEquals(expectedData(), service.performOperation());
    }
}
```

Using dependency injection with Spring Boot projects simplifies configuration and enhances productivity. Favor the use of Spring Boot's auto-configuration and starter dependencies, reducing the boilerplate code and manual configuration. Even in Spring Boot, maintain explicit configuration for complex or non-standard beans to retain clarity.

Lastly, practice minimal coupling between components, keeping them loosely coupled. Utilizing interfaces for dependencies promotes flexibility and ease of substitution, fostering a design that adheres to the Dependency Inversion Principle. For instance:

```
public interface Service {
    void execute();
}

public class ServiceImpl implements Service {
    private final Repository repository;

    public ServiceImpl(Repository repository) {
        this.repository = repository;
    }

    @Override
    public void execute() {
        repository.performOperation();
    }
}
```

Adhering to these best practices ensures that dependencies are managed in a way that supports maintainability, testability, and clear, understandable code structures. Each recommendation promotes the underlying principles of DI, aligning with core design principles such as SOLID, thus ensuring robust and scalable Spring applications.

Chapter 5

Spring Data Access

This chapter provides a comprehensive overview of managing data access in Spring applications. It begins with setting up a database and introduces the Spring JDBC module, including the use of JdbcTemplate for simplified database interactions. The chapter then explores the Spring ORM module, focusing on the integration of Hibernate and JPA with Spring Data. Readers will learn about Spring Data JPA repositories, custom repository methods, and effective transaction management. Additional topics include Spring Data REST for creating RESTful APIs, as well as best practices for achieving efficient and reliable data access within Spring applications.

5.1 Introduction to Spring Data Access

Spring Data Access is an integral component of the Spring Framework, providing robust and flexible means for interacting with a variety of data sources in a standardized manner. It abstracts the complexities of database interactions, enabling developers to focus on the core business logic of their applications without getting entangled in boilerplate code. This section provides an overview of the fundamental concepts and elements that constitute Spring Data Access, setting the stage for more advanced topics covered in subsequent sections.

At the heart of Spring Data Access are several key modules: Spring JDBC, Spring ORM, and Spring Data JPA. Each module is designed to address specific aspects of data handling and persistence. The unified programming model helps in managing relational data, effectively leveraging the power of various underlying technologies.

Spring JDBC serves as the foundation for data access and is known for its simplicity and ease of use. It encapsulates transaction management, exception handling, and resource management while providing a Template-based approach, called JdbcTemplate, to perform database operations. This abstraction allows developers to execute SQL queries, call stored procedures, and perform updates without dealing with the intricacies of JDBC.

Spring ORM builds on the capabilities of the Spring JDBC module, facilitating the integration of popular Object-Relational Mapping (ORM) frameworks such as Hibernate and JPA (Java Persistence API) with Spring. This integration simplifies the ORM framework's configuration and management, allowing seamless operations like entity lifecycle management, caching, and dirty checking. It eliminates boilerplate code and aligns the ORM frameworks within the transactional scope of Spring's transaction management model.

Spring Data JPA is a layer built on top of the JPA specification, aiming to significantly reduce the amount of boilerplate code required for data repository operations. It provides a repository abstraction that can be used to easily create and manage repositories. Notably, it supports the creation of custom query methods defined by method names, which are automatically translated into SQL queries by Spring. This level of abstraction empowers developers to build repositories that address complex query requirements with minimal effort and code.

Spring Data Access includes comprehensive **transaction management** capabilities that ensure data integrity and consistency. Transactions define a unit of work with multiple operations executed within a common transactional context. Spring simplifies transaction management by allowing it to be declaratively controlled using annotations such as @Transactional, thereby demarcating transactional boundaries in a straightforward manner.

Spring Data Access also supports **Spring Data REST**, which maps repository operations to RESTful endpoints, thereby facilitating the rapid development of data-backed RESTful web services. Without necessitating additional controller logic, repositories annotated with @RepositoryRestResource can expose CRUD operations, search methods, and even custom endpoints.

Understanding Spring Data Access necessitates familiarity with the configuration mechanisms that serve as the backbone of the framework. Annotated classes such as @Configuration, @EnableTransactionManagement, and @EnableJpaRepositories play pivotal roles in setting up application contexts. Additionally, the use of properties files or YAML files to manage database connection details ensures a clean and maintainable configuration strategy.

To illustrate the foundational aspects, consider the basic setup for enabling JDBC in a Spring application. Below is an example of a typical JdbcTemplate configuration, which might appear in a Spring @Configuration class:

```
import org.springframework.context.annotation.Bean;
import org.springframework.context.annotation.Configuration;
import org.springframework.jdbc.core.JdbcTemplate;
import org.springframework.jdbc.datasource.DriverManagerDataSource;

import javax.sql.DataSource;

@Configuration
public class DataSourceConfig {

    @Bean
    public DataSource dataSource() {
        DriverManagerDataSource dataSource = new DriverManagerDataSource();
        dataSource.setDriverClassName("com.mysql.cj.jdbc.Driver");
        dataSource.setUrl("jdbc:mysql://localhost:3306/springdb");
        dataSource.setUsername("root");
        dataSource.setPassword("password");
        return dataSource;
    }

    @Bean
    public JdbcTemplate jdbcTemplate(DataSource dataSource) {
        return new JdbcTemplate(dataSource);
    }
}
```

In this configuration, DriverManagerDataSource is instantiated and configured with database connection details. The JdbcTemplate bean is then created using this DataSource, enabling database operations to be conducted with ease. Notice how minimal and clean the configuration remains, abstracting the underlying complexity.

Spring Data Access encourages the practice of leveraging *Spring Data JPA* for advanced repository management tasks. Setting up a repository requires the definition of an interface extending JpaRepository, as illustrated in the following example:

```
import org.springframework.data.jpa.repository.JpaRepository;

public interface UserRepository extends JpaRepository<User, Long> {
```

```
    User findByUsername(String username);
}
```

Here, UserRepository extends JpaRepository, obtaining built-in CRUD functionality without additional code. The method findByUsername leverages Spring Data JPA's naming conventions to automatically construct a query based on the method name.

Spring Data Access mechanisms are bound by Spring's Dependency Injection (DI) framework, promoting loose coupling and better modularity. This ensures that data access objects (DAOs) and service layers are easy to test, extend, and maintain.

Leveraging these foundational elements empowers developers to build robust, scalable, and efficient data-access layers within their Spring applications. By understanding and utilizing the abstractions and tools provided by Spring Data Access, one can manage data interactions effectively while adhering to best practices and architectural principles.

5.2 Setting Up a Database for Spring Applications

Properly configuring a database is essential for any Spring application that handles persistent storage. This section details the steps required to set up a database to seamlessly interact with Spring applications. We'll cover the installation and configuration of PostgreSQL as our database management system (DBMS), although the principles are applicable to other relational DBMSs such as MySQL or Oracle. Additionally, we'll address how to configure the database connection in a Spring Boot application.

Installing PostgreSQL:

PostgreSQL is an open-source, powerful, and robust relational database system. To install PostgreSQL, follow these steps on a Unix-based system (similar steps apply for Windows):

- Update the local package lists from the repositories:

```
sudo apt-get update
```

- Install PostgreSQL and the PostgreSQL contrib package with additional utilities:

```
sudo apt-get install postgresql postgresql-contrib
```

- After installation, PostgreSQL should start automatically. You can check the status using:

```
sudo systemctl status postgresql
```

- Access the PostgreSQL prompt by switching to the 'postgres' user:

```
sudo -i -u postgres
```

Then start the PostgreSQL interactive terminal:

```
psql
```

Creating a Database and User:

Once PostgreSQL is installed, creating a database and user for the Spring application can be accomplished through the interactive terminal:

- Create a new database:

```
CREATE DATABASE springappdb;
```

- Create a new user with a password:

```
CREATE USER springappuser WITH PASSWORD 'securepassword';
```

- Grant necessary privileges to the user on the database:

```
GRANT ALL PRIVILEGES ON DATABASE springappdb TO
    springappuser;
```

Exit the PostgreSQL prompt by typing:

```
\q
```

Configuring the Database Connection in Spring Boot:

For a Spring Boot application to interact with the newly created PostgreSQL database, configuration settings must be added to the application.properties or application.yml file located in the src/main/resources directory.

Using application.properties, the configuration would look like this:

```
spring.datasource.url=jdbc:postgresql://localhost:5432/springappdb
spring.datasource.username=springappuser
spring.datasource.password=securepassword
spring.datasource.driver-class-name=org.postgresql.Driver

# Hibernate properties
spring.jpa.hibernate.ddl-auto=update
spring.jpa.properties.hibernate.dialect=org.hibernate.dialect.PostgreSQLDialect
```

If using application.yml, the configuration will be:

```
spring:
  datasource:
    url: jdbc:postgresql://localhost:5432/springappdb
    username: springappuser
    password: securepassword
    driver-class-name: org.postgresql.Driver

  jpa:
    hibernate:
      ddl-auto: update
    properties:
      hibernate:
        dialect: org.hibernate.dialect.PostgreSQLDialect
```

Here, the spring.datasource.url specifies the JDBC URL for PostgreSQL, spring.datasource.username and spring.datasource.password are the credentials for the database user. The driver class name is specified by spring.datasource.driver-class-name.

The Hibernate-related settings ensure proper interaction with PostgreSQL by setting the dialect to PostgreSQLDialect. The spring.jpa.hibernate.ddl-auto configuration dictates how the database schema should be managed by Hibernate. For development, update is a common option as it automatically updates the schema according to entity changes.

Verifying the Configuration:

To verify that the Spring Boot application can successfully connect to the PostgreSQL database, follow these steps:

- Ensure that the PostgreSQL service is running.
- Run the Spring Boot application using the command:

  ```
  ./mvnw spring-boot:run
  ```

  or for Gradle builds:

  ```
  ./gradlew bootRun
  ```

- Check the application logs to confirm a successful connection. You should see output similar to:

```
HikariPool-1 - Starting...
HikariPool-1 - Start completed.
```

A successful application startup verifies the proper setup of the PostgreSQL database and its integration with the Spring Boot application. Ensure to handle exceptions and errors during connection attempts to facilitate debugging and resolution.

5.3 Spring JDBC Module

The Spring JDBC module provides comprehensive support for working with relational databases. It simplifies error handling, manages connections, and abstracts away many of the repetitive programming tasks involved in database interaction. This deep integration offers a balance between flexibility and simplicity, allowing developers to effectively handle data operations without delving into excessive configuration or boilerplate code.

At the heart of the Spring JDBC module lies the JdbcTemplate class. This central class in the module handles the creation and release of database resources, translates SQL exceptions into Spring's DataAccessException hierarchy, and facilitates the execution of SQL queries and updates.

Let us examine the most salient features and functionalities provided by the JdbcTemplate class.

- **Setup and Configuration:** Setting up the JdbcTemplate requires defining a DataSource bean and then injecting it into the JdbcTemplate instance. The DataSource bean configuration can be managed through Spring's Java-based configuration or XML-based configuration. Here is an example using Java-based configuration:

```
@Configuration
public class DataSourceConfig {

    @Bean
    public DataSource dataSource() {
        DriverManagerDataSource dataSource = new DriverManagerDataSource();
        dataSource.setDriverClassName("com.mysql.cj.jdbc.Driver");
        dataSource.setUrl("jdbc:mysql://localhost:3306/mydb");
```

```
        dataSource.setUsername("username");
        dataSource.setPassword("password");
        return dataSource;
    }

    @Bean
    public JdbcTemplate jdbcTemplate(DataSource dataSource) {
        return new JdbcTemplate(dataSource);
    }
}
```

In this configuration, a DriverManagerDataSource instance is configured with the necessary database connection properties. The JdbcTemplate bean is then created by passing the DataSource bean as a parameter.

- **Basic Usage of JdbcTemplate:** The JdbcTemplate class provides methods for performing various database operations. For instance, when querying the database for a single result, the queryForObject method can be employed:

```
public User findUserById(int id) {
    String sql = "SELECT * FROM users WHERE id = ?";
    return jdbcTemplate.queryForObject(sql, new Object[]{id}, new UserRowMapper());
}
```

In this example, the queryForObject method takes a SQL query, an array of parameters, and a RowMapper object that maps the ResultSet to a Java object. The UserRowMapper class might be implemented as follows:

```
public class UserRowMapper implements RowMapper<User> {

    @Override
    public User mapRow(ResultSet rs, int rowNum) throws SQLException {
        User user = new User();
        user.setId(rs.getInt("id"));
        user.setName(rs.getString("name"));
        user.setEmail(rs.getString("email"));
        return user;
    }
}
```

The UserRowMapper class implements the RowMapper interface, providing an implementation of the mapRow method that translates a single row of the ResultSet into a User object.

- **Executing Updates:** For updating database records, the update method of the JdbcTemplate class is utilized. This method can execute an SQL update operation, such as INSERT, UPDATE, or DELETE statements:

```
public int updateUserEmail(int id, String email) {
    String sql = "UPDATE users SET email = ? WHERE id = ?";
    return jdbcTemplate.update(sql, email, id);
}
```

Here, the update method executes the given SQL statement, taking the new email and user ID as parameters. The method returns the number of rows affected by the update.

- **Batch Operations:** Batch operations can be performed using the batchUpdate method, which allows executing multiple updates in one batch to improve performance:

```
public int[] batchUpdateUsersEmails(List<User> users) {
    String sql = "UPDATE users SET email = ? WHERE id = ?";
    return jdbcTemplate.batchUpdate(sql, new BatchPreparedStatementSetter() {
        @Override
        public void setValues(PreparedStatement ps, int i) throws SQLException {
            User user = users.get(i);
            ps.setString(1, user.getEmail());
            ps.setInt(2, user.getId());
        }

        @Override
        public int getBatchSize() {
            return users.size();
        }
    });
}
```

In this example, the batchUpdate method leverages the BatchPreparedStatementSetter interface to set the parameter values for each batch entry. The getBatchSize method returns the total number of entries in the batch.

- **Error Handling and Transaction Management:** The Spring JDBC module simplifies error handling by converting SQLExceptions into a hierarchy of DataAccessException instances. This allows consistent handling of database errors across the application. For instance:

```
try {
    String sql = "SELECT * FROM users WHERE id = ?";
    User user = jdbcTemplate.queryForObject(sql, new Object[]{1}, new
        UserRowMapper());
} catch (DataAccessException e) {
```

```
    // Handle the database access error
}
```

Additionally, the JdbcTemplate can be used with Spring's transaction management support. Transaction management is typically configured via Spring's PlatformTransactionManager. Here's an example of configuring a transaction manager and using it to manage transactions:

```
@Configuration
@EnableTransactionManagement
public class AppConfig {

    @Bean
    public PlatformTransactionManager transactionManager(DataSource dataSource) {
        return new DataSourceTransactionManager(dataSource);
    }
}

@Service
public class UserService {

    @Autowired
    private JdbcTemplate jdbcTemplate;

    @Transactional
    public void updateUserDetails(User user) {
        String updateNameSql = "UPDATE users SET name = ? WHERE id = ?";
        String updateEmailSql = "UPDATE users SET email = ? WHERE id = ?";
        jdbcTemplate.update(updateNameSql, user.getName(), user.getId());
        jdbcTemplate.update(updateEmailSql, user.getEmail(), user.getId());
    }
}
```

In this configuration, the DataSourceTransactionManager bean manages transaction boundaries. Methods annotated with @Transactional are executed within a transactional context, ensuring atomicity.

- **NamedParameterJdbcTemplate:** The NamedParameterJdbcTemplate class provides additional convenience by allowing the use of named parameters instead of the traditional question mark (?) placeholders. Here's an example:

```
public User findUserByName(String name) {
    String sql = "SELECT * FROM users WHERE name = :name";
    Map<String, Object> params = new HashMap<>();
    params.put("name", name);
    return namedParameterJdbcTemplate.queryForObject(sql, params, new
            UserRowMapper());
}
```

In this instance, named parameters are mapped to values via a Map, enhancing readability and reducing the risk of parameter mismatches.

The Spring JDBC module streamlines various database tasks, providing a robust framework for data access operations while maintaining simplicity and flexibility.

5.4 Using JdbcTemplate for Data Access

JdbcTemplate is a central class in the Spring framework that simplifies the usage of JDBC and helps to avoid common issues such as resource leaks, cumbersome error handling, and redundant boilerplate code. By encapsulating the database access logic within its various methods, JdbcTemplate provides a streamlined approach for executing queries, updates, and managing prepared statements.

The basic use of JdbcTemplate involves setting it up with a DataSource and then leveraging its methods to perform database operations. Let us delve into the details of how to properly configure and use JdbcTemplate.

To begin with, ensure that you have the necessary dependencies added to your project. For instance, if you are using Maven, include the following dependencies in your pom.xml file:

```
<dependency>
    <groupId>org.springframework.boot</groupId>
    <artifactId>spring-boot-starter-jdbc</artifactId>
</dependency>
<dependency>
    <groupId>com.h2database</groupId>
    <artifactId>h2</artifactId>
    <scope>runtime</scope>
</dependency>
```

Next, configure the DataSource bean and the JdbcTemplate bean in a configuration class. Here's an example configuration using H2 in-memory database:

```
import org.springframework.context.annotation.Bean;
import org.springframework.context.annotation.Configuration;
import org.springframework.jdbc.core.JdbcTemplate;
import org.springframework.jdbc.datasource.DriverManagerDataSource;

import javax.sql.DataSource;

@Configuration
public class DataSourceConfig {

    @Bean
    public DataSource dataSource() {
        DriverManagerDataSource dataSource = new DriverManagerDataSource();
        dataSource.setDriverClassName("org.h2.Driver");
```

```
        dataSource.setUrl("jdbc:h2:mem:testdb");
        dataSource.setUsername("sa");
        dataSource.setPassword("");
        return dataSource;
    }

    @Bean
    public JdbcTemplate jdbcTemplate(DataSource dataSource) {
        return new JdbcTemplate(dataSource);
    }
}
```

With the DataSource and JdbcTemplate configured, we can move on to using JdbcTemplate for various data access operations. Below is an example of how to use JdbcTemplate to execute a simple SQL query:

```
import org.springframework.beans.factory.annotation.Autowired;
import org.springframework.jdbc.core.JdbcTemplate;
import org.springframework.stereotype.Repository;

@Repository
public class UserRepository {

    private final JdbcTemplate jdbcTemplate;

    @Autowired
    public UserRepository(JdbcTemplate jdbcTemplate) {
        this.jdbcTemplate = jdbcTemplate;
    }

    public int countUsers() {
        String sql = "SELECT COUNT(*) FROM users";
        return jdbcTemplate.queryForObject(sql, Integer.class);
    }
}
```

In the above example, queryForObject is used to execute the SQL query and retrieve a single result. JdbcTemplate provides several methods for different types of operations. Below are some commonly used methods:

- execute: Used for executing a SQL statement without returning any result.
- queryForObject: Retrieves a single result of a query.
- queryForList: Retrieves multiple rows from the database and stores them in a List.
- query: Executes a query and maps each row of the result set to a Java object using a RowMapper.
- update: Used for SQL statements that change the database state (e.g., INSERT, UPDATE, DELETE).

Let us consider an example where we need to retrieve user records from the database. We will use RowMapper to map each row to a User object:

```
import org.springframework.jdbc.core.RowMapper;

import java.sql.ResultSet;
import java.sql.SQLException;

public class UserRowMapper implements RowMapper<User> {

    @Override
    public User mapRow(ResultSet rs, int rowNum) throws SQLException {
        User user = new User();
        user.setId(rs.getInt("id"));
        user.setName(rs.getString("name"));
        user.setEmail(rs.getString("email"));
        return user;
    }
}
```

Now, we will use JdbcTemplate and UserRowMapper to retrieve users from the database:

```
import java.util.List;

@Repository
public class UserRepository {

    private final JdbcTemplate jdbcTemplate;

    @Autowired
    public UserRepository(JdbcTemplate jdbcTemplate) {
        this.jdbcTemplate = jdbcTemplate;
    }

    public List<User> findAllUsers() {
        String sql = "SELECT * FROM users";
        return jdbcTemplate.query(sql, new UserRowMapper());
    }
}
```

JdbcTemplate also facilitates the use of prepared statements, which are essential for preventing SQL injection attacks. You can use the following example to insert a new user into the database:

```
@Repository
public class UserRepository {

    private final JdbcTemplate jdbcTemplate;

    @Autowired
    public UserRepository(JdbcTemplate jdbcTemplate) {
        this.jdbcTemplate = jdbcTemplate;
    }

    public int createUser(User user) {
        String sql = "INSERT INTO users (name, email) VALUES (?, ?)";
```

```
        return jdbcTemplate.update(sql, user.getName(), user.getEmail());
    }
}
```

In this example, the update method is used with dynamic parameters to insert a new record. This not only simplifies the coding process but also enhances security by mitigating SQL injection risks.

Finally, handling transactions with JdbcTemplate is straightforward with the help of Spring's transaction management. Annotating the service method with @Transactional ensures that the database operations within that method are executed in a transactional context:

```
import org.springframework.stereotype.Service;
import org.springframework.transaction.annotation.Transactional;

@Service
public class UserService {

    private final UserRepository userRepository;

    @Autowired
    public UserService(UserRepository userRepository) {
        this.userRepository = userRepository;
    }

    @Transactional
    public void registerUser(User user) {
        userRepository.createUser(user);
        // additional operations
    }
}
```

In this example, adding @Transactional ensures that if any operation within registerUser method fails, the entire transaction will be rolled back, preserving data integrity.

By leveraging JdbcTemplate's capabilities, developers can achieve efficient and secure data access, streamline common database operations, and ensure clean and maintainable code in Spring applications.

5.5 Spring ORM Module

Spring ORM (Object-Relational Mapping) module serves as a vital component in Spring Framework's suite for data access. This module integrates with various popular ORM frameworks, providing a consistent and streamlined approach to handle database operations. The integration with ORM tools such as Hibernate, JPA, and JDO simplifies the configuration and enhances the developer's experience in managing database interactions within a Spring context.

The primary goal of the Spring ORM module is to offer a higher level of abstraction over the underlying persistence mechanisms. By doing so, it reduces the boilerplate code and enables a more declarative approach to managing data access.

Configuration and Dependency Management

To utilize the Spring ORM module, the relevant dependencies must be included in your project configuration files. For instance, when using Maven as your build tool, you need to add the following dependencies to your pom.xml file:

```
<dependency>
    <groupId>org.springframework</groupId>
    <artifactId>spring-orm</artifactId>
    <version>${spring.version}</version>
</dependency>
<dependency>
    <groupId>org.hibernate</groupId>
    <artifactId>hibernate-core</artifactId>
    <version>${hibernate.version}</version>
</dependency>
```

Setting Up a SessionFactory

One of the foundational concepts in Hibernate ORM is the SessionFactory, which provides a factory for Session instances. Within a Spring configuration, the SessionFactory bean is defined in the Spring application context. This configuration typically requires properties such as the database connection URL, username, password, dialect, and the list of annotated entity classes.

Here is an example of how to configure a SessionFactory bean using Spring's Java-based configuration:

```
@Configuration
public class HibernateConfig {

    @Bean
    public LocalSessionFactoryBean sessionFactory(DataSource dataSource) {
        LocalSessionFactoryBean sessionFactory = new LocalSessionFactoryBean();
        sessionFactory.setDataSource(dataSource);
        sessionFactory.setPackagesToScan(new String[] {"com.example.model"});

        Properties hibernateProperties = new Properties();
        hibernateProperties.setProperty("hibernate.dialect", "org.hibernate.dialect.
            MySQL5Dialect");
        hibernateProperties.setProperty("hibernate.hbm2ddl.auto", "update");

        sessionFactory.setHibernateProperties(hibernateProperties);

        return sessionFactory;
    }
```

```
}
```

In the example above, LocalSessionFactoryBean is used to set up the Hibernate SessionFactory within a Spring application. The method sessionFactory() sets the necessary Hibernate properties and scans the specified package for entity classes.

Defining Transaction Management

Transaction management is crucial for ensuring data integrity and consistency. Spring ORM module supports declarative transaction management via annotations and AOP (Aspect-Oriented Programming). By defining a transaction manager bean, developers can begin to leverage Spring's transaction support.

For example, using the HibernateTransactionManager as the transaction manager in the configuration:

```
@Configuration
@EnableTransactionManagement
public class AppConfig {

    @Bean
    public HibernateTransactionManager transactionManager(SessionFactory
         sessionFactory) {
        return new HibernateTransactionManager(sessionFactory);
    }
}
```

With the application context configured to enable transaction management via the @EnableTransactionManagement annotation, transactions can now be managed declaratively using the @Transactional annotation on service layer methods.

```
@Service
public class EmployeeService {

    @Autowired
    private EmployeeDao employeeDao;

    @Transactional
    public void saveEmployee(Employee employee) {
        employeeDao.save(employee);
    }
}
```

In the example above, the method saveEmployee() is marked with the @Transactional annotation. This ensures that the method runs within a transactional context, handling the commits and rollbacks automatically.

Mapping Entities

ORM involves mapping Java objects to database tables. This typically involves defining entity classes annotated with @Entity and other related annotations. Here is an example of an entity class mapped to a database table:

```
@Entity
@Table(name = "employees")
public class Employee {

    @Id
    @GeneratedValue(strategy = GenerationType.IDENTITY)
    @Column(name = "id")
    private Long id;

    @Column(name = "name")
    private String name;

    @Column(name = "department")
    private String department;

    // Getters and Setters
}
```

The @Entity annotation specifies that the class is an entity and is mapped to a database table. The @Table annotation specifies the name of the table. Each field is annotated with @Column to define the column mappings. The primary key is annotated with @Id and @GeneratedValue to define the generation strategy.

Repository Layer

Spring provides the HibernateTemplate class to simplify Hibernate data access code. However, the preferred approach is to leverage Spring Data JPA repositories which provide a more robust and easy-to-use abstraction.

Here is an example of a DAO implemented using Hibernate:

```
@Repository
public class EmployeeDao {

    @Autowired
    private SessionFactory sessionFactory;

    public void save(Employee employee) {
        Session session = sessionFactory.getCurrentSession();
        session.save(employee);
    }

    public Employee findById(Long id) {
        Session session = sessionFactory.getCurrentSession();
        return session.get(Employee.class, id);
    }
}
```

In this DAO, the save and findById methods use the Hibernate Session to interact with the database. By injecting the SessionFactory, we access the current session and perform database operations.

Integrating the ORM frameworks and leveraging Spring's comprehensive support for ORM tools streamline the development of data-intensive applications while ensuring clean, maintainable, and modular code.

5.6 Integrating Hibernate with Spring

Integrating Hibernate with Spring ensures streamlined data persistence in Java applications by leveraging advantages from both frameworks. This process involves configuration steps that bind Hibernate ORM with the Spring framework to facilitate efficient and scalable data transactions. We will explore the necessary configurations, Spring beans, Hibernate session management, and transaction demarcation for effective integration.

First, ensure you have the necessary dependencies in your project's build configuration file, such as Maven's pom.xml:

```
<dependency>
    <groupId>org.springframework</groupId>
    <artifactId>spring-orm</artifactId>
    <version>5.3.8</version>
</dependency>
<dependency>
    <groupId>org.hibernate</groupId>
    <artifactId>hibernate-core</artifactId>
    <version>5.5.3.Final</version>
</dependency>
<dependency>
    <groupId>javax.transaction</groupId>
    <artifactId>javax.transaction-api</artifactId>
    <version>1.3</version>
</dependency>
<dependency>
    <groupId>javax.persistence</groupId>
    <artifactId>javax.persistence-api</artifactId>
    <version>2.2</version>
</dependency>
<dependency>
    <groupId>mysql</groupId>
    <artifactId>mysql-connector-java</artifactId>
    <version>8.0.23</version>
</dependency>
```

Next, configure the application.properties file for database connectivity. This file typically resides in the src/main/resources/ directory:

```
spring.datasource.url=jdbc:mysql://localhost:3306/yourdatabase
spring.datasource.username=yourusername
spring.datasource.password=yourpassword
spring.datasource.driver-class-name=com.mysql.cj.jdbc.Driver

spring.jpa.database-platform=org.hibernate.dialect.MySQL5Dialect
spring.jpa.show-sql=true
spring.jpa.hibernate.ddl-auto=update
```

The Spring configuration class, often annotated with @Configuration, manages the creation and injection of Hibernate SessionFactory, DataSource, and related beans. Here's a sample configuration class:

```
import org.springframework.context.annotation.Bean;
import org.springframework.context.annotation.Configuration;
import org.springframework.orm.hibernate5.HibernateTransactionManager;
import org.springframework.orm.hibernate5.LocalSessionFactoryBean;
import org.springframework.transaction.annotation.EnableTransactionManagement;

import javax.sql.DataSource;
import org.springframework.boot.jdbc.DataSourceBuilder;
import java.util.Properties;

@Configuration
@EnableTransactionManagement
public class HibernateConfig {

    @Bean
    public LocalSessionFactoryBean sessionFactory() {
        LocalSessionFactoryBean sessionFactory = new LocalSessionFactoryBean();
        sessionFactory.setDataSource(dataSource());
        sessionFactory.setPackagesToScan("com.example.model");
        sessionFactory.setHibernateProperties(hibernateProperties());
        return sessionFactory;
    }

    @Bean
    public DataSource dataSource() {
        return DataSourceBuilder.create()
                .driverClassName("com.mysql.cj.jdbc.Driver")
                .url("jdbc:mysql://localhost:3306/yourdatabase")
                .username("yourusername")
                .password("yourpassword")
                .build();
    }

    private Properties hibernateProperties() {
        Properties properties = new Properties();
        properties.put("hibernate.dialect", "org.hibernate.dialect.MySQL5Dialect");
        properties.put("hibernate.show_sql", "true");
        properties.put("hibernate.format_sql", "true");
        properties.put("hibernate.hbm2ddl.auto", "update");
        return properties;
    }

    @Bean
    public HibernateTransactionManager transactionManager() {
        HibernateTransactionManager transactionManager = new
                HibernateTransactionManager();
        transactionManager.setSessionFactory(sessionFactory().getObject());
```

```
        return transactionManager;
    }
}
```

The LocalSessionFactoryBean class configures the Hibernate SessionFactory, a central component for Hibernate's operations. The dataSource bean defines the connectivity aspects to the underlying database. The hibernateProperties method encapsulates Hibernate-specific settings, and the transactionManager bean manages transactions.

Entities should be annotated with @Entity, @Table, and other relevant JPA annotations to map Java classes to database tables. Consider the following entity class as an example:

```
import javax.persistence.Entity;
import javax.persistence.Table;
import javax.persistence.Id;
import javax.persistence.GeneratedValue;
import javax.persistence.GenerationType;

@Entity
@Table(name = "employees")
public class Employee {

    @Id
    @GeneratedValue(strategy = GenerationType.IDENTITY)
    private Long id;

    private String firstName;
    private String lastName;

    // Getters and Setters
}
```

For data access implementation, create DAO beans and use the SessionFactory within transactional methods. The DAO class interacts directly with the database via Hibernate's Session interface:

```
import org.hibernate.SessionFactory;
import org.springframework.beans.factory.annotation.Autowired;
import org.springframework.stereotype.Repository;
import org.springframework.transaction.annotation.Transactional;

import java.util.List;

@Repository
public class EmployeeDAO {

    @Autowired
    private SessionFactory sessionFactory;

    @Transactional
    public void saveEmployee(Employee employee) {
        sessionFactory.getCurrentSession().saveOrUpdate(employee);
    }
```

```
    @Transactional(readOnly = true)
    public Employee getEmployeeById(Long id) {
        return sessionFactory.getCurrentSession().get(Employee.class, id);
    }

    @Transactional(readOnly = true)
    public List<Employee> getAllEmployees() {
        return sessionFactory.getCurrentSession().createQuery("from Employee",
             Employee.class).list();
    }

    @Transactional
    public void deleteEmployee(Employee employee) {
        sessionFactory.getCurrentSession().delete(employee);
    }
}
```

In this DAO class, the sessionFactory bean is injected using @Autowired. The transactional methods demonstrate basic CRUD operations: saving (saveEmployee), reading (getEmployeeById, getAllEmployees), and deleting (deleteEmployee) records in the database.

The @Transactional annotation not only simplifies transaction management but also ensures the Atomicity, Consistency, Isolation, and Durability (ACID) properties in database operations.

The final integration step involves testing the configured setup. Instantiate the ApplicationContext and invoke the DAO methods to verify the operational data access layer. A test class might look like this:

```
import org.springframework.context.annotation.AnnotationConfigApplicationContext;
import com.example.config.HibernateConfig;

public class MainApp {

    public static void main(String[] args) {
        AnnotationConfigApplicationContext context = new
             AnnotationConfigApplicationContext(HibernateConfig.class);

        EmployeeDAO employeeDAO = context.getBean(EmployeeDAO.class);

        Employee employee = new Employee();
        employee.setFirstName("John");
        employee.setLastName("Doe");

        employeeDAO.saveEmployee(employee);

        Employee emp = employeeDAO.getEmployeeById(employee.getId());
        System.out.println("Retrieved Employee: " + emp.getFirstName() + " " + emp.
             getLastName());

        context.close();
    }
}
```

Testing outputs can verify the successful integration:

```
2022-08-15 12:34:56 INFO main o.s.o.h.HibernateTransactionManager: Using DataSource [HikariDataSource (HikariPool-1)] of Hibernate SessionFactory
2022-08-15 12:34:56 INFO main o.h.h.i.QueryTranslatorFactoryInitiator: HHH000397: Using ASTQueryTranslatorFactory
2022-08-15 12:34:56 INFO main o.h.h.t.b.w.AbstractBatchImpl: HHH000010: On release of batch it still contained JDBC statements
Hibernate: insert into employees (first_name, last_name) values (?, ?)
Retrieved Employee: John Doe
```

Integrating Hibernate with Spring streamlines the complexity of Java enterprise applications by providing a robust and efficient ORM solution, essential for effective data manipulation within a Spring framework.

5.7 JPA with Spring Data

The Java Persistence API (JPA) is a specification that provides a mechanism for object-relational mapping (ORM) in Java applications. JPA allows developers to map Java objects to database tables and vice versa, facilitating the process of saving, retrieving, and managing data in a relational database. The Spring Data JPA project makes it easier to implement JPA-based repositories and access data using repository interfaces, reducing the amount of boilerplate code necessary for data access layers.

To begin using JPA with Spring Data, it is essential to include the necessary dependencies in your project. In a Maven-based project, the pom.xml file should include the following dependencies:

```
<dependency>
    <groupId>org.springframework.boot</groupId>
    <artifactId>spring-boot-starter-data-jpa</artifactId>
</dependency>
<dependency>
    <groupId>com.h2database</groupId>
    <artifactId>h2</artifactId>
    <scope>runtime</scope>
</dependency>
```

Here, the spring-boot-starter-data-jpa dependency encapsulates the necessary libraries to integrate JPA with Spring Boot, including Hibernate as the default JPA provider. The h2 dependency provides an in-memory database for rapid development and testing.

Next, configuring the database and JPA settings in application.properties is crucial. Below is a typical configuration for an H2 database:

```
spring.datasource.url=jdbc:h2:mem:testdb
spring.datasource.driverClassName=org.h2.Driver
spring.datasource.username=sa
spring.datasource.password=password
spring.jpa.hibernate.ddl-auto=update
spring.jpa.show-sql=true
```

This configuration sets up an in-memory H2 database with the JDBC URL jdbc:h2:mem:testdb. The spring.jpa.hibernate.ddl-auto=update property ensures that Hibernate automatically updates the database schema according to the JPA entity mappings. The spring.jpa.show-sql=true property instructs Spring to log the SQL statements generated by Hibernate, aiding in debugging and learning.

The primary building blocks of using JPA with Spring Data are entity classes and repository interfaces. An entity class represents a table in the database, while a repository interface provides methods to perform CRUD operations on the entities. Consider the following example of an Employee entity:

```
import javax.persistence.Entity;
import javax.persistence.GeneratedValue;
import javax.persistence.GenerationType;
import javax.persistence.Id;

@Entity
public class Employee {

    @Id
    @GeneratedValue(strategy = GenerationType.IDENTITY)
    private Long id;
    private String firstName;
    private String lastName;
    private String email;

    // Getters and setters
}
```

In this example, the Employee class is annotated with @Entity, indicating that it is a JPA entity. The id field annotated with @Id and @GeneratedValue(strategy = GenerationType.IDENTITY) marks it as the primary key with an auto-incremented value.

To perform data access operations, create a repository interface by extending the JpaRepository:

```
import org.springframework.data.jpa.repository.JpaRepository;
import org.springframework.stereotype.Repository;

@Repository
public interface EmployeeRepository extends JpaRepository<Employee, Long> {
}
```

The EmployeeRepository interface extends JpaRepository<Employee, Long>, where Employee is the entity type and Long is the type of the primary key. By extending JpaRepository, the EmployeeRepository inherits several methods for performing CRUD operations, including save(), findById(), findAll(), deleteById(), and others.

With the entity and repository defined, you can now inject EmployeeRepository into a service or controller to manage employees. For example:

```
import org.springframework.beans.factory.annotation.Autowired;
import org.springframework.stereotype.Service;

import java.util.List;

@Service
public class EmployeeService {

    @Autowired
    private EmployeeRepository employeeRepository;

    public List<Employee> getAllEmployees() {
        return employeeRepository.findAll();
    }

    public Employee getEmployeeById(Long id) {
        return employeeRepository.findById(id).orElse(null);
    }

    public Employee saveEmployee(Employee employee) {
        return employeeRepository.save(employee);
    }

    public void deleteEmployee(Long id) {
        employeeRepository.deleteById(id);
    }
}
```

The EmployeeService class defines methods to retrieve, save, and delete employees, delegating these operations to EmployeeRepository. The @Autowired annotation is used to inject an instance of EmployeeRepository into EmployeeService.

Running a Spring Boot application that uses JPA with Spring Data involves creating an entry point with the @SpringBootApplication annotation:

```
import org.springframework.boot.SpringApplication;
import org.springframework.boot.autoconfigure.SpringBootApplication;

@SpringBootApplication
public class SpringDataJpaApplication {

    public static void main(String[] args) {
        SpringApplication.run(SpringDataJpaApplication.class, args);
    }
}
```

Executing the SpringDataJpaApplication class initiates the Spring Boot application, setting up the necessary context, and configuring JPA repositories. This setup allows for seamless integration and efficient data access with minimal configuration.

Integrating JPA with Spring Data provides a powerful and streamlined approach to accessing and managing data, leveraging the strengths of both technologies to create robust and maintainable applications.

5.8 Spring Data JPA Repositories

Spring Data JPA, part of the larger Spring Data family, makes it easier to build Spring-powered applications that use JPA (Java Persistence API) for data persistence. A central concept in Spring Data JPA is the repository abstraction. This section provides an in-depth exploration of Spring Data JPA repositories, focusing on their configuration, functionalities, and practical usage patterns.

Spring Data JPA repositories simplify the data access layer implementation by encapsulating database interactions in repository interfaces. These interfaces expose CRUD operations and allow the definition of custom query methods, significantly reducing boilerplate code.

Repositories are defined by extending Spring Data JPA's Repository interfaces. The core interfaces are:

- Repository<T,ID>
- CrudRepository<T,ID>
- PagingAndSortingRepository<T,ID>
- JpaRepository<T,ID>

Here, T denotes the entity type, and ID represents the type of the entity's identifier.

To start using the Spring Data JPA repository abstraction, ensure that Spring Data JPA is included in the project dependencies and properly configured. Assuming Maven as the build tool, the relevant dependency in the pom.xml file is:

```
<dependency>
    <groupId>org.springframework.boot</groupId>
    <artifactId>spring-boot-starter-data-jpa</artifactId>
</dependency>
```

With this dependency in place, let us consider a simplified practical example involving an entity class User.

```
@Entity
public class User {
    @Id
    @GeneratedValue(strategy = GenerationType.IDENTITY)
    private Long id;
    private String username;
    private String email;

    // Getters, Setters, Constructors
}
```

Create a repository interface for the User entity by extending JpaRepository:

```
public interface UserRepository extends JpaRepository<User, Long> {
    // Custom query methods can be defined here
}
```

Spring Data JPA provides an implementation of the repository interface at runtime, allowing straightforward data access operations. For example:

```
@Service
public class UserService {

    @Autowired
    private UserRepository userRepository;

    public List<User> findAllUsers() {
        return userRepository.findAll();
    }

    public User findUserById(Long id) {
        Optional<User> user = userRepository.findById(id);
        return user.orElse(null);
    }

    public User saveUser(User user) {
        return userRepository.save(user);
    }

    public void deleteUser(Long id) {
        userRepository.deleteById(id);
    }
}
```

This example demonstrates basic CRUD operations. In addition to these methods, repositories can include custom query methods. Spring Data JPA translates method names into JPQL (Java Persistence Query Language) queries based on a predefined naming convention.

Consider the following custom query methods:

```
public interface UserRepository extends JpaRepository<User, Long> {
    List<User> findByUsername(String username);
    List<User> findByEmailContaining(String emailSubstring);
```

```
}
```

Spring Data JPA will automatically generate appropriate queries for these methods. For example, findByUsername(String username) translates to SELECT u FROM User u WHERE u.username = :username, and findByEmailContaining(String emailSubstring) translates to SELECT u FROM User u WHERE u.email LIKE %:emailSubstring%.

Another powerful feature of Spring Data JPA repositories is query annotation. The @Query annotation allows overriding default behavior by explicitly specifying JPQL or native SQL queries.

```
public interface UserRepository extends JpaRepository<User, Long> {

    @Query("SELECT u FROM User u WHERE u.email = ?1")
    User findByEmail(String email);

    @Query(value = "SELECT * FROM users WHERE username = ?1", nativeQuery
        = true)
    User findByUsernameNative(String username);
}
```

These examples manifest the flexibility offered by Spring Data JPA repositories for diverse query requirements. Furthermore, pagination and sorting are integral parts of data access in real-world applications. Spring Data JPA supports pagination and sorting through the PagingAndSortingRepository interface and the Pageable and Sort objects.

Paginated retrieval in a service class might look like this:

```
public List<User> findUsersPaginated(int page, int size) {
    Pageable pageable = PageRequest.of(page, size);
    Page<User> userPage = userRepository.findAll(pageable);
    return userPage.getContent();
}
```

Sorting users by username:

```
public List<User> findUsersSortedByUsername() {
    return userRepository.findAll(Sort.by("username").ascending());
}
```

By leveraging these capabilities, the efficiency and maintainability of the data access layer in a Spring application are greatly enhanced, aligning with best practices for modern application development.

The advantages extend beyond code reduction and auto-generation by promoting adherence to well-defined patterns and conventions, thus fostering a more structured data layer.

5.9 Custom Repository Methods

To delve deeper into Spring Data JPA, it is vital to comprehend how to define custom repository methods. While Spring Data JPA provides a wealth of query generation capabilities out of the box, there are scenarios where the provided functionality does not cater to the application's requirements. This section will explore various ways to implement custom methods in a repository, ensuring an efficient query execution process.

In Spring Data JPA, to extend the functionality of the default repository interface, we generally follow three principal techniques:

- Derived Query Methods
- JPQL (Java Persistence Query Language)
- Native Queries

These techniques provide flexibility in crafting custom queries adaptable to specific needs.

Derived Query Methods

Derived Query Methods form a convention-based approach where query generation is based on the method name's structure. The method's name is parsed by the JPA framework to generate the query automatically. This requires adherence to a strict naming convention, where the method name starts with a prefix such as findBy, readBy, or queryBy, followed by the entity's attributes.

Consider the following example:

```
public interface UserRepository extends JpaRepository<User, Long> {
    List<User> findByLastName(String lastName);
    User findByEmail(String email);
}
```

In this example, the Spring Data JPA framework translates findByLastName and findByEmail methods into appropriate SQL queries. This method is expedient but lacks the complexity needed beyond simple queries.

JPQL (Java Persistence Query Language)

JPQL is a powerful query language similar to SQL but operates on the entity level, allowing interaction with the entity objects instead of the tables directly. Custom queries can be created using the @Query annotation in the repository interface.

Example:

```
public interface UserRepository extends JpaRepository<User, Long> {

    @Query("SELECT u FROM User u WHERE u.firstName = :firstName")
    List<User> findUsersByFirstName(@Param("firstName") String firstName);

    @Query("SELECT u FROM User u WHERE u.age >= :age")
    List<User> findAdultUsers(@Param("age") int age);
}
```

The @Query annotation allows specifying a custom JPQL query directly within the repository interface. The use of the @Param annotation enables parameter binding, ensuring the query is dynamically populated with the input values.

Native Queries

Native Queries, unlike JPQL, allow using raw SQL queries which offer the most flexibility and control over the database interaction. They are particularly useful for complex queries that JPQL cannot handle efficiently. The @Query annotation with the nativeQuery attribute helps define these queries.

Example:

```
public interface UserRepository extends JpaRepository<User, Long> {

    @Query(value = "SELECT * FROM users u WHERE u.status = ?1",
           nativeQuery = true)
    List<User> findByUserStatus(String status);

    @Query(value = "SELECT * FROM users u WHERE u.created_date >= ?1",
           nativeQuery = true)
    List<User> findRecentUsers(Date createdDate);
}
```

This setup invokes SQL directly within the repository context, allowing leverage of advanced SQL functionalities like joins, subqueries, and database-specific optimizations.

Implementing Custom Repository Interfaces

When the repository requires complex logic, the best approach is to define a custom repository interface and provide its implementation. This practice is essential for maintaining a clear separation of concerns and ensuring the repository's core responsibilities remain intact.

Steps to implement:

- Define the custom repository interface.
- Provide an implementation class for the custom interface.
- Inject the custom implementation into the base repository.

Example:

Define the custom interface:

```
public interface CustomUserRepository {
    List<User> searchUsersComplexQuery(String criteria);
}
```

Provide the Implementation:

```
public class CustomUserRepositoryImpl implements CustomUserRepository {

    @PersistenceContext
    private EntityManager entityManager;

    @Override
    public List<User> searchUsersComplexQuery(String criteria) {
        String query = "SELECT u FROM User u WHERE u.criteriaField LIKE :
              criteria";
        return entityManager.createQuery(query, User.class)
                            .setParameter("criteria", "%" + criteria + "%")
                            .getResultList();
    }
}
```

Integrate with the base repository:

```
public interface UserRepository extends JpaRepository<User, Long>,
      CustomUserRepository {
    // Other query method definitions
}
```

In this scenario:

- **CustomUserRepository** defines the custom methods.
- **CustomUserRepositoryImpl** contains the logic implementation using EntityManager.
- **UserRepository** extends the base JpaRepository and includes the custom methods.

This structured approach facilitates managing custom and complex queries in a manner that adheres to the principles of clean architecture. By combining the repository mechanism with custom logic implementations, Spring Data JPA provides a comprehensive toolkit for efficient and flexible data access.

5.10 Transaction Management in Spring

Effective transaction management is essential for ensuring data integrity and consistency in any application dealing with persistent storage. In the context of Spring, transaction management provides a cohesive mechanism for defining and managing transactional boundaries. This section dives into the core concepts, configurations, and practical applications of transaction management within Spring.

Spring provides a consistent way of programming transactions across various transactional APIs such as JDBC, JPA, and Hibernate. It abstracts the underlying platform-specific transaction management operations, allowing users to manage transactions declaratively and programmatically.

At its core, Spring transaction management is built upon two complementary concepts: the **PlatformTransactionManager** and the **TransactionTemplate**. The **PlatformTransactionManager** is a central interface in Spring's transaction infrastructure, serving as a generic abstraction for Spring's transaction capability. Various implementations exist, including DataSourceTransactionManager, JpaTransactionManager, and HibernateTransactionManager, corresponding to different persistence technologies.

The **TransactionTemplate** provides a programmatic way of managing transactions without hard-coding transaction management code into the business logic. Users can configure transaction properties such as propagation behavior, isolation level, timeout, and rollback rules through the TransactionTemplate.

A detailed exploration of transaction propagation behaviors is imperative for a comprehensive understanding:

- **REQUIRED:** If a current transaction exists, the method execution will continue within that transaction. If there is no existing transaction, a new one is created.
- **REQUIRES_NEW:** Always starts a new transaction, suspending the current transaction if one exists.
- **MANDATORY:** Method must transparently join an existing transaction; otherwise, an exception is thrown.
- **SUPPORTS:** Participates in a transaction if one is present; otherwise, executes non-transactionally.

- **NOT_SUPPORTED:** Always executes non-transactionally and suspends the current transaction if one exists.
- **NEVER:** Executes non-transactionally and throws an exception if a transaction exists.
- **NESTED:** Executes within a nested transaction if an existing transaction is present, otherwise behaves like REQUIRED.

Here is an example of programmatic transaction management using TransactionTemplate:

```
import org.springframework.beans.factory.annotation.Autowired;
import org.springframework.transaction.PlatformTransactionManager;
import org.springframework.transaction.TransactionDefinition;
import org.springframework.transaction.TransactionStatus;
import org.springframework.transaction.support.DefaultTransactionDefinition;
import org.springframework.transaction.support.TransactionTemplate;

public class TransactionalService {

    @Autowired
    private PlatformTransactionManager transactionManager;

    public void executeWithTransaction() {
        DefaultTransactionDefinition def = new DefaultTransactionDefinition();
        def.setPropagationBehavior(TransactionDefinition.
              PROPAGATION_REQUIRED);

        TransactionStatus status = transactionManager.getTransaction(def);

        try {
            // business logic here

            transactionManager.commit(status);
        } catch (Exception ex) {
            transactionManager.rollback(status);
            throw ex;
        }
    }
}
```

Spring also supports declarative transaction management through annotations, which allows for cleaner and more maintainable code. Using the @Transactional annotation simplifies the declaration of transactional behavior directly at the method or class level. Here is an example:

```
import org.springframework.transaction.annotation.Transactional;
import org.springframework.stereotype.Service;

@Service
public class DeclarativeTransactionalService {

    @Transactional(propagation = Propagation.REQUIRED,
            rollbackFor = Exception.class)
    public void performTransactionalOperation() {
```

```
        // business logic that requires a transaction
    }
}
```

Key attributes of the @Transactional annotation include:

- **propagation:** Specifies the transactional propagation type (e.g., REQUIRED, REQUIRES_NEW).
- **isolation:** Defines the isolation level for the transaction (e.g., Isolation.REPEATABLE_READ).
- **timeout:** Sets the transaction timeout in seconds.
- **readOnly:** Indicates if the transaction is read-only.
- **rollbackFor:** Specifies which exceptions should trigger a rollback.

The transaction infrastructure in Spring relies on various proxy mechanisms or weaving techniques to apply transactional behavior. This can be achieved either through JDK dynamic proxies or class-based (CGLIB) proxies.

It is also crucial to configure transaction management in the Spring application context. This can be achieved via XML-based configuration or Java-based configuration using @EnableTransactionManagement. Here is an example of Java-based configuration:

```
import org.springframework.context.annotation.Bean;
import org.springframework.context.annotation.Configuration;
import org.springframework.transaction.PlatformTransactionManager;
import org.springframework.transaction.annotation.EnableTransactionManagement;
import org.springframework.transaction.support.TransactionTemplate;

@Configuration
@EnableTransactionManagement
public class TransactionManagementConfig {

    @Bean
    public PlatformTransactionManager transactionManager() {
        // instantiation of a specific PlatformTransactionManager,
        // e.g., JpaTransactionManager, DataSourceTransactionManager, etc.
        return new JpaTransactionManager(entityManagerFactory());
    }

    @Bean
    public TransactionTemplate transactionTemplate(PlatformTransactionManager
            transactionManager) {
        return new TransactionTemplate(transactionManager);
    }

    // other bean definitions
```

```
    // e.g., EntityManagerFactory bean
}
```

Understanding transaction management is vital for ensuring data consistency and reliability in Spring applications. Proper configuration and usage of transactional annotations and templates help prevent issues such as dirty reads, non-repeatable reads, and phantom reads. Moreover, considering propagation attributes and isolation levels ensures that transactions behave as intended within varying contexts and dependencies.

5.11 Spring Data REST

Spring Data REST is a powerful module within the Spring ecosystem that facilitates the creation of RESTful web services directly from your data access repositories. This module effectively abstracts the complexity involved in building RESTful APIs, enabling developers to focus more on the business logic rather than wiring up the CRUD operations manually. It automatically exposes your Spring Data repositories as RESTful endpoints without requiring boilerplate code. As you progress through this section, comprehensive understanding and step-by-step guidance will be provided to leverage Spring Data REST efficiently.

Spring Data REST is built on top of several Spring projects, including Spring Data JPA for repositories, Spring MVC for RESTful endpoints, and the Jackson library for JSON binding and conversion. Before diving into the practical aspects, it's important to ensure that the relevant dependencies are included in your pom.xml.

```
<dependency>
    <groupId>org.springframework.boot</groupId>
    <artifactId>spring-boot-starter-data-rest</artifactId>
</dependency>
<dependency>
    <groupId>org.springframework.boot</groupId>
    <artifactId>spring-boot-starter-data-jpa</artifactId>
</dependency>
<dependency>
    <groupId>com.h2database</groupId>
    <artifactId>h2</artifactId>
    <scope>runtime</scope>
</dependency>
```

Once the dependencies are included, setting up the project to use Spring Data REST involves minimal configuration. By annotating your entities and repository interfaces appropriately, Spring Data REST will handle the exposure of your data endpoints.

Consider a simple entity class Book:

```
package com.example.demo.domain;

import javax.persistence.Entity;
import javax.persistence.GeneratedValue;
import javax.persistence.GenerationType;
import javax.persistence.Id;

@Entity
public class Book {

    @Id
    @GeneratedValue(strategy = GenerationType.AUTO)
    private Long id;

    private String title;
    private String author;

    // Getters and setters omitted for brevity
}
```

Next, define a repository interface for this entity:

```
package com.example.demo.repository;

import com.example.demo.domain.Book;
import org.springframework.data.repository.CrudRepository;

public interface BookRepository extends CrudRepository<Book, Long> {
}
```

With these two classes in place, you will have the entity Book and its repository BookRepository. To enable Spring Data REST, only a small amount of configuration is typically required in your main application class.

```
package com.example.demo;

import org.springframework.boot.SpringApplication;
import org.springframework.boot.autoconfigure.SpringBootApplication;

@SpringBootApplication
public class DemoApplication {
    public static void main(String[] args) {
        SpringApplication.run(DemoApplication.class, args);
    }
}
```

Running the application will automatically expose RESTful endpoints for the Book entity. Common endpoints include:

- GET /books -> Retrieves a list of all books

- GET /books/id -> Retrieves a book by its ID
- POST /books -> Creates a new book
- PUT /books/id -> Updates an existing book by its ID
- DELETE /books/id -> Deletes a book by its ID

To test these endpoints, you can use tools such as Postman or curl commands:

```
# Retrieve all books
curl -X GET http://localhost:8080/books

# Retrieve a specific book by ID
curl -X GET http://localhost:8080/books/1

# Create a new book
curl -X POST http://localhost:8080/books -H "Content-Type: application/json" -d '{"
    title": "Spring in Action", "author": "Craig Walls"}'

# Update an existing book
curl -X PUT http://localhost:8080/books/1 -H "Content-Type: application/json" -d '{"
    title": "Spring Boot in Action", "author": "Craig Walls"}'

# Delete a book by ID
curl -X DELETE http://localhost:8080/books/1
```

Spring Data REST also provides a rich framework for paging and sorting. To retrieve a paginated list of books, you can simply append the page, size, and sort parameters to your request:

```
GET /books?page=0&size=5&sort=title,asc
```

Spring Data REST handles associations between entities out of the box. If your Book entity has a relationship with another entity, such as Category, configuring Spring Data REST to expose these relationships is straightforward. Consider extending the Book entity to include a reference to a Category entity:

```
@Entity
public class Book {

    @Id
    @GeneratedValue(strategy = GenerationType.AUTO)
    private Long id;

    private String title;
    private String author;

    @ManyToOne
    @JoinColumn(name = "category_id")
    private Category category;

    // Getters and setters omitted for brevity
}
```

You should also define the Category entity and its corresponding repository:

```
@Entity
public class Category {

    @Id
    @GeneratedValue(strategy = GenerationType.AUTO)
    private Long id;

    private String name;

    // Getters and setters omitted for brevity
}
```

```
package com.example.demo.repository;

import com.example.demo.domain.Category;
import org.springframework.data.repository.CrudRepository;

public interface CategoryRepository extends CrudRepository<Category, Long> {
}
```

Spring Data REST will automatically expose the relationships and allow traversal between entities. For example, accessing /books/1/category might retrieve the category associated with a given book.

By leveraging these functionalities, developers can efficiently and effectively build robust RESTful services using Spring Data REST with minimal boilerplate and configuration.

5.12 Best Practices for Data Access in Spring

Implementing effective data access in Spring applications demands attention to detail and adherence to a set of best practices that ensure robustness, scalability, and maintainability. This section elucidates several key practices for achieving these goals when working with data access in Spring.

- **1. Prefer JdbcTemplate or Spring Data Repositories:** Spring's JdbcTemplate and Spring Data Repositories abstract much of the boilerplate code required for data access, reducing redundancy and errors. Using these frameworks enhances productivity and facilitates smoother integration with different data stores.
- **2. Use Named Parameters:** Opt for named parameters in SQL

queries to improve readability and maintainability. Spring supports named parameters through the NamedParameterJdbcTemplate class. This approach makes your queries clearer and less prone to errors compared to positional parameters.

```
NamedParameterJdbcTemplate namedParameterJdbcTemplate = new
    NamedParameterJdbcTemplate(dataSource);

String sql = "SELECT * FROM employees WHERE first_name = :firstName
    AND last_name = :lastName";
Map<String, Object> params = new HashMap<>();
params.put("firstName", "John");
params.put("lastName", "Doe");

List<Employee> employees = namedParameterJdbcTemplate.query(sql, params,
    new EmployeeRowMapper());
```

- **3. Leverage Connection Pooling:** Efficient data access requires optimal management of database connections. Always use a connection pooling library like HikariCP, which provides high performance and reliability. Configure your DataSource to utilize connection pooling to reduce overhead and improve application responsiveness.

```
@Bean
public DataSource dataSource() {
    HikariConfig config = new HikariConfig();
    config.setJdbcUrl("jdbc:mysql://localhost:3306/mydb");
    config.setUsername("username");
    config.setPassword("password");
    config.setMaximumPoolSize(20);

    return new HikariDataSource(config);
}
```

- **4. Implement Proper Exception Handling:** Spring's data access framework translates database-specific exceptions into a consistent set of DataAccessException, providing a more holistic error handling approach. Ensure you catch and appropriately handle these exceptions to provide meaningful feedback to users and log relevant information for debugging.

```
try {
    jdbcTemplate.update("INSERT INTO employees (first_name, last_name)
        VALUES (?, ?)", "John", "Doe");
} catch (DataAccessException e) {
    // Log the exception and provide user-friendly feedback.
    logger.error("Error occurred while accessing the database", e);
}
```

- **5. Optimize Database Queries:** Carefully design your queries to improve performance. Avoid fetching more data than necessary and make use of database indexes. Consider batch updates and use join queries appropriately. Profiling and optimizing slow queries can greatly enhance application performance.

- **6. Use Lazy Loading with Caution:** Hibernate and JPA support lazy loading which defers the loading of an object until it is specifically requested. While this can lead to performance optimization, misuse can cause LazyInitializationException. It is crucial to manage your sessions properly, particularly in web applications where detached entities can lead to issues.

- **7. Transaction Management:** Always use transactions to ensure data integrity and consistency. Spring provides robust transaction management capabilities. Use the @Transactional annotation to declare transaction boundaries clearly. This ensures that either all operations within the boundary are completed successfully or none are, adhering to the ACID principles.

```
@Service
public class EmployeeService {

    @Autowired
    private EmployeeRepository employeeRepository;

    @Transactional
    public void saveEmployeeWithDependents(Employee employee) {
        employeeRepository.save(employee);
        // Further dependent operations
    }
}
```

- **8. Properly Handle Connection Closures:** When working directly with JdbcTemplate or DataSource, ensure connections are closed properly to prevent resource leaks. Spring's JdbcTemplate takes care of this, but always double-check in custom scenarios.

- **9. Use Projections and DTOs for Complex Queries:** For complex queries that return a combination of different entities or non-entity data, utilize projections or Data Transfer Objects (DTOs) to encapsulate query results. This avoids loading unnecessary data and simplifies handling in the application.

```
@Query("SELECT new com.example.dto.EmployeeDTO(e.firstName, d.
    departmentName) FROM Employee e JOIN e.department d WHERE d.
    departmentId = :deptId")
List<EmployeeDTO> findEmployeesByDepartment(@Param("deptId") Long
    deptId);
```

- **10. Cache Frequently Accessed Data:** To reduce load on the database and improve performance, consider caching frequently accessed or static data. Spring supports various caching solutions like EhCache, Redis, etc. Use @Cacheable, @CachePut, and @CacheEvict annotations to manage caching efficiently.

```
@Cacheable("employeeCache")
public Employee findEmployeeById(Long id) {
    return employeeRepository.findById(id).orElse(null);
}
```

Always validate the necessity and configuration of any caching mechanism to prevent stale data issues.

These guidelines are designed to help you create efficient, scalable, and maintainable data access layers in your Spring applications. Employing these best practices ensures your application can handle current requirements and scale gracefully as demand grows.

Chapter 6

Spring MVC Framework

This chapter covers the Spring MVC framework, which is essential for developing web applications in Spring. Starting with the architecture of Spring MVC, it explains how to set up a project and configure the DispatcherServlet. The chapter guides readers through defining controllers, mapping requests, handling form submissions, and performing data binding and validation. It delves into view resolution mechanisms, working with JSPs, and integrating Thymeleaf. Additionally, it addresses developing RESTful web services and implementing exception handling within the Spring MVC framework.

6.1 Introduction to Spring MVC

Spring MVC (Model-View-Controller) is a highly versatile and powerful framework within the larger Spring Framework. It facilitates the development of robust, maintainable, and scalable web applications by adhering to the Model-View-Controller design pattern. This section introduces the foundational concepts of Spring MVC, setting the stage for more advanced topics in subsequent sections.

At its core, Spring MVC serves as a request-driven framework, which means it primarily addresses web requests: parsing inputs, processing business logic, and rendering appropriate views. The DispatcherServlet plays a pivotal role in this architecture by acting as the front controller. This architecture separates the application's concerns into clear, manageable segments.

The Model-View-Controller architecture is divided into three distinct parts:

- **Model:** This represents the application's data and business logic. It is responsible for retrieving and manipulating data from the database and encapsulates the core logic necessary for the application's functionality. In Spring MVC, the model is often a simple Java object or a collection of objects.
- **View:** This is the representation of the data. The view is concerned with rendering the model to the user interface. Views in Spring MVC are resolved by a ViewResolver and are typically JSPs, Thymeleaf templates, or any other rendering technology supported by Spring.
- **Controller:** This component handles the user input, processes it, and returns the appropriate model and view. The controller acts as an intermediary between the model and the view, receiving web requests, handling user input, invoking business logic, and directing output to the view layer.

The interaction between these three components can be understood as follows: a user sends a request to the server, the DispatcherServlet intercepts it and delegates it to a specific controller. The controller processes the request, interacts with the model to retrieve data, and selects a view for rendering. The view then generates the HTML response to be returned to the client.

To visualize a basic flow within the Spring MVC framework, consider the following high-level steps:

1. A user sends an HTTP request to the web application.
2. The request is first intercepted by the **DispatcherServlet**, which is configured in the web.xml or using Java-based configuration.
3. The DispatcherServlet consults the **HandlerMapping** to determine the appropriate controller based on the URL pattern of the request.
4. The request is then forwarded to the selected **Controller**. The controller processes the request using business logic, potentially retrieving or updating data via the model.

5. The controller returns a **ModelAndView** object, which encapsulates both the model data and the view name.

6. The **ViewResolver** resolves the logical view name to a specific view implementation (e.g., a JSP file).

7. The view renders the content using the model data and generates an HTTP response.

8. The DispatcherServlet sends the response back to the client.

A key feature of Spring MVC is its inherent extensibility. The framework is designed with multiple extension points that can be customized to meet specific business requirements. Examples include custom data binders, validation frameworks, and view resolvers. Moreover, Spring MVC seamlessly integrates with other parts of the Spring ecosystem, including Spring Security, Spring Data, and Spring Boot, providing a cohesive environment for enterprise application development.

Consider the task of setting up a simple Spring MVC project. Here, the configuration of the DispatcherServlet typically involves web.xml, but with Spring Boot, this configuration can be accomplished through Java classes:

```
import org.springframework.web.servlet.support.
    AbstractAnnotationConfigDispatcherServletInitializer;

public class MyWebAppInitializer extends
    AbstractAnnotationConfigDispatcherServletInitializer {
    @Override
    protected Class<?>[] getRootConfigClasses() {
        return new Class[] { AppConfig.class };
    }

    @Override
    protected Class<?>[] getServletConfigClasses() {
        return new Class[] { WebConfig.class };
    }

    @Override
    protected String[] getServletMappings() {
        return new String[] { "/" };
    }
}
```

In this example, MyWebAppInitializer sets up the DispatcherServlet, mapping it to the root URL. By specifying AppConfig and WebConfig, we separate the configuration of the root context (which may include global beans like data sources) from the web context (which typically includes MVC-related beans).

Furthermore, Spring MVC controllers are relatively straightforward to define. A simple controller handling basic requests might look like this:

```
import org.springframework.stereotype.Controller;
import org.springframework.ui.Model;
import org.springframework.web.bind.annotation.GetMapping;

@Controller
public class HomeController {
    @GetMapping("/")
    public String home(Model model) {
        model.addAttribute("message", "Welcome to Spring MVC!");
        return "home";
    }
}
```

In this HomeController, the @Controller annotation marks the class as a Spring MVC controller. The @GetMapping annotation maps HTTP GET requests to the home method, which processes the request by adding an attribute to the model and returning the view name "home". The view resolver will then map this view name to an actual view implementation, typically a JSP or a Thymeleaf template, which will render the final output.

The flexibility, scalability, and integration capabilities make Spring MVC a preferred choice for building modern web applications. As we progress through this chapter, we'll delve into each architectural component and configuration aspect in more detail, ensuring that you have a comprehensive understanding of how to leverage Spring MVC effectively in your projects.

6.2 Spring MVC Architecture

The architecture of the Spring MVC framework is designed following the Model-View-Controller (MVC) design pattern, which separates the application into three interconnected components. This modular understanding promotes separation of concerns, making large-scale applications more manageable, maintainable, and testable.

The core components of the Spring MVC architecture include the following:

- **DispatcherServlet**
- **Controller**
- **Model**

- **View**
- **ViewResolver**

DispatcherServlet acts as the central component, responsible for handling all incoming HTTP requests. It delegates control to specific controllers as defined by URL mappings in the application's configuration. The DispatcherServlet is defined in the web.xml file or through annotation-based configuration.

To illustrate the operation of DispatcherServlet, consider the following XML configuration:

```
<servlet>
    <servlet-name>dispatcher</servlet-name>
    <servlet-class>org.springframework.web.servlet.DispatcherServlet</servlet-class>
    <load-on-startup>1</load-on-startup>
</servlet>
<servlet-mapping>
    <servlet-name>dispatcher</servlet-name>
    <url-pattern>/</url-pattern>
</servlet-mapping>
```

Here, the url-pattern element specifies that all incoming requests should be routed through the DispatcherServlet.

Controller components contain the business logic of the application and handle user input. They interpret user inputs, map them to the appropriate service methods, and add the resultant data to the model. Controllers are typically annotated with @Controller and @RequestMapping annotations for defining request handling methods.

```
@Controller
public class HomeController {

    @RequestMapping(value = "/", method = RequestMethod.GET)
    public String home(Model model) {
        model.addAttribute("message", "Welcome to Spring MVC Framework!");
        return "home";
    }
}
```

In the example above, the HomeController maps the root URL ("/") to the home method. The method adds data to the model and returns the view name "home".

Model components hold the data for the application. Data obtained from service methods or directly from controllers is placed into models. This data can then be accessed in the view layer for rendering.

The integration of model data is often achieved through the Model interface, as seen in the HomeController example above.

View is responsible for rendering the model data. Views can be implemented using various technologies such as JSP, Thymeleaf, or PDF. The view name returned by the controller is resolved to a specific view file by the ViewResolver.

A simple JSP view example named home.jsp might look as follows:

```
<%@ taglib uri="http://java.sun.com/jsp/jstl/core" prefix="c" %>
<!DOCTYPE html>
<html>
<head>
    <title>Home Page</title>
</head>
<body>
    <h2>${message}</h2>
</body>
</html>
```

In this JSP file, the message attribute from the model is accessed using the JSTL c tag library and displayed in an <h2> HTML element.

ViewResolver is a component that resolves view names to actual view pages. Spring MVC provides several implementations of the ViewResolver interface, such as InternalResourceViewResolver for JSP and ThymeleafViewResolver for Thymeleaf.

View resolver configuration typically appears in the Spring configuration file.

```
@Bean
public InternalResourceViewResolver viewResolver() {
    InternalResourceViewResolver resolver = new InternalResourceViewResolver();
    resolver.setPrefix("/WEB-INF/views/");
    resolver.setSuffix(".jsp");
    return resolver;
}
```

In this configuration, the viewResolver bean is set up with a prefix and suffix for resolving view page names. If the controller returns "home" as a view name, the full path "/WEB-INF/views/home.jsp" will be used to render the view.

The entire flow of a typical Spring MVC application can be summarized as follows:

1. A client sends an HTTP request to the web application.
2. The DispatcherServlet receives the request and consults the handler mappings to match the URL to a corresponding controller.
3. The matched controller method processes the request, interacts with the service layer, and returns a view name and model data.

4. The DispatcherServlet consults the ViewResolver to translate the view name to an actual view.

5. The view renders the model data and the response is sent back to the client.

This structured flow ensures that each component focuses on a specific responsibility, conforming to the principles of the MVC pattern and leading to a clearer, more modular application architecture.

6.3 Setting Up a Spring MVC Project

To set up a Spring MVC project, we will follow a systematic approach that includes initializing a Spring project and configuring the essential components required for the Spring MVC framework to function seamlessly. This section will guide you through the detailed steps necessary to establish a foundational Spring MVC project.

Step 1: Initialize a Spring Project

1. Utilize Spring Initializr to create a new project. Spring Initializr is a web-based tool that simplifies the process of bootstrapping a new Spring application. Navigate to https://start.spring.io/. 2. Configure the project metadata:

- **Project**: Select *Maven Project*.
- **Language**: Choose *Java*.
- **Spring Boot**: Select an appropriate version, preferably the latest stable release.
- **Project Metadata**: Define the Group, Artifact, Name, Description, Package name, Packaging, and Java version.
  - **Group**: com.example
  - **Artifact**: spring-mvc-example
  - **Name**: Spring MVC Example
  - **Description**: Demo project for Spring MVC
  - **Package name**: com.example.springmvc
  - **Packaging**: jar

- **Java**: 11

3. Add dependencies necessary for a Spring MVC project:

- **Spring Web**: Provides fundamental features to build web applications.
- **Thymeleaf**: For web page and view rendering.
- **Spring Boot DevTools**: Offers development-time conveniences.
- **Lombok** (Optional): Simplifies coding by reducing boilerplate code.

4. Generate the project by clicking the *Generate* button. This will download a zip file containing the base structure of your Spring MVC project. Extract the contents of the zip file to a preferred directory.

Step 2: Import the Project into an IDE

1. Open your Integrated Development Environment (IDE), such as IntelliJ IDEA or Eclipse. 2. Import the generated Maven project:

- In IntelliJ IDEA: *File* → *Open* → Select the extracted project directory.
- In Eclipse: *File* → *Import* → *Existing Maven Projects* → Next → Browse and select the project root directory.

3. Wait for the IDE to resolve dependencies and set up the project. This may take a few minutes.

Step 3: Configure Project Structure

The project's directory structure will include several critical files and directories. Key among them are:

```
spring-mvc-example/
 src/
    main/
       java/
          com/
             example/
                springmvc/
       resources/
       webapp/
          WEB-INF/
    test/
```

```
mvnw
mvnw.cmd
pom.xml
README.md
```

Key directories and configurations include:

- **src/main/java**: This directory contains all Java source files. By default, it will include the main application entry point.
- **src/main/resources**: This directory stores various configuration files. Ensure that the application.properties (or application.yml) files reside here for application-specific settings.
- **src/main/webapp/WEB-INF**: This directory holds the web application configuration files, including JSP pages or other view-related resources.
- **pom.xml**: This is the Maven configuration file where dependencies and build configuration are managed.

Step 4: Configure the DispatcherServlet

The DispatcherServlet acts as the central point for handling all HTTP requests and responses. It is necessary to configure the web.xml file or use Java-based configuration to register the DispatcherServlet.

Using Java-based configuration:

```
package com.example.springmvc;

import org.springframework.boot.SpringApplication;
import org.springframework.boot.autoconfigure.SpringBootApplication;
import org.springframework.boot.web.servlet.ServletRegistrationBean;
import org.springframework.context.annotation.Bean;
import org.springframework.web.servlet.DispatcherServlet;

@SpringBootApplication
public class SpringMvcExampleApplication {

    public static void main(String[] args) {
        SpringApplication.run(SpringMvcExampleApplication.class, args);
    }

    @Bean
    public ServletRegistrationBean<DispatcherServlet> dispatcherServlet() {
        DispatcherServlet dispatcherServlet = new DispatcherServlet();
        ServletRegistrationBean<DispatcherServlet> registrationBean = new
                ServletRegistrationBean<>(dispatcherServlet, "/");
```

```
        registrationBean.setName("dispatcher");
        return registrationBean;
    }
}
```

Step 5: Define Application Properties

In the src/main/resources/application.properties file, configure any application-specific settings. For instance:

```
server.port=8080
spring.mvc.view.prefix=/WEB-INF/views/
spring.mvc.view.suffix=.jsp
```

Step 6: Define a Simple Controller

Create a simple controller to handle HTTP requests. This can be done by defining a Java class annotated with @Controller. For example:

```
package com.example.springmvc.controller;

import org.springframework.stereotype.Controller;
import org.springframework.ui.Model;
import org.springframework.web.bind.annotation.GetMapping;

@Controller
public class HomeController {

    @GetMapping("/")
    public String home(Model model) {
        model.addAttribute("message", "Welcome to Spring MVC!");
        return "home";
    }
}
```

Step 7: Create a View

In the src/main/webapp/WEB-INF/views/ directory, create a JSP file named home.jsp:

```
<%@ taglib uri="http://java.sun.com/jsp/jstl/core" prefix="c" %>
<!DOCTYPE html>
<html xmlns="http://www.w3.org/1999/xhtml">
<head>
    <title>Spring MVC Example</title>
</head>
<body>
    <h1>${message}</h1>
</body>
</html>
```

Step 8: Run the Application

Finally, run the Spring Boot application. Both IntelliJ IDEA and Eclipse offer integrated mechanisms to run Spring Boot applications directly. Alternatively, you can use Maven on the command line:

```
./mvnw spring-boot:run
```

Access the application by navigating to http://localhost:8080/ in a web browser. You should see the message "Welcome to Spring MVC!"

This comprehensive setup establishes a solid foundation for a Spring MVC project, enabling further customization and development of web applications.

6.4 Understanding DispatcherServlet

In the context of Spring MVC, the DispatcherServlet plays a pivotal role as it acts as the front controller for the web application. The primary function of the DispatcherServlet is to manage and delegate requests to the appropriate handlers, ensuring a clear separation of concerns and promoting a clean and maintainable code base.

At a high level, the DispatcherServlet follows the Front Controller design pattern. It intercepts incoming HTTP requests, delegates the requests to suitable handler methods, and finally returns a response. The DispatcherServlet itself does not handle requests directly but relies on various components configured in the Spring application context to process these requests.

Initialization and Configuration

The DispatcherServlet is configured through the web.xml file in a traditional Spring MVC project. With the introduction of Spring Boot, the configuration can be achieved through annotations and code-based configuration.

Example of web.xml configuration:

```
<servlet>
    <servlet-name>dispatcher</servlet-name>
    <servlet-class>org.springframework.web.servlet.DispatcherServlet</servlet-
         class>
    <load-on-startup>1</load-on-startup>
</servlet>

<servlet-mapping>
    <servlet-name>dispatcher</servlet-name>
```

```
    <url-pattern>/</url-pattern>
</servlet-mapping>
```

In modern Spring Boot applications, the DispatcherServlet is automatically configured. However, it can be customized further if required.

```
import org.springframework.boot.web.servlet.ServletRegistrationBean;
import org.springframework.context.annotation.Bean;
import org.springframework.context.annotation.Configuration;

@Configuration
public class WebConfig {

    @Bean
    public ServletRegistrationBean<DispatcherServlet> dispatcherRegistration(
            DispatcherServlet dispatcherServlet) {
        ServletRegistrationBean<DispatcherServlet> registration = new
                ServletRegistrationBean<>(dispatcherServlet);
        registration.addUrlMappings("/");
        return registration;
    }
}
```

Request Handling Workflow

When an HTTP request is received by the DispatcherServlet, it follows a series of steps to process the request:

- **Receive Request**: The DispatcherServlet receives a request and acts as the initial entry point.
- **Locate Handler**: It consults the HandlerMapping to determine the appropriate handler method based on the request URL.
- **Invoke Handler**: The handler method, typically a controller method annotated with @RequestMapping or other request mapping annotations, is invoked.
- **Process Response**: The handler method processes the request and returns a ModelAndView object or another return type such as @ResponseBody.
- **View Resolution**: If a ModelAndView object is returned, the ViewResolver resolves the view name to an actual view, such as a JSP or a Thymeleaf template.
- **Render View**: The resolved view is rendered, and the final HTML output is sent back to the client.

Components Involved

Several key components work in conjunction with the DispatcherServlet to handle a request effectively:

- **Handler Mapping**: Determines which controller will handle the request. Examples include RequestMappingHandlerMapping and SimpleUrlHandlerMapping.
- **Handler Adapter**: Executes the appropriate handler method. Examples include RequestMappingHandlerAdapter and HttpRequestHandlerAdapter.
- **View Resolver**: Resolves logical view names returned by controllers to actual view implementations. Examples include InternalResourceViewResolver for JSPs and ThymeleafViewResolver for Thymeleaf templates.
- **Exception Resolver**: Handles exceptions thrown during request processing, translating them into adequate responses. Examples include DefaultHandlerExceptionResolver and SimpleMappingExceptionResolver.

Example of a simple controller with mapped request handling:

```
import org.springframework.stereotype.Controller;
import org.springframework.web.bind.annotation.GetMapping;
import org.springframework.web.servlet.ModelAndView;

@Controller
public class HomeController {

    @GetMapping("/")
    public ModelAndView home() {
        ModelAndView mav = new ModelAndView("home");
        mav.addObject("message", "Welcome to the home page!");
        return mav;
    }
}
```

Advantages of DispatcherServlet

- **Centralized Control**: Provides a single point of entry to manage all web requests.
- **Flexible Configuration**: Supports flexible configuration through annotations, XML, and Java classes.

- **Extensibility**: Easily extensible by adding custom handler mappings, view resolvers, and other components.
- **Separation of Concerns**: Promotes separation of application layers by clearly defining the roles of controllers, services, and views.

DispatcherServlet Customization

Though the default configuration is sufficient for most scenarios, customization can be achieved by extending DispatcherServlet or providing custom implementations of the support classes.

Example of customizing DispatcherServlet initialization:

```
import org.springframework.web.servlet.DispatcherServlet;

import javax.servlet.ServletConfig;
import javax.servlet.ServletException;

public class CustomDispatcherServlet extends DispatcherServlet {

    @Override
    protected void initFrameworkServlet() throws ServletException {
        // Custom initialization code here
        super.initFrameworkServlet();
    }
}
```

This enables developers to inject additional behaviors at servlet initialization if needed. Additionally, Spring's configuration flexibility allows the injection of custom handler mappings or exception resolvers to suit specific application requirements.

The DispatcherServlet is indispensable for any Spring MVC-based application due to its role in orchestrating request processing, delegating to appropriate controllers, and rendering views efficiently. By understanding its mechanisms and properly configuring the supporting components, developers can leverage the full potential of the Spring MVC framework to build robust, maintainable web applications.

6.5 Defining Controllers in Spring MVC

In the Spring MVC framework, a controller plays a pivotal role in managing application flow. Controllers are responsible for processing user requests, building the necessary model data, and returning the appropriate view for display. A controller class in Spring MVC can be either a POJO (Plain Old Java Object) annotated with @Controller or @RestController, depending on the type of web application being developed. This section provides a detailed overview of defining controllers, annotating methods to handle requests, and employing various components to support the request-handling process.

@Controller is a specialization of the @Component annotation allowing for automatic detection through classpath scanning. The @RestController is a convenience annotation that combines @Controller and @ResponseBody, simplifying the creation of RESTful endpoints.

A basic example of a controller class is illustrated as follows:

```
package com.example.demo.controller;

import org.springframework.stereotype.Controller;
import org.springframework.web.bind.annotation.GetMapping;
import org.springframework.web.bind.annotation.RequestMapping;

@Controller
@RequestMapping("/home")
public class HomeController {

    @GetMapping
    public String showHomePage() {
        return "home";
    }
}
```

Here, the @Controller annotation designates HomeController as a Spring MVC controller. The @RequestMapping annotation defines a base URL path for the controller. Within the HomeController class, the showHomePage() method is annotated with @GetMapping, indicating that it will handle HTTP GET requests sent to /home. This method returns the logical view name home, which the view resolver will use to render the appropriate view.

Handling HTTP POST requests typically involves form submissions. For example:

```
package com.example.demo.controller;

import org.springframework.stereotype.Controller;
import org.springframework.web.bind.annotation.PostMapping;
import org.springframework.web.bind.annotation.RequestMapping;
import org.springframework.web.bind.annotation.RequestParam;
import org.springframework.ui.Model;
```

```
@Controller
@RequestMapping("/form")
public class FormController {

    @PostMapping("/submit")
    public String handleFormSubmission(@RequestParam("username") String
        username,
                                       @RequestParam("password") String
                                           password,
                                       Model model) {
        model.addAttribute("username", username);
        model.addAttribute("password", password);
        return "formSuccess";
    }
}
```

In this example, FormController handles POST requests at the URL /form/submit. The method handleFormSubmission() takes two parameters, username and password, captured from the form submission via @RequestParam. These parameters are added to the Model, enabling data passing to the view formSuccess.

For complex applications, controllers often need to handle various request types and URL mappings. Spring MVC supports method-level request mapping annotations like @GetMapping, @PostMapping, @PutMapping, @DeleteMapping, among others, to facilitate this. This approach provides enhanced clarity and fine-grained control over request handling.

A more detailed example includes path variables and exception handling:

```
package com.example.demo.controller;

import org.springframework.stereotype.Controller;
import org.springframework.web.bind.annotation.*;
import org.springframework.ui.Model;
import org.springframework.http.HttpStatus;
import org.springframework.web.server.ResponseStatusException;

@Controller
@RequestMapping("/products")
public class ProductController {

    @GetMapping("/{id}")
    public String getProductById(@PathVariable("id") Long id, Model model) {
        Product product = findProductById(id);
        if (product == null) {
            throw new ResponseStatusException(HttpStatus.NOT_FOUND, "
```

```
                Product not found");
        }
        model.addAttribute("product", product);
        return "productDetail";
    }

    private Product findProductById(Long id) {
        // Simulate a method to find a product by its ID (to be implemented).
        return null; // Replace with actual retrieval logic.
    }
}
```

In the example above, ProductController includes a getProductById() method that handles GET requests for a specific product. The method uses @PathVariable to capture the product ID from the URL. If the product is not found, a ResponseStatusException is thrown, which results in a 404 Not Found status. This showcases handling exceptions within controller methods concisely.

By utilizing these annotations appropriately, developers can create robust controllers that manage web requests efficiently, simplifying the development of web applications using the Spring MVC framework.

6.6 Mapping Requests to Controllers

Request mapping in Spring MVC is a critical concept to understand, as it connects various web requests received by the DispatcherServlet to the appropriate controller methods designed to handle them. In the Spring MVC framework, controllers can be mapped to URLs using annotations, enabling cleaner, more decoupled code.

The primary annotation for mapping requests in Spring MVC is @RequestMapping. This annotation can be placed at both the class level and the method level. At the class level, it defines the base URI that applies to all handler methods within the controller. At the method level, it specifies the specific endpoint URIs.

Consider the following example of a simple controller class:

```
import org.springframework.stereotype.Controller;
import org.springframework.web.bind.annotation.RequestMapping;
import org.springframework.web.bind.annotation.RequestMethod;

@Controller
@RequestMapping("/home")
public class HomeController {
```

```
    @RequestMapping(method = RequestMethod.GET)
    public String index() {
        return "home";
    }

    @RequestMapping(value = "/contact", method = RequestMethod.GET)
    public String contact() {
        return "contact";
    }
}
```

In this example, the HomeController is mapped to handle requests to /home as its base URI. The method index() will handle GET requests to /home, while the method contact() will handle GET requests to /home-/contact.

The @RequestMapping annotation provides numerous attributes to describe the request pattern, such as:

- **method**: Constrains the HTTP methods (GET, POST, etc.) this method handles.
- **params**: Specifies request parameters for method mapping. Useful for more fine-grained control.
- **headers**: Allows matching of request headers.
- **consumes**: Limits the media types the method consumes.
- **produces**: Limits the media types the method produces.

For example, to map a method to handle POST requests only with specific parameters, headers, and request/response content types, the annotation would be used as follows:

```
@RequestMapping(value = "/submit", method = RequestMethod.POST,
        params = "action=save",
        headers = "content-type=application/json",
        consumes = "application/json", produces = "application/json")
public @ResponseBody String handlePost(@RequestBody String payload) {
    // ... handle the request
    return "{\"status\": \"success\"}";
}
```

Here, the handlePost method is designed to process POST requests targeted at /submit with an action=save parameter and a content-type header of application/json. It consumes and produces JSON media types.

Path Variables and Request Parameters

Spring MVC also supports extraction of parts of the URI as parameters via @PathVariable and @RequestParam annotations respectively.

The @PathVariable annotation is used to extract templated parts of the URI. For instance:

```
@RequestMapping(value = "/user/{userId}", method = RequestMethod.GET)
public @ResponseBody User getUser(@PathVariable("userId") int userId) {
    // Fetch the user based on userId
    User user = userService.findById(userId);
    return user;
}
```

In this example, the userId part of the URI /user/{userId} is extracted and passed as a method parameter.

The @RequestParam annotation is used to extract query parameters from the URI:

```
@RequestMapping(value = "/search", method = RequestMethod.GET)
public @ResponseBody List<User> searchUsers(@RequestParam("name") String
    name) {
    // Search for users based on the provided name
    List<User> users = userService.searchByName(name);
    return users;
}
```

This makes it possible to extract the name query parameter from a request like /search?name=John.

Media Type Handling

Spring MVC facilitates the handling of specific media types through the consumes and produces attributes of @RequestMapping. This is essential for RESTful APIs providing different representations.

For scenarios demanding method differentiation based on media type, set the consumes and produces properties as shown:

```
@RequestMapping(value = "/update", method = RequestMethod.POST,
    consumes = "application/json", produces = "application/json")
public @ResponseBody ResponseEntity<String> update(@RequestBody User user
    ) {
    // Process the JSON representation of User
    userService.updateUser(user);
    return new ResponseEntity<>("{\"status\":\"updated\"}", HttpStatus.OK);
}
```

```
@RequestMapping(value = "/update", method = RequestMethod.POST,
    consumes = "application/xml", produces = "application/xml")
public @ResponseBody ResponseEntity<String> updateXml(@RequestBody User
    user) {
    // Process the XML representation of User
    userService.updateUser(user);
    return new ResponseEntity<>("<status>updated</status>", HttpStatus.OK
        );
}
```

The two update methods handle POST requests to /update but differentiate based on whether the request consumes JSON or XML.

Handling Multiple Request Methods

Spring MVC allows mapping multiple HTTP methods for the same URI within a single method definition using the method attribute of @RequestMapping:

```
@RequestMapping(value = "/test", method = {RequestMethod.GET,
    RequestMethod.POST})
public @ResponseBody String handleGetAndPost() {
    return "Handled both GET and POST";
}
```

Combining Annotations

It is possible to combine different annotations to handle more complex scenarios:

```
@RequestMapping(value = "/items/{id}", method = RequestMethod.GET,
    headers = "Accept=application/json")
public @ResponseBody Item getItemJson(@PathVariable("id") long id) {
    return itemService.getItemById(id);
}

@RequestMapping(value = "/items/{id}", method = RequestMethod.GET,
    headers = "Accept=application/xml")
public @ResponseBody Item getItemXml(@PathVariable("id") long id) {
    return itemService.getItemById(id);
}
```

Here, two methods handle the GET requests to /items/{id} for different expected response media types.

The precise use of @RequestMapping and associated attributes enables fine-grained control in mapping requests to controller methods, allowing architects and developers to build robust and maintainable web applications.

6.7 Handling Form Submissions

Handling form submissions is a critical aspect of web application development. Spring MVC provides robust support for handling form data, including binding form data to Java objects, validating user input, and processing data submissions. This section will detail the steps necessary to handle form submissions effectively using Spring MVC.

To begin with, the HTML form must be properly structured to send data to the Spring MVC controller. Consider the following example of an HTML form that submits user information:

```
<form action="/submitUserInfo" method="post">
    <label for="username">Username:</label>
    <input type="text" id="username" name="username">
    <br>
    <label for="age">Age:</label>
    <input type="number" id="age" name="age">
    <br>
    <input type="submit" value="Submit">
</form>
```

In this form, the 'action' attribute specifies the URL '/submitUserInfo' where the form data will be sent upon submission, and the 'method' attribute specifies that the data should be sent using the POST method. Each input field has a 'name' attribute that corresponds to the property name in the Java object where the data will be populated.

Next, the Spring MVC controller must have a method mapped to handle the form submission. Here is an example of a controller class with a method to process the form data:

```
import org.springframework.stereotype.Controller;
import org.springframework.web.bind.annotation.GetMapping;
import org.springframework.web.bind.annotation.PostMapping;
import org.springframework.web.bind.annotation.RequestMapping;
import org.springframework.web.bind.annotation.RequestParam;
import org.springframework.ui.Model;

@Controller
@RequestMapping("/user")
public class UserController {

    @GetMapping("/form")
    public String showForm() {
        // return the form view
        return "userForm";
    }
```

```
    @PostMapping("/submitUserInfo")
    public String submitUserInfo(@RequestParam("username") String username,
                                 @RequestParam("age") int age,
                                 Model model) {
        // Process the form data
        model.addAttribute("username", username);
        model.addAttribute("age", age);

        // return the result view
        return "userResult";
    }
}
```

In this example, the '@Controller' annotation denotes that this class is a Spring MVC controller. The '@RequestMapping("/user")' annotation maps the URLs that start with '/user' to this controller. The 'showForm' method is mapped to the '/form' URL using '@GetMapping' and returns the view name for the form, which is 'userForm'.

The 'submitUserInfo' method is mapped to '/submitUserInfo' using '@PostMapping'. It includes '@RequestParam' annotations to extract form data parameters and populate method arguments. The extracted data is then added to the 'Model' object for rendering in the view. The method returns 'userResult', which is the view name to display the form submission result.

For data binding, Spring MVC can automatically bind form data to Java objects. This is achieved by creating a command object that represents the data structure. Consider the following 'User' class:

```
public class User {
    private String username;
    private int age;

    // Getters and Setters
    public String getUsername() {
        return username;
    }

    public void setUsername(String username) {
        this.username = username;
    }

    public int getAge() {
        return age;
    }

    public void setAge(int age) {
        this.age = age;
    }
```

```
}
```

The controller can then use this 'User' class as a command object:

```
import org.springframework.stereotype.Controller;
import org.springframework.web.bind.annotation.ModelAttribute;
import org.springframework.web.bind.annotation.PostMapping;
import org.springframework.web.bind.annotation.RequestMapping;
import org.springframework.ui.Model;

@Controller
@RequestMapping("/user")
public class UserController {

    @PostMapping("/submitUserInfo")
    public String submitUserInfo(@ModelAttribute User user, Model model) {
        // Process the form data
        model.addAttribute("user", user);

        // return the result view
        return "userResult";
    }
}
```

In this version of the controller, the '@ModelAttribute' annotation is used to bind the form data to a 'User' object. The form data is automatically populated into the 'User' object with corresponding properties. This technique simplifies the extraction of form data and avoids manual parsing of individual parameters.

Furthermore, validation of form data is essential to ensure that the submitted data conforms to the application's requirements. Spring MVC supports validation through JSR-303/JSR-380 annotations using the javax.validation package. To enable validation, include the following dependency in the 'pom.xml' file:

```
<dependency>
    <groupId>org.springframework.boot</groupId>
    <artifactId>spring-boot-starter-validation</artifactId>
</dependency>
```

Next, add validation annotations to the 'User' class:

```
import javax.validation.constraints.Min;
import javax.validation.constraints.NotBlank;

public class User {
    @NotBlank(message = "Username is mandatory")
    private String username;

```

```
    @Min(value = 18, message = "Age must be at least 18")
    private int age;

    // Getters and Setters
}
```

The controller must be updated to handle validation results:

```
import org.springframework.stereotype.Controller;
import org.springframework.validation.BindingResult;
import org.springframework.web.bind.annotation.ModelAttribute;
import org.springframework.web.bind.annotation.PostMapping;
import org.springframework.web.bind.annotation.RequestMapping;
import org.springframework.ui.Model;

import javax.validation.Valid;

@Controller
@RequestMapping("/user")
public class UserController {

    @PostMapping("/submitUserInfo")
    public String submitUserInfo(@Valid @ModelAttribute User user,
          BindingResult result, Model model) {
        if (result.hasErrors()) {
            // return the form view with validation errors
            return "userForm";
        }

        // Process the form data
        model.addAttribute("user", user);

        // return the result view
        return "userResult";
    }
}
```

In this implementation, the '@Valid' annotation is used to trigger validation on the 'User' object, and 'BindingResult' is used to capture any validation errors. The method checks if there are validation errors with 'result.hasErrors()' and returns the form view if errors are present. This ensures that validation feedback can be provided to users before processing the data.

6.8 Data Binding and Validation

Within the Spring MVC framework, data binding and validation are critical for ensuring that the data received from client inputs, such as form submissions, is properly mapped to model objects and validated for correctness. This section explores the principles and implementation techniques for data binding and validation, providing robust strategies for developing reliable web applications.

The process of data binding in Spring MVC involves the automatic conversion of incoming HTTP request parameters to Java objects, facilitating efficient manipulation and usage within the application. By leveraging the Formatter and Converter interfaces, Spring MVC offers flexible mechanisms to handle type conversion during the binding process.

```
import org.springframework.core.convert.converter.Converter;

public class StringToDateConverter implements Converter<String, Date> {
    @Override
    public Date convert(String source) {
        SimpleDateFormat sdf = new SimpleDateFormat("yyyy-MM-dd");
        try {
            return sdf.parse(source);
        } catch (ParseException e) {
            throw new IllegalArgumentException("Invalid date format");
        }
    }
}
```

The StringToDateConverter shown here converts a String representation of a date into a Date object. To register this converter, it must be added to the application's configuration.

```
import org.springframework.context.annotation.Configuration;
import org.springframework.format.FormatterRegistry;
import org.springframework.web.servlet.config.annotation.WebMvcConfigurer;

@Configuration
public class WebConfig implements WebMvcConfigurer {
    @Override
    public void addFormatters(FormatterRegistry registry) {
        registry.addConverter(new StringToDateConverter());
    }
}
```

Validation in Spring MVC is closely coupled with the data binding mechanism. The framework uses the Java Bean Validation API (JSR-380), which introduces annotations that specify validation rules directly on the model fields.

```
import javax.validation.constraints.NotNull;
import javax.validation.constraints.Size;

public class User {
    @NotNull
    @Size(min = 1, max = 20)
    private String username;

    @NotNull
    @Size(min = 8)
    private String password;

    // getters and setters
}
```

The @NotNull and @Size annotations ensure that the username and password fields are not null and enforce size constraints. To trigger validation during form submission, the model must be annotated with @Valid in the controller method parameter.

```
import org.springframework.stereotype.Controller;
import org.springframework.ui.Model;
import org.springframework.validation.BindingResult;
import org.springframework.web.bind.annotation.PostMapping;

import javax.validation.Valid;

@Controller
public class UserController {

    @PostMapping("/register")
    public String registerUser(@Valid User user, BindingResult result, Model
            model) {
        if (result.hasErrors()) {
            return "registrationForm";
        }
        // Process the valid user
        return "redirect:/success";
    }
}
```

The BindingResult captures any validation errors, which can be evaluated to determine the appropriate response. When there are validation errors, the method returns to the registration form, preserving the error messages within the form view.

```
<form th:action="@{/register}" th:object="${user}" method="post">
    <div>
        <label>Username:</label>
```

```
        <input type="text" th:field="*{username}" />
        <span th:if="${#fields.hasErrors('username')}" th:errors="*{username}"
            >Invalid Username</span>
    </div>
    <div>
        <label>Password:</label>
        <input type="password" th:field="*{password}" />
        <span th:if="${#fields.hasErrors('password')}" th:errors="*{password}">
            Invalid Password</span>
    </div>
    <button type="submit">Register</button>
</form>
```

Within the Thymeleaf template, the th:object attribute is bound to the user model attribute, and the th:field attribute specifies the form fields. The th:if and th:errors attributes are used to display validation messages next to the respective fields when errors are present.

Data validation can be further extended by creating custom validation annotations. This entails writing a custom annotation and a validator class.

```
import javax.validation.Constraint;
import javax.validation.Payload;
import java.lang.annotation.Retention;
import java.lang.annotation.RetentionPolicy;
import java.lang.annotation.Target;
import java.lang.annotation.ElementType;

@Constraint(validatedBy = CustomValidator.class)
@Target(ElementType.FIELD)
@Retention(RetentionPolicy.RUNTIME)
public @interface CustomValidation {
    String message() default "Default validation message";
    Class<?>[] groups() default {};
    Class<? extends Payload>[] payload() default {};
}
```

```
import javax.validation.ConstraintValidator;
import javax.validation.ConstraintValidatorContext;

public class CustomValidator implements ConstraintValidator<CustomValidation,
     String> {
    @Override
    public void initialize(CustomValidation constraintAnnotation) {
    }

    @Override
    public boolean isValid(String value, ConstraintValidatorContext context) {
        return value != null && value.matches("[a-zA-Z0-9]+");
    }
```

```
}
```

The CustomValidation annotation specifies the validation constraints, and the CustomValidator implements the logic to validate that the field contains only alphanumeric characters.

Integrating both data binding and validation within the Spring MVC framework allows developers to create web applications that handle user data securely and effectively. Ensuring that data conforms to expected formats and constraints is crucial for maintaining application integrity and providing a reliable user experience.

6.9 Using View Resolvers

In the Spring MVC framework, the ViewResolver is a key component responsible for resolving view names to actual view implementations. Upon receiving a request and processing it, a controller returns a logical view name. The ViewResolver's job is to map this logical view name to a specific view, such as a JSP file or a Thymeleaf template, that will render the response.

Spring MVC provides several implementations of the ViewResolver interface, with the most common ones being InternalResourceViewResolver, BeanNameViewResolver, XmlViewResolver, and ThymeleafViewResolver. Understanding how to configure and use these resolvers allows you to effectively manage how different views are resolved and rendered in your application.

InternalResourceViewResolver

The InternalResourceViewResolver resolves view names to URLs by prepending a prefix and appending a suffix to the view name. This is particularly useful when working with JSPs. Below is an example configuration for an InternalResourceViewResolver:

```
@Configuration
public class MvcConfig implements WebMvcConfigurer {

    @Bean
    public InternalResourceViewResolver viewResolver() {
        InternalResourceViewResolver resolver = new
              InternalResourceViewResolver();
        resolver.setPrefix("/WEB-INF/views/");
        resolver.setSuffix(".jsp");
        return resolver;
```

```
    }
}
```

Given this configuration, if a controller returns "home" as the view name:

```
@RequestMapping("/home")
public String home() {
    return "home";
}
```

The InternalResourceViewResolver will resolve "home" to "/WEB-INF/views/home.jsp".

ThymeleafViewResolver

Integrating Thymeleaf with Spring MVC requires configuring ThymeleafViewResolver. First, add the Thymeleaf dependencies to your pom.xml:

```
<dependency>
    <groupId>org.thymeleaf</groupId>
    <artifactId>thymeleaf-spring5</artifactId>
    <version>3.0.11.RELEASE</version>
</dependency>
```

Then configure the ThymeleafViewResolver, along with the ThymeleafTemplateEngine and SpringResourceTemplateResolver:

```
@Bean
public SpringResourceTemplateResolver templateResolver() {
    SpringResourceTemplateResolver templateResolver = new
          SpringResourceTemplateResolver();
    templateResolver.setPrefix("/WEB-INF/templates/");
    templateResolver.setSuffix(".html");
    templateResolver.setTemplateMode(TemplateMode.HTML);
    templateResolver.setCacheable(true);
    return templateResolver;
}

@Bean
public SpringTemplateEngine templateEngine() {
    SpringTemplateEngine templateEngine = new SpringTemplateEngine();
    templateEngine.setTemplateResolver(templateResolver());
    templateEngine.setEnableSpringELCompiler(true);
    return templateEngine;
}

@Bean
public ThymeleafViewResolver viewResolver() {
    ThymeleafViewResolver resolver = new ThymeleafViewResolver();
```

```
    resolver.setTemplateEngine(templateEngine());
    resolver.setOrder(1);
    return resolver;
}
```

With this configuration, if a controller returns "dashboard" as the view name:

```
@RequestMapping("/dashboard")
public String dashboard() {
    return "dashboard";
}
```

The ThymeleafViewResolver will resolve "dashboard" to "/WEB-INF/templates/dashboard.html".

Configuring Multiple View Resolvers

Spring MVC allows configuring multiple view resolvers. In such cases, it's crucial to specify their order using the setOrder method. The lowest order value has the highest priority. Here is an example configuration with both InternalResourceViewResolver and ThymeleafViewResolver:

```
@Bean
public ThymeleafViewResolver thymeleafViewResolver() {
    ThymeleafViewResolver resolver = new ThymeleafViewResolver();
    resolver.setTemplateEngine(templateEngine());
    resolver.setOrder(1);
    return resolver;
}

@Bean
public InternalResourceViewResolver internalResourceViewResolver() {
    InternalResourceViewResolver resolver = new InternalResourceViewResolver();
    resolver.setPrefix("/WEB-INF/views/");
    resolver.setSuffix(".jsp");
    resolver.setOrder(2);
    return resolver;
}
```

In this configuration, Thymeleaf views will be resolved first due to the higher priority (lower order value), and JSP views will serve as a fall-back.

Custom ViewResolver

Creating a custom ViewResolver involves implementing the ViewResolver interface. This allows you to tailor view resolution mechanisms to specific requirements. Below is an example:

```
public class CustomViewResolver implements ViewResolver {
    @Override
    public View resolveViewName(String viewName, Locale locale) throws
        Exception {
        if (viewName.startsWith("json")) {
            MappingJackson2JsonView jsonView = new
                MappingJackson2JsonView();
            return jsonView;
        } else {
            InternalResourceView view = new InternalResourceView("/WEB-INF/
                views/" + viewName + ".jsp");
            return view;
        }
    }
}
```

In this custom implementation, views starting with "json" will be resolved to JSON views, while others will default to JSP views. Register the custom view resolver as follows:

```
@Bean
public ViewResolver customViewResolver() {
    return new CustomViewResolver();
}
```

This section elaborates on the essential configurations and usage of view resolvers in Spring MVC. By managing and customizing view resolution effectively, developers can control the rendering of responses in a flexible and maintainable manner.

```
/home -> /WEB-INF/views/home.jsp
/dashboard -> /WEB-INF/templates/dashboard.html
```

6.10 Working with JSPs in Spring MVC

JavaServer Pages (JSPs) are a technology used to create dynamically generated web content. JSPs allow for the embedding of Java code within HTML pages, making it possible to generate dynamic content based on application data. In the context of Spring MVC, JSPs are frequently used as view components to render model data and present it to the user. This section delves into how to effectively work with JSPs within the Spring MVC framework, covering topics such as configuring view resolvers, defining and using JSPs, and understanding the various JSP tags and expressions.

Configuring View Resolvers

To use JSPs as the view technology in a Spring MVC application, it is essential to configure a view resolver bean in the Spring configuration. A view resolver maps logical view names returned by controllers to actual JSP files. One of the most common view resolvers is InternalResourceViewResolver. Below is an example of how to configure this view resolver in a Spring configuration file:

```
<bean class="org.springframework.web.servlet.view.InternalResourceViewResolver
    ">
    <property name="prefix" value="/WEB-INF/views/" />
    <property name="suffix" value=".jsp" />
</bean>
```

This configuration indicates that all view names returned by controllers will have /WEB-INF/views/ prefixed and .jsp suffixed. For instance, if a controller returns the view name "home", the resolver will look for a JSP file at /WEB-INF/views/home.jsp.

Defining and Using JSPs

To define a JSP, create a .jsp file under the directory specified in the view resolver's prefix. For instance, create home.jsp in the WEB-INF/views directory. Below is an example of a simple JSP file:

```
<%@ page language="java" contentType="text/html; charset=UTF-8"
    pageEncoding="UTF-8"%>
<!DOCTYPE html>
<html>
<head>
    <title>Home Page</title>
</head>
<body>
    <h1>Welcome to the Home Page</h1>
    <p>Hello, ${user}!</p>
</body>
</html>
```

In this example, ${user} is an expression that will be replaced by the value of the user attribute from the model.

Using JSP Tag Libraries

JSP Tag Libraries (JSTL) provide a set of custom tags that simplify the authoring of JSPs. They include tags for common tasks such as iteration, conditionals, and formatting. To use JSTL, add the following directives at the top of your JSP file:

```
<%@ taglib uri="http://java.sun.com/jsp/jstl/core" prefix="c" %>
<%@ taglib uri="http://java.sun.com/jsp/jstl/fmt" prefix="fmt" %>
```

Below is an example of a JSP file using JSTL to iterate over a list of items:

```
<%@ page language=”java” contentType=”text/html; charset=UTF-8”
    pageEncoding=”UTF-8”%>
<%@ taglib uri=”http://java.sun.com/jsp/jstl/core” prefix=”c” %>
<!DOCTYPE html>
<html>
<head>
    <title>Item List</title>
</head>
<body>
    <h1>Items</h1>
    <ul>
        <c:forEach var=”item” items=”${itemList}”>
            <li>${item}</li>
        </c:forEach>
    </ul>
</body>
</html>
```

In this example, itemList is a collection of items passed from the controller's model, and the c:forEach tag iterates over each item, displaying it in an unordered list (<ul>).

Handling Form Submissions with JSPs

JSPs can also be used to create and handle form submissions in Spring MVC applications. Below is an illustration of a JSP form:

```
<%@ page language=”java” contentType=”text/html; charset=UTF-8”
    pageEncoding=”UTF-8”%>
<!DOCTYPE html>
<html>
<head>
    <title>Form Submission</title>
</head>
<body>
    <h1>Submit Form</h1>
    <form action=”submitForm” method=”post”>
        Name: <input type=”text” name=”name” /><br/>
        Age: <input type=”text” name=”age” /><br/>
        <input type=”submit” value=”Submit” />
    </form>
</body>
</html>
```

The corresponding controller might look like this:

```
@Controller
public class FormController {
```

```
    @RequestMapping(value = "/submitForm", method = RequestMethod.POST)
    public String submitForm(@RequestParam("name") String name,
                             @RequestParam("age") int age,
                             Model model) {
        model.addAttribute("name", name);
        model.addAttribute("age", age);
        return "formSuccess"; // Redirect to formSuccess.jsp
    }
}
```

The formSuccess.jsp file could then display the submitted form data:

```
<%@ page language="java" contentType="text/html; charset=UTF-8"
    pageEncoding="UTF-8"%>
<!DOCTYPE html>
<html>
<head>
    <title>Form Success</title>
</head>
<body>
    <h1>Form Submission Successful</h1>
    <p>Name: ${name}</p>
    <p>Age: ${age}</p>
</body>
</html>
```

In this example, the form data submitted to /submitForm is captured by the FormController and displayed on the formSuccess page.

Working with JSPs in Spring MVC involves configuring view resolvers, defining JSPs, utilizing JSTL for simplifying JSP authoring, and handling form submissions. Understanding these components enhances the ability to develop dynamic and responsive web applications using the Spring MVC framework. The provided examples illustrate how to seamlessly integrate JSPs with Spring MVC, ensuring a cohesive and functional web application structure.

6.11 Integrating Thymeleaf with Spring MVC

Thymeleaf is a modern server-side Java template engine for web and standalone environments. To integrate Thymeleaf with Spring MVC, follow these steps to ensure a smooth and effective integration process that is both performant and maintainable.

- **Adding Thymeleaf Dependency**

To use Thymeleaf in a Spring MVC project, the Thymeleaf dependency must be added to the project's pom.xml file. Below is an example configuration for a Maven project:

```
<dependency>
    <groupId>org.thymeleaf</groupId>
    <artifactId>thymeleaf-spring5</artifactId>
    <version>3.0.12.RELEASE</version>
</dependency>
```

Ensure that the version number corresponds to the latest release version compatible with your Spring framework version.

- **Configuring Thymeleaf Template Resolver**

After adding the Thymeleaf dependency, configure the template resolver. The template resolver is responsible for finding and loading the Thymeleaf templates. This configuration typically resides in a Spring configuration class annotated with @Configuration.

```
import org.springframework.context.annotation.Bean;
import org.springframework.context.annotation.Configuration;
import org.thymeleaf.spring5.SpringTemplateEngine;
import org.thymeleaf.spring5.view.ThymeleafViewResolver;
import org.thymeleaf.templateresolver.ClassLoaderTemplateResolver;
import org.thymeleaf.templateresolver.ITemplateResolver;

@Configuration
public class ThymeleafConfig {

    @Bean
    public ITemplateResolver templateResolver() {
        ClassLoaderTemplateResolver templateResolver = new
            ClassLoaderTemplateResolver();
        templateResolver.setPrefix("templates/");
        templateResolver.setSuffix(".html");
        templateResolver.setTemplateMode("HTML");
        templateResolver.setCharacterEncoding("UTF-8");
        templateResolver.setCacheable(false);
        return templateResolver;
    }

    @Bean
    public SpringTemplateEngine templateEngine(ITemplateResolver
        templateResolver) {
        SpringTemplateEngine templateEngine = new SpringTemplateEngine();
        templateEngine.setTemplateResolver(templateResolver);
        return templateEngine;
    }
```

```
    @Bean
    public ThymeleafViewResolver viewResolver(SpringTemplateEngine
        templateEngine) {
        ThymeleafViewResolver viewResolver = new ThymeleafViewResolver();
        viewResolver.setTemplateEngine(templateEngine);
        viewResolver.setCharacterEncoding("UTF-8");
        return viewResolver;
    }
}
```

In the above configuration, the ClassLoaderTemplateResolver is used, which loads templates from the classpath. The templates are expected to be located in the templates/ directory with an .html extension. The SpringTemplateEngine manages the template processing, and ThymeleafViewResolver resolves view names into Thymeleaf templates.

- **Creating Thymeleaf Templates**

With the Thymeleaf configuration in place, create HTML templates in the specified directory. Consider the following Thymeleaf template named index.html:

```
<!DOCTYPE html>
<html xmlns:th="http://www.thymeleaf.org">
<head>
    <meta charset="UTF-8">
    <title>Welcome Page</title>
</head>
<body>
    <h1>Welcome to Thymeleaf Integration with Spring MVC</h1>
    <p th:text="'Hello, ' + ${name} + '!'">Fallback text</p>
</body>
</html>
```

This template uses the th:text attribute to dynamically insert the value of the name variable passed from the Spring controller.

- **Defining a Controller to Use Thymeleaf Templates**

Define a Spring MVC controller that handles requests and returns the name of the Thymeleaf template to be rendered. Below is an example controller:

```
import org.springframework.stereotype.Controller;
import org.springframework.ui.Model;
import org.springframework.web.bind.annotation.GetMapping;
```

```
@Controller
public class MainController {

    @GetMapping("/")
    public String index(Model model) {
        model.addAttribute("name", "Spring MVC User");
        return "index";
    }
}
```

In this controller, the index method handles GET requests to the root URL ("/"). It adds the name attribute to the model, which will be accessible within the Thymeleaf template, and returns the template name "index".

- **Running and Testing the Application**

Once everything is set up correctly, run the Spring application to test the Thymeleaf integration. You should see the Thymeleaf template rendered correctly at the specified endpoint. The page should display "Welcome to Thymeleaf Integration with Spring MVC" and "Hello, Spring MVC User!".

By following these steps, Thymeleaf can be effectively integrated into a Spring MVC project, providing a powerful and flexible mechanism for rendering server-side views. The combination of Thymeleaf's expressive template language and Spring MVC's robust architecture facilitates the development of maintainable and dynamic web applications.

6.12 RESTful Web Services with Spring MVC

Restful web services play a crucial role in modern web application development by allowing different systems to communicate with each other over HTTP. The Spring MVC framework provides robust support for creating RESTful web services, allowing developers to design APIs that support CRUD operations through standard HTTP methods. In this section, we will explore how to define RESTful web services using Spring MVC, including setting up controllers, handling requests, and serializing responses.

Defining a RESTful Controller

In Spring MVC, a RESTful controller is typically annotated with @RestController and the request mappings are defined using @RequestMapping or its composed annotations such as @GetMapping, @PostMapping, @PutMapping, and @DeleteMapping. Here is an example of a simple RESTful controller for managing a collection of entities:

```
import org.springframework.web.bind.annotation.*;

import java.util.ArrayList;
import java.util.List;

@RestController
@RequestMapping("/api/articles")
public class ArticleController {

    private List<Article> articles = new ArrayList<>();

    @GetMapping
    public List<Article> getAllArticles() {
        return articles;
    }

    @GetMapping("/{id}")
    public Article getArticleById(@PathVariable int id) {
        return articles.stream()
                .filter(article -> article.getId() == id)
                .findFirst()
                .orElse(null);
    }

    @PostMapping
    public Article createArticle(@RequestBody Article article) {
        articles.add(article);
        return article;
    }

    @PutMapping("/{id}")
    public Article updateArticle(@PathVariable int id, @RequestBody Article
        updatedArticle) {
        for (int i = 0; i < articles.size(); i++) {
            if (articles.get(i).getId() == id) {
                articles.set(i, updatedArticle);
                return updatedArticle;
            }
        }
        return null;
    }

    @DeleteMapping("/{id}")
    public void deleteArticle(@PathVariable int id) {
        articles.removeIf(article -> article.getId() == id);
    }
```

```
}
```

Handling Requests and Responses

Mapping incoming HTTP requests to appropriate handler methods is straightforward in Spring MVC using annotations. For example, @GetMapping maps a GET request to a method, @PostMapping maps a POST request, and so on. Path variables can be extracted using the @PathVariable annotation, and request bodies can be bound to method parameters using the @RequestBody annotation.

Serialization and Deserialization

Spring MVC uses the Jackson library by default to automatically convert Java objects to JSON and vice versa. When a request is made with the content type application/json, Spring MVC handles the deserialization. Similarly, the response is serialized to JSON when the return type of a method is a Java object.

Consider the following Article class used in the controller shown above:

```
public class Article {

    private int id;
    private String title;
    private String content;

    // Getters and Setters

    public int getId() {
        return id;
    }

    public void setId(int id) {
        this.id = id;
    }

    public String getTitle() {
        return title;
    }

    public void setTitle(String title) {
        this.title = title;
    }

    public String getContent() {
        return content;
    }

    public void setContent(String content) {
        this.content = content;
```

```
    }
}
```

Error Handling in RESTful Services

Implementing effective error handling is essential in RESTful services. Spring MVC offers robust exception handling mechanisms, including the @ExceptionHandler annotation and ControllerAdvice to handle exceptions globally.

```
import org.springframework.http.HttpStatus;
import org.springframework.http.ResponseEntity;
import org.springframework.web.bind.annotation.ControllerAdvice;
import org.springframework.web.bind.annotation.ExceptionHandler;
import org.springframework.web.bind.annotation.ResponseStatus;

@ControllerAdvice
public class GlobalExceptionHandler {

    @ExceptionHandler(ArticleNotFoundException.class)
    @ResponseStatus(HttpStatus.NOT_FOUND)
    public ResponseEntity<String> handleArticleNotFound(
            ArticleNotFoundException ex) {
        return new ResponseEntity<>("Article not found: " + ex.getMessage(),
              HttpStatus.NOT_FOUND);
    }

    // Additional exception handlers can be added here
}
```

Testing RESTful Web Services

Testing RESTful web services can be performed using various tools. One practical method is to use MockMvc, which allows tests to be executed against the controller's HTTP layer.

```
import static org.springframework.test.web.servlet.request.
    MockMvcRequestBuilders.*;
import static org.springframework.test.web.servlet.result.MockMvcResultMatchers
    .*;
import static org.springframework.test.web.servlet.setup.MockMvcBuilders.*;

import org.junit.jupiter.api.Test;
import org.springframework.beans.factory.annotation.Autowired;
import org.springframework.boot.test.autoconfigure.web.servlet.WebMvcTest;
import org.springframework.test.web.servlet.MockMvc;

@WebMvcTest(ArticleController.class)
public class ArticleControllerTest {

    @Autowired
```

```
    private MockMvc mockMvc;

    @Test
    public void shouldReturnAllArticles() throws Exception {
        mockMvc.perform(get("/api/articles"))
                .andExpect(status().isOk())
                .andExpect(content().contentType("application/json"));
    }

    // Additional test methods for other endpoints
}
```

Through these practices and mechanisms, the development of robust, maintainable, and efficient RESTful web services with Spring MVC is facilitated. This system seamlessly handles both simple CRUD operations and complex business logic, ensuring a scalable architecture for modern API-driven applications.

```
GET /api/articles HTTP/1.1
Host: example.com
Accept: application/json

HTTP/1.1 200 OK
Content-Type: application/json
Content-Length: ...

[
    {
        "id": 1,
        "title": "First Article",
        "content": "Content of the first article"
    },
    {
        "id": 2,
        "title": "Second Article",
        "content": "Content of the second article"
    }
]
```

6.13 Exception Handling in Spring MVC

Exception handling is a critical aspect of any robust web application. The Spring MVC framework provides several mechanisms to manage exceptions systematically, ensuring that the user experience is not disrupted by unexpected errors.

Spring MVC offers multiple methodologies for handling exceptions, ranging from simple try-catch blocks to more sophisticated techniques using @ExceptionHandler methods, @ControllerAdvice, and even custom HandlerExceptionResolver. This section will explore these methods in detail, providing clear and practical examples to aid comprehension.

The simplest form of exception handling in any Java application is the try-catch block. While effective for localized error handling, it does not scale well for larger applications due to code clutter and complexity.

```
@RequestMapping("/demo")
public String demoMethod(Model model) {
    try {
        // logic that may throw an exception
    } catch (Exception e) {
        model.addAttribute("errorMessage", "An error occurred: " + e.getMessage
            ());
        return "errorPage";
    }
    return "successPage";
}
```

While the try-catch approach can be used, Spring MVC recommends adopting a more modular and maintainable strategy. The @ExceptionHandler annotation is a more elegant solution tailored to handle exceptions in a specific controller.

```
@Controller
public class DemoController {

    @RequestMapping("/demo")
    public String demoMethod() {
        // logic that may throw an exception
        throw new RuntimeException("Unexpected error");
    }

    @ExceptionHandler(RuntimeException.class)
    public String handleRuntimeException(RuntimeException e, Model model) {
        model.addAttribute("errorMessage", "An error occurred: " + e.getMessage
            ());
        return "errorPage";
    }
}
```

In the above code, @ExceptionHandler is used to define a method that handles RuntimeException. When such an exception occurs in demoMethod, control is transferred to handleRuntimeException, which prepares the error message and returns the name of the error view.

For more centralized exception handling, @ControllerAdvice can be used. This annotation allows the definition of global exception handlers that can apply to multiple controllers.

```
@ControllerAdvice
public class GlobalExceptionHandler {

    @ExceptionHandler(Exception.class)
    public String handleAllExceptions(Exception e, Model model) {
        model.addAttribute("errorMessage", "General error occurred: " + e.
            getMessage());
        return "errorPage";
    }

    @ExceptionHandler(NullPointerException.class)
    public String handleNullPointerException(NullPointerException e, Model
        model) {
        model.addAttribute("errorMessage", "Null Pointer Exception: " + e.
            getMessage());
        return "nullPointerErrorPage";
    }
}
```

Here, the GlobalExceptionHandler class annotated with @ControllerAdvice encompasses handlers for different types of exceptions. The handleAllExceptions method catches any Exception, while the handleNullPointerException method specifically targets NullPointerException.

Another powerful feature provided by Spring MVC is the HandlerExceptionResolver interface, which allows for resolving exceptions in a custom manner. This interface can be particularly useful when exception handling logic needs to be reused across various components or modules.

```
public class CustomExceptionResolver implements HandlerExceptionResolver {

    @Override
    public ModelAndView resolveException(HttpServletRequest request,
        HttpServletResponse response, Object handler, Exception ex) {
        ModelAndView modelAndView = new ModelAndView("errorPage");
        modelAndView.addObject("errorMessage", ex.getMessage());
        return modelAndView;
    }
}
```

To register this CustomExceptionResolver, it must be added to the Spring configuration.

```
@Configuration
public class WebConfig implements WebMvcConfigurer {

    @Override
    public void configureHandlerExceptionResolvers(List<
        HandlerExceptionResolver> resolvers) {
```

```
        resolvers.add(new CustomExceptionResolver());
    }
}
```

Spring MVC also provides built-in exception handling mechanisms, among which is the DefaultHandlerExceptionResolver that resolves standard Spring exceptions and translates them into HTTP status codes.

Integrating exception handling with RESTful web services is equally critical. For REST controllers, exceptions can be handled differently, mainly by returning appropriate HTTP response statuses and body content. The @RestControllerAdvice annotation serves a similar purpose as @ControllerAdvice, but is tailored for @RestController-annotated classes.

```
@RestControllerAdvice
public class RestGlobalExceptionHandler {

    @ExceptionHandler(Exception.class)
    public ResponseEntity<String> handleAllExceptions(Exception e) {
        return new ResponseEntity<>("General error: " + e.getMessage(),
            HttpStatus.INTERNAL_SERVER_ERROR);
    }

    @ExceptionHandler(ResourceNotFoundException.class)
    public ResponseEntity<String> handleResourceNotFound(
        ResourceNotFoundException e) {
        return new ResponseEntity<>("Resource not found: " + e.getMessage(),
            HttpStatus.NOT_FOUND);
    }
}
```

This example demonstrates handling exceptions in a RESTful context, where handleAllExceptions and handleResourceNotFound methods return ResponseEntity objects with appropriate HTTP status codes and error messages.

Through these mechanisms, Spring MVC offers a comprehensive and flexible system for managing exceptions in Java-based web applications. By leveraging @ExceptionHandler, @ControllerAdvice, HandlerExceptionResolver, and related annotations, developers can create more maintainable and user-friendly applications that gracefully handle unexpected conditions.

Chapter 7

Spring Boot

This chapter introduces Spring Boot, highlighting its features and advantages for simplifying Spring application development. It covers setting up a Spring Boot project, utilizing the Spring Boot Initializr, and understanding auto-configuration. The chapter explains how to create simple applications, use Spring Boot starters, and manage externalized configurations. Additionally, it explores tools like Spring Boot Actuator for monitoring and Spring Boot DevTools for development enhancements. The chapter concludes with testing Spring Boot applications and deploying them efficiently.

7.1 Introduction to Spring Boot

Spring Boot, an extension of the Spring framework, is designed to simplify the initial setup and development of new Spring applications. It provides a set of conventions and default configurations to rapidly create stand-alone, production-ready applications with minimal configuration.

One of the primary objectives of Spring Boot is to reduce the complexity of configuring a Spring application. Traditional Spring requires extensive configuration, often through XML files or numerous Java configuration classes. Spring Boot alleviates this by offering a suite of pre-configured templates, known as auto-configuration, which automatically sets up standard Spring components based on the dependencies you include in your project.

Spring Boot embraces *convention over configuration*. This means it comes with sensible defaults, so you do not have to define every parameter and wiring explicitly unless you need to customize them. This approach significantly reduces boilerplate code and speeds up the development process.

To facilitate the rapid creation of applications, Spring Boot provides a built-in web server, allowing developers to focus on coding the application's business logic rather than configuring underlying services. Spring Boot supports both Tomcat and Jetty as embedded servers. By embedding the web server, Spring Boot makes it straightforward to package the application as a self-contained JAR file.

The core features of Spring Boot include:

- **Auto-configuration:** Automatically configures Spring and third-party libraries based on the beans available in the classpath.
- **Standalone Spring applications:** Spring Boot allows the creation of standalone Spring applications with an embedded server. This means no need to deploy WAR files to an external web server.
- **Production-ready features:** Includes a comprehensive set of tools and extensions to monitor and manage applications, such as Spring Boot Actuator.
- **Spring Boot CLI:** A command-line interface that can be used to develop Spring Boot applications using Groovy.
- **Spring Initializr:** A web-based tool and a related API to quickly generate a Spring Boot project with the dependencies you need.
- **Microservices support:** Easily develop microservices using Spring Boot with Cloud-native features.

To give a concrete example of the simplicity Spring Boot brings, consider a basic Spring Boot application. Below is a minimal Spring Boot application that starts up a web server and serves a simple REST endpoint:

```
import org.springframework.boot.SpringApplication;
import org.springframework.boot.autoconfigure.SpringBootApplication;
import org.springframework.web.bind.annotation.GetMapping;
import org.springframework.web.bind.annotation.RestController;
```

```
@SpringBootApplication
public class MySpringBootApplication {

    public static void main(String[] args) {
        SpringApplication.run(MySpringBootApplication.class, args);
    }
}

@RestController
class MyController {

    @GetMapping("/hello")
    public String hello() {
        return "Hello, World!";
    }
}
```

When executed, this simple example starts an embedded web server (typically Tomcat by default), maps the root URL path '/hello' to the 'hello' function, which just returns a plain text string "Hello, World!". You can run this application without any additional configuration files or complex setup.

Additionally, Spring Boot integrates seamlessly with popular build tools like Maven and Gradle. For instance, to set up the necessary dependencies using Maven, the pom.xml file would include:

```
<dependencies>
    <dependency>
        <groupId>org.springframework.boot</groupId>
        <artifactId>spring-boot-starter-web</artifactId>
    </dependency>
</dependencies>
```

The spring-boot-starter-web dependency encompasses essential libraries for developing web applications, including Spring MVC, JSON processing, and an embedded Tomcat server.

Another notable feature is the Spring Boot Actuator, which provides a comprehensive toolset for monitoring and managing Spring Boot applications. Actuator includes several built-in endpoints that offer various metrics, health checks, and application environment details, facilitating the maintenance and operation of the application in a production environment.

Spring Boot is designed to work effortlessly out-of-the-box, but it also provides you with the flexibility to customize configurations when necessary. For example, if the default embedded server does not meet particular requirements, it can be replaced with another server such as Jetty or Undertow with relative ease.

In the next sections, we will delve deeper into these features, beginning with setting up a Spring Boot project and exploring the streamlined development experience that Spring Boot offers.

7.2 Features and Advantages of Spring Boot

Spring Boot provides several powerful features and advantages that simplify the development of Spring applications. These features facilitate rapid development, production-ready environments, and minimize boilerplate configuration, thus enhancing developer productivity and application maintainability.

Convention over Configuration and Opinionated Defaults

One of the core principles of Spring Boot is "Convention over Configuration", which means that the framework provides sensible defaults for developers to follow. This approach reduces the need for extensive configuration files, enabling a quicker setup for new projects. Spring Boot's opinionated defaults ensure that the framework's configurations are aligned with common industry best practices, accelerating the development process.

Spring Boot Starters

Spring Boot Starters are a set of convenient dependency descriptors that you can use to include a group of relevant dependencies. For instance, if you want to create a web application, you can use spring-boot-starter-web, which includes dependencies such as Spring MVC, Jackson (for JSON processing), and Tomcat (as the default embedded container).

```
<dependency>
    <groupId>org.springframework.boot</groupId>
    <artifactId>spring-boot-starter-web</artifactId>
</dependency>
```

Using starters simplifies the dependency management in your Maven or Gradle build files, making it easier to manage your project's dependencies.

Auto-Configuration

Spring Boot's auto-configuration capability automatically configures your Spring application based on the dependencies you have added. For instance, if you have added H2 Database and Spring Data JPA in your classpath, Spring Boot will automatically set up a data source, an entity manager, and other related configurations without any additional configuration.

```
import org.springframework.boot.SpringApplication;
import org.springframework.boot.autoconfigure.SpringBootApplication;

@SpringBootApplication
public class MyApplication {
    public static void main(String[] args) {
        SpringApplication.run(MyApplication.class, args);
    }
}
```

Embedded Servers

Spring Boot supports embedded servers such as Tomcat, Jetty, and Undertow. By using embedded servers, developers can package their Spring Boot applications as executable JAR files and run them independently without the need for a separate application server.

```
$ java -jar myapplication.jar
```

This feature simplifies deployment, as the application and its server are bundled together, ensuring consistency between development and production environments.

Production-Ready Features

Spring Boot includes several production-ready features that simplify monitoring and management. The Spring Boot Actuator provides a range of endpoints for health checks, metrics, and environment information.

```
management:
  endpoints:
    web:
      exposure:
        include: "*"
```

This configuration exposes all actuator endpoints, making it easier to monitor and maintain the health of your application in production environments.

Externalized Configuration

Externalized configuration allows you to manage your application's configuration properties outside of the application code. Using property files, YAML files, environment variables, and command-line arguments, you can externalize configuration and manage different configurations for various environments (e.g., development, testing, production).

```
server:
  port: 8081
spring:
  datasource:
    url: jdbc:h2:mem:testdb
    username: sa
    password: password
```

By leveraging externalized configuration, you can ensure that your application is flexible and adaptable to different deployment contexts without modifying the source code.

Spring Boot DevTools

Spring Boot DevTools is a set of development tools that enhance the development experience. Features include automatic restarts, live reload, and configurations for efficient development.

```
<dependency>
    <groupId>org.springframework.boot</groupId>
    <artifactId>spring-boot-devtools</artifactId>
    <optional>true</optional>
</dependency>
```

Simplified Testing

Spring Boot simplifies testing by providing test dependencies and annotations. The @SpringBootTest annotation allows for comprehensive integration tests that load the complete application context.

```
import org.springframework.boot.test.context.SpringBootTest;
import org.junit.jupiter.api.Test;

@SpringBootTest
class MyApplicationTests {
    @Test
    void contextLoads() {
    }
}
```

Comprehensive Documentation and Community Support

Spring Boot boasts comprehensive documentation and a vibrant community. The extensive documentation covers all aspects of the framework, with numerous examples, and is kept up-to-date with each release. The community surrounding Spring Boot is active, providing various resources such as tutorials, forums, and Stack Overflow support to facilitate learning and troubleshooting.

These features contribute to the ease of developing and maintaining Spring applications, making Spring Boot a preferred choice for modern application development.

7.3 Setting Up a Spring Boot Project

Setting up a Spring Boot project involves a series of steps that lay the foundation for robust application development. These steps include creating a project structure, initializing the project using the Spring Boot Initializr, and configuring the necessary dependencies. Below, we delve into these steps in detail to ensure a comprehensive understanding.

To begin, navigate to https://start.spring.io/, the official Spring Boot Initializr. This tool simplifies the creation of a new Spring Boot project by generating the necessary boilerplate code and configurations. The interface allows you to select various project parameters, including the build system, language, and dependencies.

Configure the project metadata. Set the *Group* field to com.example and the *Artifact* field to demo. The *Group* and *Artifact* fields constitute the project's coordinates in the Maven repository, uniquely identifying the project.

Choose the build system. For instance, select Maven as the build tool by setting *Packaging* to jar and *Java* version to 11. This ensures the generated project is compatible with Java 11 and packaged as a JAR file.

Specify dependencies. For example, include the Spring Web, Spring Data JPA, and H2 Database dependencies. These selections ensure your project supports web functionalities, data persistence with JPA, and an in-memory database for development purposes. Below is a Maven pom.xml file reflecting these choices:

```
<project xmlns="http://maven.apache.org/POM/4.0.0" xmlns:xsi="http://www.
    w3.org/2001/XMLSchema-instance" xsi:schemaLocation="http://maven.
    apache.org/POM/4.0.0 http://maven.apache.org/xsd/maven-4.0.0.xsd">
  <modelVersion>4.0.0</modelVersion>

  <groupId>com.example</groupId>
  <artifactId>demo</artifactId>
```

```xml
    <version>0.0.1-SNAPSHOT</version>
    <packaging>jar</packaging>

    <name>demo</name>
    <description>Demo project for Spring Boot</description>
    <parent>
        <groupId>org.springframework.boot</groupId>
        <artifactId>spring-boot-starter-parent</artifactId>
        <version>2.5.4</version>
        <relativePath/> <!-- lookup parent from repository -->
    </parent>

    <properties>
        <java.version>11</java.version>
    </properties>

    <dependencies>
        <dependency>
            <groupId>org.springframework.boot</groupId>
            <artifactId>spring-boot-starter-web</artifactId>
        </dependency>
        <dependency>
            <groupId>org.springframework.boot</groupId>
            <artifactId>spring-boot-starter-data-jpa</artifactId>
        </dependency>
        <dependency>
            <groupId>com.h2database</groupId>
            <artifactId>h2</artifactId>
            <scope>runtime</scope>
        </dependency>
        <dependency>
            <groupId>org.springframework.boot</groupId>
            <artifactId>spring-boot-starter-test</artifactId>
            <scope>test</scope>
        </dependency>
    </dependencies>

    <build>
        <plugins>
            <plugin>
                <groupId>org.springframework.boot</groupId>
                <artifactId>spring-boot-maven-plugin</artifactId>
            </plugin>
        </plugins>
    </build>

</project>
```

Once the dependencies are selected, click the Generate button to download the project archive. Extract the archive to your desired directory.

Open the project in your preferred Integrated Development Environment (IDE), such as IntelliJ IDEA, Eclipse, or Visual Studio Code. Import the project as a Maven project to manage dependencies automatically. In IntelliJ IDEA, you can do this by selecting File → Open... and choosing the project's root directory containing the pom.xml file. IntelliJ IDEA will recognize the project structure and prompt to import the Maven dependencies.

Examine the project structure. The default structure generated by Spring Boot Initializr follows a standard Maven project setup:

```
demo
  src
    main
      java
        com
          example
            demo
              DemoApplication.java
      resources
        static
        templates
        application.properties
    test
      java
        com.example.demo
          DemoApplicationTests.java
  .gitignore
  HELP.md
  mvnw
  mvnw.cmd
  pom.xml
  README.md
```

The **src** directory contains application source code and resources. The **main** subdirectory is divided into **java** and **resources** directories. The **java** directory contains the primary application code, organized by package. The initial DemoApplication.java serves as the entry point for the Spring Boot application:

```
package com.example.demo;

import org.springframework.boot.SpringApplication;
import org.springframework.boot.autoconfigure.SpringBootApplication;

@SpringBootApplication
public class DemoApplication {

    public static void main(String[] args) {
        SpringApplication.run(DemoApplication.class, args);
    }

}
```

The main method leverages the SpringApplication.run method

to launch the application context. The @SpringBootApplication annotation is a composite annotation that includes @Configuration, @EnableAutoConfiguration, and @ComponentScan, providing a succinct way to initialize the application.

The **resources** directory accommodates static assets, templates, and property files. The application.properties file is critical for configuring various aspects of the Spring Boot application, such as the database connection, server port, logging levels, and more.

Initiate the Spring Boot application by running the main method of DemoApplication.java. In IntelliJ IDEA, this can be achieved by clicking the green run button adjacent to the main method declaration. Alternatively, if using the command line, navigate to the project's root directory and execute:

```
./mvnw spring-boot:run
```

Upon successful execution, the application will start an embedded server (by default, Tomcat) and be accessible at http://localhost:8080. The console output will indicate a successful startup:

```
2023-01-01 00:00:00.000  INFO 12345 --- [           main] com.example.demo.DemoApplication         : Started DemoApplication in 2.345 seconds
```

The setup of a Spring Boot project provides a solid foundation for subsequent development activities. By leveraging the Spring Boot Initializr, managing dependencies through Maven, configuring core properties, and understanding the generated project structure, developers can effectively initiate the development of robust, maintainable applications.

7.4 Spring Boot Initializr

The Spring Boot Initializr is a crucial tool designed to streamline the initial setup of a Spring Boot project. Serving as a web-based wizard, it simplifies the generation of a new Spring Boot application by providing a user-friendly interface for configuration. This section delves into the functionalities and usage of the Spring Boot Initializr, ensuring a thorough understanding of how to employ it effectively to bootstrap your projects.

To access the Spring Boot Initializr, navigate to the URL https://start.spring.io. The webpage presents you with several configuration options to fine-tune the parameters of your new Spring Boot project. These options can be categorized as follows: Project, Language, Spring Boot

Version, Project Metadata, Packaging, Java Version, Dependencies.

Project: This option lets you choose between Maven and Gradle. Maven is selected by default as it is a widely used project management and build automation tool. However, if you prefer to use Gradle, which offers faster builds due to its incremental build methodology, you can select it here.

Language: The Initializr supports three languages: Java, Kotlin, and Groovy. Java is the default selection and the most commonly used language in Spring projects. Kotlin, offering concise syntax and enhanced null safety, is gaining popularity. Groovy, known for its simplicity and dynamic features, is also available but less frequently used.

Spring Boot Version: It is paramount to choose a stable and appropriate Spring Boot version for your project. The Initializr typically recommends a stable release for production-ready applications. Ensure compatibility with your development environment and dependencies when selecting the version.

Project Metadata: This section includes several fields:

- **Group:** Defines the group ID for your project, typically structured as a reverse domain name, e.g., "com.example".
- **Artifact:** Represents the artifact ID, essentially the name of the project.
- **Name:** Specifies the name of the project, generally the same as the Artifact.
- **Description:** A brief description of the project's purpose.
- **Package Name:** Automatically generated based on the Group and Artifact fields but can be customized.

Packaging: You can choose between "Jar" and "War." Selecting "Jar" is common for Spring Boot applications that run standalone, while "War" is chosen if deploying to an external application server.

Java Version: It is critical to select the Java version compatible with your environment and dependencies. The Initializr usually recommends the latest LTS (Long Term Support) version for stability and support.

Dependencies: One of the most significant advantages of Spring Boot Initializr is the ability to select various dependencies, called "starters," to include in your project from the outset. These starters simplify dependency management by aggregating commonly used libraries and frameworks. The dependencies are conveniently categorized for ease of selection. For instance:

- **Core:** Includes essential components like Spring Boot DevTools, Lombok for boilerplate code reduction, and Spring Configuration Processor.
- **Web:** Encompasses libraries for building web applications, such as Spring Web, Spring WebFlux for reactive programming, and Rest Repositories.
- **Template Engines:** Contains libraries like Thymeleaf and Freemarker for server-side rendering of HTML templates.
- **SQL:** Includes Spring Data JPA, JDBC, and various database connectors (e.g., MySQL, PostgreSQL).
- **NoSQL:** Provides connectors for NoSQL databases, such as MongoDB, Cassandra, and Redis.
- **Security:** Features Spring Security for implementing authentication and authorization.
- **Developer Tools:** Offers tools such as Spring Boot DevTools for improving developer productivity.
- **Operations:** Includes Spring Boot Actuator for monitoring and managing applications.
- **Cloud:** Features libraries for building cloud-native applications, such as Spring Cloud.

Upon configuration of these parameters, clicking the "Generate" button prompts the download of a compressed archive containing the project scaffold. Extracting this archive reveals a fully functional Spring Boot project structure, configured according to the specifications set in the Initializr.

The following is a simple demonstration of generating and initializing a new Spring Boot project using Maven and Java, selecting Spring Web as a dependency.

```
curl https://start.spring.io/starter.zip \
  -d dependencies=web \
```

```
    -d language=java \
    -d bootVersion=2.5.4 \
    -d groupId=com.example \
    -d artifactId=demo \
    -d name=demo \
    -d description="Demo project for Spring Boot" \
    -d packageName=com.example.demo \
    -d packaging=jar \
    -d javaVersion=11 \
    -o demo.zip
```

Extract the downloaded demo.zip file:

```
unzip demo.zip -d demo
cd demo
```

The project directory structure is generated as follows:

```
demo/
  mvnw
  mvnw.cmd
  pom.xml
  src/
    main/
      java/
        com/
          example/
            demo/
              DemoApplication.java
      resources/
        application.properties
        static/
    test/
      java/
        com/
          example/
            demo/
              DemoApplicationTests.java
```

This directory structure includes the following key components:

- mvnw: Maven wrapper script for Unix.
- mvnw.cmd: Maven wrapper script for Windows.
- pom.xml: The Maven configuration file, containing information about the project's dependencies and configurations.
- src/main/java: The source directory for Java code.
- src/main/resources: Contains static resources, configuration files, and templates.
- src/test/java: Holds the test cases.

The automatically generated DemoApplication.java serves as the entry point of the Spring Boot application:

```
package com.example.demo;

import org.springframework.boot.SpringApplication;
import org.springframework.boot.autoconfigure.SpringBootApplication;

@SpringBootApplication
public class DemoApplication {
    public static void main(String[] args) {
        SpringApplication.run(DemoApplication.class, args);
    }
}
```

To execute the application, use the following Maven command:

```
./mvnw spring-boot:run
```

The application starts, and you can navigate to http://localhost:8080 to verify successful execution.

7.5 Spring Boot Auto-Configuration

Spring Boot's auto-configuration feature simplifies the configuration process required to set up a Spring application. It aims to automatically configure your Spring application based on the included jar dependencies, minimizing the need for developers to manually configure beans that are commonly used in Spring applications.

Auto-configuration is enacted through the EnableAutoConfiguration annotation or the more encompassing SpringBootApplication annotation, which is typically used. The SpringBootApplication annotation is a convenience annotation that combines EnableAutoConfiguration, ComponentScan, and Configuration annotations.

```
@SpringBootApplication
public class DemoApplication {
    public static void main(String[] args) {
        SpringApplication.run(DemoApplication.class, args);
    }
}
```

When the application starts, Spring Boot scans for available libraries and looks for spring.factories files under the META-INF directory to determine which auto-configuration classes to activate. These auto-configuration classes are typically mapped to certain conditions using the @Conditional annotations ensuring that certain beans are only created if a particular library or other condition is present.

Auto-configuration attempts to guess and configure beans you are likely to need. For example, if you have a HSQLDB database in your classpath, and you don't have any manual DataSource defined, Spring Boot auto-configures an in-memory database for you.

In practical terms, this means that for many common use cases, you can get a fully configured Spring application with minimal effort. For instance:

```
@RestController
public class HelloController {
    @GetMapping("/hello")
    public String sayHello() {
        return "Hello, World!";
    }
}
```

In the example above, if you add Spring Web dependency, Spring Boot will automatically configure an embedded Tomcat server and register the HelloController bean, allowing it to serve HTTP requests.

Customization and Exclusions

While auto-configuration simplifies development, there might be scenarios requiring custom configurations or exclusion of certain auto-configurations. This can be achieved through various means:

- **Using** spring.autoconfigure.exclude **property:**

  This property can be set in the application.properties or application.yml file to exclude specific auto-configuration classes.

```
spring.autoconfigure.exclude=org.springframework.boot.autoconfigure.
    jdbc.DataSourceAutoConfiguration
```

- **Using the** exclude **attribute of** EnableAutoConfiguration **annotation:**

```
@SpringBootApplication(exclude = { DataSourceAutoConfiguration.
    class })
public class DemoApplication {
    public static void main(String[] args) {
        SpringApplication.run(DemoApplication.class, args);
    }
}
```

- **Conditional Annotations:**

  Additional customization can be achieved using Spring's various conditional annotations such as ConditionalOnClass, ConditionalOnMissingBean, and others. These annotations are often used within auto-configuration classes to conditionally create beans based on the presence or absence of specific classes or beans in the classpath.

```
@Configuration
@ConditionalOnClass(DataSource.class)
public class DataSourceConfig {
    @Bean
    @ConditionalOnMissingBean
    public DataSource dataSource() {
        return new HikariDataSource();
    }
}
```

@ConditionalOnClass(DataSource.class) ensures that this configuration class will only be instantiated if the DataSource class is present in the classpath, and @ConditionalOnMissingBean ensures that a new DataSource bean is only created if one does not already exist.

These mechanisms provide developers with the flexibility to augment or override the auto-configuration without losing the capability to quickly spin up new services or applications using the defaults provided by Spring Boot.

Internals of Auto-Configuration

Internally, auto-configuration classes are loaded via the spring.factories file located in the META-INF directory. This is where fully qualified names of auto-configuration classes are listed. Here's an example of the spring.factories file:

```
org.springframework.boot.autoconfigure.EnableAutoConfiguration=\
org.springframework.boot.autoconfigure.jdbc.DataSourceAutoConfiguration,\
org.springframework.boot.autoconfigure.orm.jpa.HibernateJpaAutoConfiguration,\
org.springframework.boot.autoconfigure.web.servlet.WebMvcAutoConfiguration
```

Each listed class in the spring.factories file is a candidate for auto-configuration. They employ various conditional checks to determine their applicability in the current context.

Debugging Auto-Configuration

Spring Boot provides an actuator endpoint that helps in understanding which auto-configuration classes were applied and which were not. You can enable the actuator to expose the /actuator/conditions endpoint by including the following dependency:

```
<dependency>
    <groupId>org.springframework.boot</groupId>
    <artifactId>spring-boot-starter-actuator</artifactId>
</dependency>
```

Once enabled, accessing http://localhost:8080/actuator/conditions will provide detailed information about auto-configuration including reasons why certain configurations were or were not applied.

The auto-configuration feature in Spring Boot represents a powerful mechanism to eliminate boilerplate and accelerate application development. With sensible defaults and the ability to layer custom configurations over auto-configured beans, Spring Boot combines flexibility with rapid development potential.

7.6 Creating Simple Applications with Spring Boot

Spring Boot radically simplifies the process of developing and running a new Spring application. To create a simple Spring Boot application, it is essential to understand the fundamentals of Spring Boot's architecture and how it streamlines configuration. We will develop a basic web application and illustrate the key components, from setting up the project structure to final execution.

Setting Up the Project Structure

Using Spring Boot Initializr (covered in a previous section), generated project files include the main entry point for the Spring Boot application, typically a single class annotated with @SpringBootApplication. This annotation is pivotal as it combines three crucial annotations: @Configuration, @EnableAutoConfiguration, and @ComponentScan.

An example structure might look as follows:

```
@SpringBootApplication
public class MySpringBootApplication {
    public static void main(String[] args) {
        SpringApplication.run(MySpringBootApplication.class, args);
    }
}
```

Creating a Basic REST Controller

To create a RESTful web service, we need to define a controller class. In Spring Boot, this is done using the @RestController annotation, which itself is a combination of @Controller and @ResponseBody:

```
@RestController
public class HelloWorldController {

    @RequestMapping("/")
    public String home() {
        return "Hello, Spring Boot!";
    }
}
```

Here, @RequestMapping("/") maps the home method to the root URL. When users navigate to the root URL of our application, the "Hello, Spring Boot!" string is returned as a web response.

Running the Application

Run the application by executing the main method in MySpringBootApplication. Spring Boot configurations will be automatically applied, and the embedded Tomcat server starts up by default on port 8080 (unless configured otherwise).

```
2023-05-01 10:33:00.123  INFO 10172 --- [           main] o.s.b.w.embedded.tomcat.TomcatWebServer  : Tomcat started on port(s): 8080 (http) with context path ''
2023-05-01 10:33:00.130  INFO 10172 --- [           main] com.example.MySpringBootApplication      : Started MySpringBootApplication in 2.139 seconds (JVM running for 3.003)
```

Navigating to http://localhost:8080 will render the text "Hello, Spring Boot!", verifying that our application is live.

Adding Custom Configurations

Spring Boot allows seamless integration of custom configurations using application.properties or application.yml files located in the src/main/resources directory. For example, setting a custom port:

```
server.port=9090
```

After restarting the application, the embedded server will listen on port 9090.

Connecting to a Database

For database operations, we often use Spring Data JPA alongside Spring Boot. Add the necessary dependencies in pom.xml:

```
<dependency>
    <groupId>org.springframework.boot</groupId>
    <artifactId>spring-boot-starter-data-jpa</artifactId>
</dependency>
```

```
<dependency>
    <groupId>com.h2database</groupId>
    <artifactId>h2</artifactId>
    <scope>runtime</scope>
</dependency>
```

Next, configure the database connection in application.properties:

```
spring.datasource.url=jdbc:h2:mem:testdb
spring.datasource.driverClassName=org.h2.Driver
spring.datasource.username=sa
spring.datasource.password=password
spring.jpa.database-platform=org.hibernate.dialect.H2Dialect
```

Create an entity class and repository:

```
@Entity
public class User {
    @Id
    @GeneratedValue(strategy = GenerationType.AUTO)
    private Long id;
    private String name;

    // getters and setters
}

public interface UserRepository extends JpaRepository<User, Long> {
}
```

Define a service and expose it via a REST controller:

```
@Service
public class UserService {

    @Autowired
    private UserRepository userRepository;

    public User saveUser(User user) {
        return userRepository.save(user);
    }

    public List<User> getAllUsers() {
        return userRepository.findAll();
    }
}

@RestController
@RequestMapping("/users")
public class UserController {

    @Autowired
    private UserService userService;
```

```
    @PostMapping
    public User createUser(@RequestBody User user) {
        return userService.saveUser(user);
    }

    @GetMapping
    public List<User> getUsers() {
        return userService.getAllUsers();
    }
}
```

These setups connect to the H2 in-memory database and provide endpoints to create and retrieve user entities.

Testing the Application

Automate testing using Spring Boot's support for JUnit. Add dependencies to pom.xml:

```
<dependency>
    <groupId>org.springframework.boot</groupId>
    <artifactId>spring-boot-starter-test</artifactId>
    <scope>test</scope>
</dependency>
```

Create a test class:

```
@RunWith(SpringRunner.class)
@SpringBootTest
public class UserControllerTest {

    @Autowired
    private MockMvc mockMvc;

    @MockBean
    private UserService userService;

    @Test
    public void testCreateUser() throws Exception {
        User user = new User();
        user.setName("John Doe");

        Mockito.when(userService.saveUser(ArgumentMatchers.any(User.class))).
              thenReturn(user);

        mockMvc.perform(MockMvcRequestBuilders.post("/users")
                .contentType(MediaType.APPLICATION_JSON)
                .content("{\"name\":\"John Doe\"}"))
                .andExpect(MockMvcResultMatchers.status().isOk())
                .andExpect(MockMvcResultMatchers.jsonPath("$.name").value("
                    John Doe"));
```

```
    }
}
```

This test validates the user creation endpoint, ensuring responses are as expected.

Through this comprehensive setup and execution, creating simple applications with Spring Boot provides practical illustrations and ensures foundational principles are implemented effectively.

7.7 Spring Boot Starters

Spring Boot starters are a crucial feature that streamlines the bootstrapping process of a Spring-based application. They serve as convenient dependency descriptors added within a Spring Boot project to easily incorporate various libraries and frameworks. The primary purpose of starters is to eliminate the need for manual dependency management, thereby accelerating the development process. This section delves into the mechanism and details of Spring Boot starters, elucidating their components and functionality.

Overview of Starters

Spring Boot starters are essentially a set of pre-configured Maven or Gradle dependencies that bundle commonly used libraries and frameworks. These starters relieve developers from the burden of individually specifying and managing dependencies. Each starter encapsulates a particular functionality or feature set. For example, the spring-boot-starter-web includes dependencies for building web applications, such as Spring MVC and embedded Tomcat.

Here is an example of adding a typical Spring Boot starter using Maven:

```
<dependency>
    <groupId>org.springframework.boot</groupId>
    <artifactId>spring-boot-starter-web</artifactId>
</dependency>
```

For Gradle, the equivalent would be:

```
implementation 'org.springframework.boot:spring-boot-starter-web'
```

Commonly Used Starters

Spring Boot provides an extensive suite of starters. Some of the most frequently used ones include:

- **spring-boot-starter-web**: Facilitates the creation of web applications. It includes Spring MVC, embedded Tomcat (by default), Jackson for JSON processing, and validation libraries.
- **spring-boot-starter-data-jpa**: Assists in building applications with Spring Data JPA and Hibernate as the default JPA provider.
- **spring-boot-starter-security**: Integrates Spring Security for securing applications.
- **spring-boot-starter-actuator**: Provides production-ready features like metrics and monitoring.
- **spring-boot-starter-test**: Contains testing libraries, including JUnit, Hamcrest, and Mockito.

Advantages of Using Starters

The use of starters simplifies dependency management and enhances productivity. The advantages include:

- **Ease of Configuration**: Starters auto-configure the application based on the included dependencies, reducing boilerplate code.
- **Consistent Versions**: Ensures compatibility by managing a consistent version set of dependencies.
- **Reduced Time to Market**: Accelerates development by abstracting complexities associated with dependency management.

Creating Custom Starters

In scenarios where the predefined starters do not meet specific requirements, developers can create custom starters. This involves defining a new project that includes the necessary dependencies and configuration classes.

```
<project xmlns="http://maven.apache.org/POM/4.0.0"
        xmlns:xsi="http://www.w3.org/2001/XMLSchema-instance"
        xsi:schemaLocation="http://maven.apache.org/POM/4.0.0
                            http://maven.apache.org/xsd/maven-4.0.0.xsd">
    <modelVersion>4.0.0</modelVersion>
    <groupId>com.example</groupId>
    <artifactId>custom-starter</artifactId>
    <version>1.0.0</version>
```

```
    <dependencies>
        <dependency>
            <groupId>org.springframework.boot</groupId>
            <artifactId>spring-boot-starter</artifactId>
        </dependency>
        <!-- Additional dependencies go here -->
    </dependencies>
</project>
```

By packaging and publishing this project as a JAR, it can be reused across multiple applications.

Insight Into Dependency Resolution

Spring Boot manages dependency versions through a collective bill of materials (BOM) file. These BOM files ensure that the dependencies specified within starters are compatible with each other. For instance, the Spring Boot framework uses the spring-boot-dependencies BOM to centralize version management. When a starter dependency is declared, it implicitly includes the compatible versions of transitive dependencies defined in the BOM.

Here is an example of how dependency versions are managed using a BOM in Maven:

```
<dependencyManagement>
    <dependencies>
        <dependency>
            <groupId>org.springframework.boot</groupId>
            <artifactId>spring-boot-dependencies</artifactId>
            <version>2.5.4</version>
            <type>pom</type>
            <scope>import</scope>
        </dependency>
    </dependencies>
</dependencyManagement>
```

For Gradle, the usage of BOM is supported from version 5.0 onward:

```
dependencyManagement {
    imports {
        mavenBom "org.springframework.boot:spring-boot-dependencies:2.5.4"
    }
}
```

Ensuring that all dependencies across a project align with the versions defined in the BOM centralizes compatibility and simplifies maintenance efforts.

The modular nature of Spring Boot starters thus facilitates a streamlined and efficient approach to constructing a robust Spring-based application. By leveraging starters, developers can focus on writing business logic without the overhead of dependency management intricacies, improving both development speed and application stability.

7.8 Externalized Configuration in Spring Boot

Externalized configuration is a fundamental feature in Spring Boot that allows externalizing the configuration of an application from the code, enabling applications to be run in different environments without requiring code changes. Spring Boot provides a useful and versatile way to inject external properties from various sources like properties files, YAML files, environment variables, and command-line arguments.

A core aspect of externalized configuration in Spring Boot is the application.properties or application.yml file. Typically, these files are located in the src/main/resources directory of a Spring Boot project. The properties defined in these files can determine how the Spring Boot application behaves at runtime.

```
# application.properties
server.port=8081
spring.datasource.url=jdbc:mysql://localhost:3306/mydb
spring.datasource.username=root
spring.datasource.password=secret
```

In the above example, the application.properties file sets the server port and the database connection details. When the application starts, Spring Boot reads these properties and applies them automatically.

Spring Boot also supports YAML files for configuration. YAML stands for "YAML Ain't Markup Language," a data serialization standard particularly friendly to configuration files due to its readability and structure.

```
# application.yml
server:
  port: 8082
spring:
  datasource:
    url: jdbc:mysql://localhost:3306/mydb
    username: root
    password: secret
```

In this YAML configuration example, indentation is crucial as it signifies the nesting of keys, making the configuration clear and hierarchical.

Spring Boot allows overriding these configurations through environment variables and command-line arguments without changing the properties file. Environment variables can be particularly useful in a Continuous Integration/Continuous Delivery (CI/CD) pipeline, where environment-specific parameters can be injected dynamically.

To use an environment variable, prefix the property name with SPRING_ and replace dots with underscores:

```
SPRING_DATASOURCE_URL=jdbc:mysql://localhost:3306/proddb
```

Command-line arguments can also override properties. When running a Spring Boot application as a JAR, one can pass arguments using the – prefix:

```
java -jar myapp.jar --server.port=9090 --spring.datasource.username=admin
```

Combining these configuration methodologies makes the application flexible and easily adaptable.

Spring Boot also supports custom configuration properties using the @ConfigurationProperties annotation. This is particularly useful for grouping related properties together. To implement this, create a properties class:

```
import org.springframework.boot.context.properties.ConfigurationProperties;
import org.springframework.stereotype.Component;

@Component
@ConfigurationProperties(prefix = "myapp")
public class MyAppProperties {
    private String apiUrl;
    private int timeout;

    // getters and setters
    public String getApiUrl() {
        return apiUrl;
    }

    public void setApiUrl(String apiUrl) {
        this.apiUrl = apiUrl;
    }

    public int getTimeout() {
        return timeout;
    }

    public void setTimeout(int timeout) {
```

```
        this.timeout = timeout;
    }
}
```

This properties class can then be used in application properties or YAML files:

```
# application.properties
myapp.apiUrl=https://api.example.com
myapp.timeout=5000
```

To use these properties in the application, simply auto-wire the MyAppProperties bean wherever needed:

```
import org.springframework.beans.factory.annotation.Autowired;
import org.springframework.web.bind.annotation.GetMapping;
import org.springframework.web.bind.annotation.RestController;

@RestController
public class MyAppController {

    @Autowired
    private MyAppProperties myAppProperties;

    @GetMapping("/settings")
    public String getSettings() {
        return "API URL: " + myAppProperties.getApiUrl() +
               ", Timeout: " + myAppProperties.getTimeout();
    }
}
```

Spring Boot's environment abstraction, Environment, can also be used directly to access properties. This enables programmatic retrieval of configuration properties.

```
import org.springframework.beans.factory.annotation.Autowired;
import org.springframework.core.env.Environment;
import org.springframework.web.bind.annotation.GetMapping;
import org.springframework.web.bind.annotation.RestController;

@RestController
public class EnvController {

    @Autowired
    private Environment environment;

    @GetMapping("/envdetails")
    public String getEnvDetails() {
        String apiUrl = environment.getProperty("myapp.apiUrl");
        String timeout = environment.getProperty("myapp.timeout");
        return "API URL: " + apiUrl + ", Timeout: " + timeout;
```

```
    }
}
```

When running, the properties will be resolved and used as configured:

API URL: https://api.example.com, Timeout: 5000

These techniques collectively contribute to a robust and flexible externalized configuration mechanism in Spring Boot, simplifying the management of environment-specific settings and enhancing the application's adaptability during deployment.

7.9 Spring Boot Actuator

Spring Boot Actuator provides a set of tools for monitoring and managing Spring Boot applications. It exposes various endpoints that help in understanding the runtime behavior and health of the application. Actuator is instrumental in gaining insights into the application's operational metrics and enables easier debugging and maintenance.

Spring Boot Actuator includes several built-in endpoints that are available out of the box. These endpoints cover a wide range of functionalities such as health check, metrics, environment properties, and application info. To use these endpoints, it is essential to include the Actuator dependency in the pom.xml or build.gradle file.

```
<dependency>
    <groupId>org.springframework.boot</groupId>
    <artifactId>spring-boot-starter-actuator</artifactId>
</dependency>
```

```
implementation 'org.springframework.boot:spring-boot-starter-actuator'
```

By default, most Actuator endpoints are not exposed over HTTP. To expose these endpoints, configuration in the application.properties or application.yml file is necessary. Endpoints can be exposed individually, or a common base path can be provided for all endpoints.

```
management.endpoints.web.exposure.include=*
management.endpoints.web.base-path=/actuator
```

```
management:
  endpoints:
    web:
      exposure:
```

```
    include: "*"
  base-path: /actuator
```

The key endpoints provided by Actuator include:

- **Health Endpoint (/health)**: Provides information about the application's health status. The health status can be extended to include various checks like database connectivity, disk space availability, and more.

- **Info Endpoint (/info)**: Displays arbitrary application information. Custom application details can be added to the info endpoint through configuration.

- **Metrics Endpoint (/metrics)**: Offers metrics data about the application's performance, such as memory usage, CPU usage, JVM metrics, and others.

- **Trace Endpoint (/trace)** (deprecated in Spring Boot 2.x): Provides HTTP request trace information.

- **Beans Endpoint (/beans)**: Lists all the Spring Beans in the application context and their dependencies.

- **Env Endpoint (/env)**: Displays current environment properties and configurations.

- **Loggers Endpoint (/loggers)**: View and configure log levels at runtime.

- **HTTP Trace Endpoint (/httptrace)**: Similar to trace endpoint but provides more detailed tracing of HTTP requests and responses.

Here is an example usage of the Health and Metrics endpoints. Assuming the default base path is set to /actuator, these endpoints can be accessed as follows:

```
/actuator/health
{
  "status": "UP",
  "components": {
    "db": {
      "status": "UP",
      "details": {
        "database": "H2",
        "result": 1
      }
    },
    "diskSpace": {
      "status": "UP",
      "details": {
        "total": 499963174912,
        "free": 310221823488,
        "threshold": 10485760
      }
    }
  }
}
/actuator/metrics
{
  "names": [
    "jvm.buffer.count",
    "jvm.buffer.memory.used",
    "jvm.buffer.total.capacity",
    "jvm.gc.memory.allocated",
    "jvm.gc.memory.promoted",
    ...
  ]
}
```

Customizing Actuator endpoints involves developing additional health indicators, metrics, and info contributors. For example, to create a custom health indicator that checks if a specific service is available, implement the HealthIndicator interface.

```
import org.springframework.boot.actuate.health.Health;
import org.springframework.boot.actuate.health.HealthIndicator;
import org.springframework.stereotype.Component;

@Component
public class CustomServiceHealthIndicator implements HealthIndicator {

    @Override
    public Health health() {
        boolean serviceUp = checkMyServiceHealth();
        if (serviceUp) {
            return Health.up().withDetail("service", "Available").build();
        }
        return Health.down().withDetail("service", "Unavailable").build();
    }

    private boolean checkMyServiceHealth() {
        // Logic to check health of the service
        return true;
    }
```

```
}
```

To contribute custom information to the /info endpoint, create a bean that implements the InfoContributor interface.

```
import org.springframework.boot.actuate.info.Info;
import org.springframework.boot.actuate.info.InfoContributor;
import org.springframework.stereotype.Component;

import java.util.HashMap;
import java.util.Map;

@Component
public class CustomInfoContributor implements InfoContributor {

    @Override
    public void contribute(Info.Builder builder) {
        Map<String, Object> customInfo = new HashMap<>();
        customInfo.put("version", "1.0.0");
        customInfo.put("description", "This is a custom info endpoint contribution
             .");
        builder.withDetails(customInfo);
    }
}
```

Actuator also provides integration with various monitoring systems such as Prometheus, Grafana, and others by making use of the Micrometer library, which is included as a transitive dependency of Spring Boot Actuator. This allows for exporting metrics to external monitoring and alerting systems.

The inclusion of Spring Boot Actuator in an application empowers developers and operations teams with valuable insights and management capabilities, enabling more robust and maintainable applications.

7.10 Spring Boot DevTools

Spring Boot DevTools is an essential feature introduced to improve the development workflow by providing rapid feedback and productivity enhancements. DevTools offers several useful features, such as automatic restarts, live reload, property defaults, and configurations that are particularly beneficial during the development phase. This section will discuss these features in detail and demonstrate how to set up and utilize them effectively.

To add DevTools to a Spring Boot project, include the following dependency in your pom.xml for Maven projects:

```
<dependency>
    <groupId>org.springframework.boot</groupId>
    <artifactId>spring-boot-devtools</artifactId>
    <optional>true</optional>
</dependency>
```

For Gradle projects, add the following to the dependencies block in build.gradle:

```
dependencies {
    developmentOnly("org.springframework.boot:spring-boot-devtools")
}
```

Automatic Restarts

One of the most significant features of Spring Boot DevTools is the capability to automatically restart the application whenever files on the classpath change. This can drastically reduce the time required for developers to see the effects of their changes. The restart functionality is designed to watch for file modifications, typically in the target/classes for Maven or build/classes/java/main for Gradle, and trigger an application restart.

```
Restarting application...
Application restarted successfully.
```

By default, static resources such as .html files located under src/main/resources/static are not included in the restart trigger. However, they can be reloaded with a browser refresh.

Live Reload

Spring Boot DevTools integrates with the LiveReload protocol. LiveReload is a standard used to refresh the web browser when files in the project change. To use LiveReload, you need to run a LiveReload server, and, optionally, a browser extension like LiveReload that listens for reload changes.

Add the LiveReload button from the extensions to your browser, and when enabled, any changes will immediately reflect without manual intervention. This helps to see front-end changes on the go.

Global Settings

DevTools provides global settings that allow you to configure the default behavior across all of your Spring Boot projects. This is done by creating a .spring-boot-devtools.properties file in the user's home directory:

```
restart.include.company-commonlibs=/company-commonlibs[\\d\\.]*\\.jar
restart.exclude.company-excludes=/company-excludes[\\d\\.]*\\.jar
```

For example, the above configuration includes JARs that match company-commonlibs and excludes JARs that match company-excludes from triggering a restart.

Property Defaults

Spring Boot DevTools automatically applies sensible development-time configuration properties, modifying behaviors such as caching and template reloading:

- spring.thymeleaf.cache=false - Thymeleaf templates are not cached, allowing immediate reflection of template changes.
- spring.freemarker.cache=false - Freemarker templates are not cached.
- spring.groovy.template.cache=false - Groovy templates are not cached.
- spring.mustache.cache=false - Mustache templates are not cached.
- spring.mvc.log-resolved-exception=true - All handled exceptions are always logged.

Such properties enhance the development experience by removing the need to restart or rebuild the application for each change.

Remote Debugging

While DevTools is primarily a local development enhancement tool, remote debugging can also be configured for deployment in a development environment. Use the following properties in application.properties or application.yml to enable remote debugging:

```
# Enable remote debugging
spring.devtools.remote.secret=mysecret
# The remote debug server port
spring.devtools.remote.context-path=/remote
```

Ensure that the environment where the remote debugging is enabled is secure, as the remote server can execute code on your application.

Disabling Restart

There are scenarios where a restart might not be desirable, such as when debugging and needing to maintain the application's state. To disable the automatic restart feature, include the following property in application properties:

```
spring.devtools.restart.enabled=false
```

This setting prevents the application from automatic restarts, allowing developers to use other debugging techniques without interruption.

Spring Boot DevTools significantly contributes to an efficient development process. By reducing the development cycle time and offering features like automatic restarts, live reload, and sensible property defaults, DevTools minimizes the overhead typically associated with traditional development practices. Integrating DevTools into your workflow ensures a seamless and productive development experience, allowing developers to focus on implementing features and resolving issues more efficiently.

7.11 Spring Boot Testing

Testing is an integral part of the software development lifecycle, and Spring Boot provides a wide array of tools and frameworks to aid and streamline the testing process. This section delves into different testing strategies and the specific support provided by Spring Boot for comprehensive testing.

Spring Boot simplifies the setup for tests using annotations and helper classes. A typical Spring Boot application should be tested at multiple levels: unit tests, integration tests, and end-to-end (E2E) tests. We will cover the essentials of writing and running these tests in a Spring Boot environment.

Unit Tests: The goal of unit testing is to test individual parts of the application (usually methods) in isolation. Mockito is often used in conjunction with Spring Boot for unit testing due to its ability to create mock objects.

Here is a simple example of a unit test using JUnit and Mockito:

```
import static org.mockito.Mockito.*;
import static org.junit.jupiter.api.Assertions.*;

import org.junit.jupiter.api.Test;
import org.mockito.InjectMocks;
```

```
import org.mockito.Mock;
import org.mockito.junit.jupiter.MockitoExtension;
import org.junit.jupiter.api.extension.ExtendWith;

@ExtendWith(MockitoExtension.class)
public class UserServiceTest {

    @Mock
    private UserRepository userRepository;

    @InjectMocks
    private UserService userService;

    @Test
    public void testGetUserById() {
        User mockUser = new User(1L, "John Doe");
        when(userRepository.findById(1L)).thenReturn(Optional.of(mockUser));

        User user = userService.getUserById(1L);
        assertEquals("John Doe", user.getName());
    }
}
```

In the snippet above, we use Mockito and JUnit 5 to create and inject mocks. The @Mock annotation is used to create a mock repository, and @InjectMocks is used to inject the mock into the service.

Integration Tests: These tests focus on the interaction between multiple parts of the application, ensuring that they work together as expected. Spring Boot provides the @SpringBootTest annotation, which loads the complete application context for integration tests.

Below is an example of an integration test in Spring Boot:

```
import org.junit.jupiter.api.Test;
import org.springframework.beans.factory.annotation.Autowired;
import org.springframework.boot.test.context.SpringBootTest;
import org.springframework.boot.test.web.client.TestRestTemplate;
import org.springframework.http.ResponseEntity;

import static org.junit.jupiter.api.Assertions.*;

@SpringBootTest(webEnvironment = SpringBootTest.WebEnvironment.
    RANDOM_PORT)
public class UserControllerIntegrationTest {

    @Autowired
    private TestRestTemplate restTemplate;

    @Test
    public void testGetUser() {
```

```
        ResponseEntity<User> response = restTemplate.getForEntity("/users/1",
            User.class);
        User user = response.getBody();
        assertEquals("John Doe", user.getName());
    }
}
```

In this example, the @SpringBootTest annotation starts the entire Spring application context. The webEnvironment=SpringBootTest.WebEnvironment.RANDOM_PORT attribute starts the embedded server at a random port.

MockMvc for Controller Tests: Spring Boot provides the MockMvc framework to test web layer components without needing to start up the full HTTP server.

```
import static org.springframework.test.web.servlet.request.
    MockMvcRequestBuilders.get;
import static org.springframework.test.web.servlet.result.MockMvcResultMatchers.
    status;
import static org.springframework.test.web.servlet.result.MockMvcResultMatchers.
    jsonPath;

import org.junit.jupiter.api.Test;
import org.springframework.beans.factory.annotation.Autowired;
import org.springframework.boot.test.autoconfigure.web.servlet.WebMvcTest;
import org.springframework.test.web.servlet.MockMvc;

@WebMvcTest(UserController.class)
public class UserControllerTest {

    @Autowired
    private MockMvc mockMvc;

    @Test
    public void testGetUser() throws Exception {
        mockMvc.perform(get("/users/1"))
                .andExpect(status().isOk())
                .andExpect(jsonPath("$.name").value("John Doe"));
    }
}
```

The @WebMvcTest annotation is specialized for testing MVC controllers. This annotation only loads the controller beans and uses MockMvc to mimic HTTP requests and responses.

Test Slices: For more fine-grained tests, Spring Boot includes "test slices". Slices load only a part of the application configuration, making tests faster and more focused. Examples include @DataJpaTest for JPA repositories and @WebMvcTest for the web layer.

```
import org.junit.jupiter.api.Test;
import org.springframework.beans.factory.annotation.Autowired;
import org.springframework.boot.test.autoconfigure.orm.jpa.DataJpaTest;
import static org.assertj.core.api.Assertions.assertThat;

@DataJpaTest
public class UserRepositoryTest {

    @Autowired
    private UserRepository userRepository;

    @Test
    public void testFindByUserId() {
        User user = userRepository.findById(1L).orElse(null);
        assertThat(user).isNotNull();
        assertThat(user.getName()).isEqualTo("John Doe");
    }
}
```

Spring Boot Actuator Integration: The Actuator endpoints can also be included in the testing strategy. Testing custom health indicators or metrics can be achieved by making requests to the Actuator endpoints and verifying the responses.

```
import org.junit.jupiter.api.Test;
import org.springframework.beans.factory.annotation.Autowired;
import org.springframework.boot.test.context.SpringBootTest;
import org.springframework.boot.test.web.client.TestRestTemplate;
import org.springframework.http.ResponseEntity;
import static org.assertj.core.api.Assertions.assertThat;

@SpringBootTest(webEnvironment = SpringBootTest.WebEnvironment.
    RANDOM_PORT)
public class ActuatorIntegrationTest {

    @Autowired
    private TestRestTemplate restTemplate;

    @Test
    public void testHealthEndpoint() {
        ResponseEntity<String> response = restTemplate.getForEntity("/
            actuator/health", String.class);
        assertThat(response.getStatusCode().is2xxSuccessful()).isTrue();
        assertThat(response.getBody()).contains("\"status\":\"UP\"");
    }
}
```

By leveraging the powerful orchestration between Spring Boot features and relevant testing frameworks, software systems can achieve a robust and maintainable approach to automated testing, ensuring comprehensive coverage of their functionality while mitigating potential regressions and defects.

7.12 Deploying Spring Boot Applications

Deploying a Spring Boot application involves several steps that ensure the application runs efficiently and reliably in a production environment. This section details the process of packaging your Spring Boot application, preparing it for different environments, and deploying it to various platforms.

Packaging a Spring Boot Application

Spring Boot applications can be packaged as executable JAR (Java ARchive) or WAR (Web Application Archive) files. The executable JAR format is the most straightforward and is suitable for applications that run independently. WAR packaging, on the other hand, is used when deploying to traditional application servers such as Apache Tomcat or Jetty.

To package the application as an executable JAR, include the following configuration in your pom.xml for a Maven project:

```
<build>
    <plugins>
        <plugin>
            <groupId>org.springframework.boot</groupId>
            <artifactId>spring-boot-maven-plugin</artifactId>
        </plugin>
    </plugins>
</build>
```

For a Gradle project, ensure your build.gradle has the following plugin:

```
plugins {
    id 'org.springframework.boot' version '2.5.4'
}
```

To package your application, run the following command:

```
mvn clean package
```

or for Gradle:

```
gradle build
```

This generates a JAR file in the target (Maven) or build/libs (Gradle) directory.

Deploying to a Standalone Server

A Spring Boot application packaged as a JAR can be deployed to a standalone server simply by running the JAR file. This can be done using the following command in the terminal:

```
java -jar target/myapp-0.0.1-SNAPSHOT.jar
```

To ensure your application starts automatically upon server reboot, you can configure it as a service in Linux. Create a new service file, e.g., /etc/systemd/system/myapp.service, and include the following content:

```
[Unit]
Description=My Spring Boot Application
After=syslog.target

[Service]
User=yourusername
ExecStart=/usr/bin/java -jar /path/to/myapp-0.0.1-SNAPSHOT.jar
SuccessExitStatus=143

[Install]
WantedBy=multi-user.target
```

Enable and start the service with the following commands:

```
sudo systemctl enable myapp
sudo systemctl start myapp
```

Deploying to Cloud Platforms

Spring Boot applications can also be deployed to various cloud platforms, including AWS, Azure, Google Cloud Platform, and others.

Amazon Web Services (AWS)

- **Elastic Beanstalk**: AWS Elastic Beanstalk is a platform-as-a-service (PaaS) solution that facilitates deploying and scaling web applications. Create an Elastic Beanstalk application and upload your JAR or WAR file through the AWS Management Console.

- **EC2 Instances**: For greater control, deploy your application on an EC2 instance. Follow the packaging steps, transfer the JAR file to EC2 using SCP or similar tools, and configure it as a service.

Microsoft Azure

- **Azure App Services**: A fully managed platform, Azure App Services simplifies deploying Spring Boot applications. Create a new web app, select the Java runtime stack, and deploy your JAR file via FTP or using the Azure CLI.

```
az webapp create --resource-group myResourceGroup --plan
    myAppServicePlan --name myApp --runtime "JAVA|11-java11"
az webapp deployment source config-zip --resource-group myResourceGroup
    --name myApp --src target/myapp-0.0.1-SNAPSHOT.jar
```

- **Azure Kubernetes Service (AKS)**: For containerized deployments, build a Docker image of your Spring Boot application and push it to Azure Container Registry (ACR). Deploy the application using Kubernetes.

```
docker build -t myapp .
docker tag myapp <acr-name>.azurecr.io/myapp
docker push <acr-name>.azurecr.io/myapp
kubectl apply -f deployment.yaml
```

Google Cloud Platform (GCP)

- **App Engine**: Google App Engine supports Spring Boot applications effortlessly. Create an app.yaml configuration file and deploy using the Google Cloud SDK.

```
runtime: java
env: standard
entrypoint: java -jar myapp-0.0.1-SNAPSHOT.jar
```

  Deploy the application using:

```
gcloud app deploy
```

- **Google Kubernetes Engine (GKE)**: Similar to AKS, deploy your Spring Boot application as a Docker container.

Deploying to Containers

Containers ensure consistency across different environments. Docker is the most prevalent containerization technology. To containerize a Spring Boot application, create a Dockerfile in the root directory of your project:

```
FROM openjdk:11-jre
ARG JAR_FILE=target/myapp-0.0.1-SNAPSHOT.jar
COPY ${JAR_FILE} app.jar
ENTRYPOINT ["java", "-jar", "/app.jar"]
```

Build and run the Docker image:

```
docker build -t myapp .
docker run -p 8080:8080 myapp
```

For orchestrating containers in a cluster, Kubernetes is widely used. Define deployment and service configurations in YAML files, and use kubectl to manage them.

```
apiVersion: apps/v1
kind: Deployment
metadata:
  name: myapp-deployment
spec:
  replicas: 3
  selector:
    matchLabels:
      app: myapp
  template:
    metadata:
      labels:
        app: myapp
    spec:
      containers:
      - name: myapp
        image: myapp:latest
        ports:
        - containerPort: 8080
---
apiVersion: v1
kind: Service
metadata:
  name: myapp-service
spec:
  selector:
    app: myapp
  ports:
    - protocol: TCP
      port: 80
      targetPort: 8080
  type: LoadBalancer
```

Deploy the application with:

```
kubectl apply -f deployment.yaml
kubectl apply -f service.yaml
```

Each deployment strategy has its nuances and suitability depending on the application's requirements, scalability needs, and operational context. Understanding these detailed steps allows for efficient deployment to meet production-grade demands.

Chapter 8

Spring Security

This chapter delves into Spring Security, covering its core concepts and setup within a Spring project. It explains the configuration of authentication and authorization mechanisms, including the implementation of UserDetailsService. The chapter addresses customizing login and logout processes, securing web applications and RESTful services, and applying method-level security. Additionally, it explores the integration of OAuth2 and the handling of security exceptions, concluding with best practices for ensuring robust security in Spring applications.

8.1 Introduction to Spring Security

Spring Security is a comprehensive and extensible security framework that provides authentication, authorization, and protection against common attacks in enterprise Java applications. It is the de facto standard for securing Spring-based applications. Leveraging Spring Security involves understanding its architecture, core concepts, and methodologies for configuring and employing its features effectively.

Spring Security operates primarily through a series of filter chains. Each filter in the chain provides a specific type of functionality, such as authentication or authorization. This chain allows for both pre-built and custom filters to be employed in a highly modular manner.

The primary components of Spring Security include:

- **Authentication**: The process of verifying the identity of the user or system making a request.
- **Authorization**: The determination of whether an authenticated user has the necessary permissions to perform an action or access a resource.
- **Security Context**: Maintains the security information (principally user details) relevant to the current security operation.
- **Filters**: These are the building blocks of the security infrastructure within Spring Security, each responsible for specific aspects of security processing.
- **UserDetailsService**: An interface used for retrieving user-related data, integral to the authentication process.

Authentication

Authentication within Spring Security is usually handled by AuthenticationManager, which actively processes user credentials and determines if the user is authenticated. The most common implementation of AuthenticationManager is ProviderManager, which delegates the actual authentication process to a configured list of AuthenticationProviders.

```
@Override
protected void configure(AuthenticationManagerBuilder auth) {
    auth.inMemoryAuthentication()
        .withUser("user")
        .password(passwordEncoder().encode("password"))
        .roles("USER")
        .and()
        .withUser("admin")
        .password(passwordEncoder().encode("admin"))
        .roles("ADMIN");
}
```

This example demonstrates an in-memory authentication setup where user credentials are statically defined within the configuration. The passwordEncoder method ensures that passwords are encoded properly before storing them in memory.

Authorization

Authorization is the verification process for what authenticated users are allowed to do. In Spring Security, authorization can be configured by either annotations or within the XML configuration. The most essential type of annotation is @Secured.

```
@Secured("ROLE_ADMIN")
public void adminOnlyMethod() {
    // implementation details
}
```

This annotation indicates that only users with the role of "ROLE_ADMIN" can invoke the adminOnlyMethod. Spring Security backends this method of authorization using SecurityContext to hold authentication and granted authority.

Security Context

The SecurityContext contains authentication and possibly granted roles information for the current authentication object. A typical workflow in web applications sees the SecurityContext populated with the incoming request's authentication details (like username and password). This SecurityContext will then be available through the application for verifying authentication and authorization.

The SecurityContextHolder is a helper utility that facilitates interaction with the SecurityContext.

```
Authentication auth = SecurityContextHolder.getContext().getAuthentication();
String name = auth.getName(); // get logged in username
```

Security Filters

Filters are used to ensure requests flowing into the application are sanitized, authenticated, and authorized. The most critical filter is UsernamePasswordAuthenticationFilter, which is responsible for processing login forms by capturing and validating username and password.

```
<http>
    <intercept-url pattern="/admin/**" access="hasRole('ROLE_ADMIN')" />
    <form-login
        login-page="/login"
        default-target-url="/home"
        authentication-failure-url="/login?error"
        username-parameter="username"
        password-parameter="password"/>
    <logout
        logout-success-url="/login?logout" />
</http>
```

This XML configuration defines rules for URL patterns and access, along with specifics for the login page, default page after a successful login, and handling of authentication failures.

UserDetailsService

UserDetailsService is an interface that enables customized retrieval of user information for authentication. This is particularly valuable when abstracting the data source, whether it be a database, LDAP, or other storage systems.

```
@Service
public class CustomUserDetailsService implements UserDetailsService {
    @Override
    public UserDetails loadUserByUsername(String username) throws
         UsernameNotFoundException {
        User user = userRepository.findByUsername(username);
        if (user == null) {
            throw new UsernameNotFoundException("User not found");
        }
        return new org.springframework.security.core.userdetails.User(user.
             getUsername(), user.getPassword(), getAuthorities(user));
    }

    private Collection<? extends GrantedAuthority> getAuthorities(User user) {
        List<GrantedAuthority> authorities = new ArrayList<>();
        for (Role role : user.getRoles()) {
            authorities.add(new SimpleGrantedAuthority(role.getName()));
        }
        return authorities;
    }
}
```

In this sample configuration, the UserDetailsService implementation fetches user details from a repository, processes roles, and forms a UserDetails object used by Spring Security to manage and authenticate users.

Implementing and understanding these core components prepares you to delve deeper into more advanced configurations and customizations central to building a secure Spring-based application.

8.2 Core Concepts of Spring Security

Spring Security is a comprehensive framework that provides authentication, authorization, and protection against common security exploits. Understanding its core concepts is essential for leveraging the full potential of the framework.

At the heart of Spring Security are several fundamental components that work together to enforce security policies. These include the Authentication and Authorization processes, the SecurityContext, various filters, and the UserDetails service.

Authentication refers to the process of verifying the identity of a user or system. In Spring Security, this is achieved using the AuthenticationManager interface, which processes authentication requests. The actual implementation typically delegates to a series of AuthenticationProviders to perform the authentication.

```
@Autowired
private UserDetailsService userDetailsService;

@Autowired
public void configureGlobal(AuthenticationManagerBuilder auth) throws
    Exception {
  auth.userDetailsService(userDetailsService).passwordEncoder(
        passwordEncoder());
}
```

In the above example, an AuthenticationManagerBuilder is used to configure an AuthenticationManager that retrieves user details from a UserDetailsService and encodes passwords using a specified PasswordEncoder.

Authorization determines whether an authenticated user has the required permissions to access a specific resource. Spring Security uses AccessDecisionManager and AccessDecisionVoters to make authorization decisions based on the user's roles or authorities.

```
http
    .authorizeRequests()
        .antMatchers("/admin/**").hasRole("ADMIN")
        .antMatchers("/user/**").hasRole("USER")
        .anyRequest().authenticated();
```

Here, the authorizeRequests() method is used to define which URL patterns are available to users with specific roles.

The **SecurityContext** is a storage mechanism for security information. The SecurityContextHolder is responsible for holding the SecurityContext, which contains the currently authenticated user's details. The context can be accessed throughout the application to perform security checks.

```
Authentication authentication = SecurityContextHolder.getContext().
    getAuthentication();
```

```
String currentPrincipalName = authentication.getName();
```

In this snippet, the name of the currently authenticated user is retrieved from the SecurityContext.

Filters play a critical role in Spring Security by intercepting requests and applying security logic. The framework uses a chain of servlet filters to manage security-related operations. Key filters include the UsernamePasswordAuthenticationFilter, which processes form-based login, and the BasicAuthenticationFilter, which handles HTTP basic authentication.

```
http
    .addFilterBefore(new CustomFilter(), UsernamePasswordAuthenticationFilter.
         class);
```

In this example, a custom filter is added to the security filter chain before the UsernamePasswordAuthenticationFilter.

The **UserDetailsService** interface is a core component for retrieving user-related data. Implementations of this interface provide user information, such as username, password, and authorities, which are used during authentication.

```
@Service
public class CustomUserDetailsService implements UserDetailsService {

    @Autowired
    private UserRepository userRepository;

    @Override
    public UserDetails loadUserByUsername(String username) throws
         UsernameNotFoundException {
        User user = userRepository.findByUsername(username);
        if (user == null) {
            throw new UsernameNotFoundException("User not found");
        }
        return new org.springframework.security.core.userdetails.User(user.
             getUsername(), user.getPassword(), user.getAuthorities());
    }
}
```

Here, a custom UserDetailsService implementation retrieves user details from a repository and converts them into a UserDetails object.

Spring Security includes a series of other essential concepts, such as **password encoding**, **remember-me authentication**, and the use of **security annotations** to manually secure methods. Password encoding involves transforming plain text passwords into a secure format before storage. Remember-me authentication extends user sessions beyond the default timeframe. Security annotations, such as @Secured and @PreAuthorize, provide fine-grained control over access at the method level.

```
@Secured("ROLE_ADMIN")
public void adminMethod() {
    // method logic
}

@PreAuthorize("hasRole('ROLE_USER')")
public void userMethod() {
    // method logic
}
```

These annotations, when applied to methods, ensure that only users with the appropriate roles can execute the methods.

Understanding these core concepts is vital for effectively using Spring Security to protect applications. Knowledge of authentication and authorization, the SecurityContext, filters, and the UserDetails service lays the groundwork for more advanced security configurations.

8.3 Setting Up Spring Security in a Spring Project

The initial step to integrate Spring Security into a Spring project involves including the necessary dependencies and configuring the security framework appropriately. This section provides a meticulous walkthrough for setting up Spring Security, from dependency management to configuration adjustments.

Spring Security relies on various libraries and modules to function correctly. To integrate these into your project, it is essential to incorporate the appropriate dependencies. For a Maven project, you need to add the following dependencies to your pom.xml file:

```
<dependency>
    <groupId>org.springframework.boot</groupId>
    <artifactId>spring-boot-starter-security</artifactId>
</dependency>
<dependency>
    <groupId>org.springframework.security</groupId>
    <artifactId>spring-security-test</artifactId>
```

```
    <scope>test</scope>
</dependency>
```

For a Gradle project, append the following lines to your build.gradle file:

```
implementation 'org.springframework.boot:spring-boot-starter-security'
testImplementation 'org.springframework.security:spring-security-test'
```

Once the dependencies are included, Spring Boot automatically recognizes and includes Spring Security in your application context. The next step requires configuring Spring Security to align with your application-specific security requirements. This is predominantly handled within a class that extends WebSecurityConfigurerAdapter. The following code illustrates a fundamental configuration:

```
import org.springframework.security.config.annotation.web.builders.HttpSecurity;
import org.springframework.security.config.annotation.web.configuration.
    EnableWebSecurity;
import org.springframework.security.config.annotation.web.configuration.
    WebSecurityConfigurerAdapter;

@EnableWebSecurity
public class SecurityConfig extends WebSecurityConfigurerAdapter {

    @Override
    protected void configure(HttpSecurity http) throws Exception {
        http
            .authorizeRequests()
                .antMatchers("/", "/home").permitAll()
                .anyRequest().authenticated()
                .and()
            .formLogin()
                .loginPage("/login")
                .permitAll()
                .and()
            .logout()
                .permitAll();
    }
}
```

In the configure method, we define security configurations for HTTP requests. Key components include:

- authorizeRequests(): Configures URL access restrictions. The sample permits access to "/" and "/home" for all users, while securing all other endpoints to authenticated users.
- formLogin(): Customizes the login page configuration—specifying that the login page can be accessed by anyone.

- logout(): Enables the logout functionality and permits all users to access the logout endpoint.

Customizing the security filter chain may require additional configurations. To define users and their roles in-memory, use the configure method accepting an AuthenticationManagerBuilder parameter:

```
import org.springframework.context.annotation.Configuration;
import org.springframework.security.config.annotation.authentication.builders.
    AuthenticationManagerBuilder;
import org.springframework.security.config.annotation.web.configuration.
    EnableWebSecurity;
import org.springframework.security.config.annotation.web.configuration.
    WebSecurityConfigurerAdapter;

@Configuration
@EnableWebSecurity
public class SecurityConfig extends WebSecurityConfigurerAdapter {

    @Override
    protected void configure(AuthenticationManagerBuilder auth) throws
        Exception {
        auth.inMemoryAuthentication()
                .withUser("user").password("{noop}password").roles("USER")
                .and()
                .withUser("admin").password("{noop}admin").roles("USER", "
                    ADMIN");
    }
}
```

This example demonstrates how to define two users, user and admin, with respective roles and credentials using in-memory authentication. The setting page.title() ensures that the passwords are stored in plain text, indicated by the "noop" prefix.

To secure a RESTful service, adjust the HttpSecurity configuration to handle CSRF (Cross-Site Request Forgery) appropriately and ensure stateless sessions:

```
@Override
protected void configure(HttpSecurity http) throws Exception {
    http
        .csrf().disable()
        .authorizeRequests()
            .antMatchers("/api/public").permitAll()
            .antMatchers("/api/private").authenticated()
            .and()
        .sessionManagement()
            .sessionCreationPolicy(SessionCreationPolicy.STATELESS)
            .and()
```

```
        .httpBasic();
}
```

This configuration disables CSRF protection (commonly employed for non-browser clients), ensures public access to "/api/public", requires authentication for "/api/private", enforces stateless session management, and utilizes basic HTTP authentication.

Integrating a custom user details service involves implementing the UserDetailsService interface and loading user-specific data. Create a class named CustomUserDetailsService:

```
import org.springframework.security.core.userdetails.UserDetails;
import org.springframework.security.core.userdetails.UserDetailsService;
import org.springframework.security.core.userdetails.UsernameNotFoundException
    ;
import org.springframework.stereotype.Service;

@Service
public class CustomUserDetailsService implements UserDetailsService {

    @Override
    public UserDetails loadUserByUsername(String username) throws
            UsernameNotFoundException {
        // Custom logic to load user by username
        return null;
    }
}
```

Then wire this service into your security configuration:

```
import org.springframework.beans.factory.annotation.Autowired;
import org.springframework.context.annotation.Bean;
import org.springframework.context.annotation.Configuration;
import org.springframework.security.config.annotation.authentication.builders.
    AuthenticationManagerBuilder;
import org.springframework.security.config.annotation.web.configuration.
    EnableWebSecurity;
import org.springframework.security.config.annotation.web.configuration.
    WebSecurityConfigurerAdapter;
import org.springframework.security.crypto.bcrypt.BCryptPasswordEncoder;
import org.springframework.security.crypto.password.PasswordEncoder;

@Configuration
@EnableWebSecurity
public class SecurityConfig extends WebSecurityConfigurerAdapter {

    @Autowired
    private CustomUserDetailsService customUserDetailsService;

    @Override
```

```
    protected void configure(AuthenticationManagerBuilder auth) throws
        Exception {
        auth.userDetailsService(customUserDetailsService)
            .passwordEncoder(passwordEncoder());
    }

    @Bean
    public PasswordEncoder passwordEncoder() {
        return new BCryptPasswordEncoder();
    }
}
```

This configuration specifies a custom user details service and uses BCrypt for password encoding. The PasswordEncoder bean ensures robust password security by hashing passwords using the BCrypt algorithm.

Careful adjustments to these configurations and an in-depth understanding of the underlying mechanics are crucial to effectively securing a Spring application. Enabling the required dependencies, constructing a coherent security configuration, and comprehensively testing the security setup are vital steps in this process.

8.4 Configuring Authentication

Authentication is a pivotal aspect of application security, ensuring that only legitimate users gain access to the protected resources. In Spring Security, authentication is the process of verifying the credentials of a user. This section details the steps to configure authentication from various sources, like in-memory, JDBC, LDAP, and custom implementations.

To begin with, Spring Security requires defining a security configuration class, extending WebSecurityConfigurerAdapter. This class allows you to override the configure methods to set up authentication.

```
import org.springframework.context.annotation.Configuration;
import org.springframework.security.config.annotation.authentication.builders.
    AuthenticationManagerBuilder;
import org.springframework.security.config.annotation.web.configuration.
    EnableWebSecurity;
import org.springframework.security.config.annotation.web.configuration.
    WebSecurityConfigurerAdapter;

@Configuration
@EnableWebSecurity
```

```
public class SecurityConfig extends WebSecurityConfigurerAdapter {

    @Override
    protected void configure(AuthenticationManagerBuilder auth) throws
        Exception {
        // Configuration will be done here
    }
}
```

In-Memory Authentication

In-memory authentication involves hardcoding user details directly within the configuration class. This is useful for simple applications or for testing purposes.

```
@Override
protected void configure(AuthenticationManagerBuilder auth) throws Exception {
    auth.inMemoryAuthentication()
        .withUser("user").password("{noop}password").roles("USER")
        .and()
        .withUser("admin").password("{noop}admin").roles("ADMIN");
}
```

In this example, we use the `inMemoryAuthentication()` method to add users with their credentials and roles. The `noop` password encoder is specified to indicate no encoding is used. For production, a robust password encoder must be utilized.

JDBC Authentication

JDBC authentication integrates with a database to authenticate users. Spring Security provides a default schema, but it can be customized.

First, configure a data source and then utilize `jdbcAuthentication()` method.

```
import javax.sql.DataSource;
import org.springframework.beans.factory.annotation.Autowired;

@Autowired
private DataSource dataSource;

@Override
protected void configure(AuthenticationManagerBuilder auth) throws Exception {
    auth.jdbcAuthentication()
        .dataSource(dataSource)
        .usersByUsernameQuery("select username, password, enabled from users
            where username = ?")
        .authoritiesByUsernameQuery("select username, authority from authorities
            where username = ?");
}
```

This configuration fetches user details from the users table and authorities from the authorities table based on the provided SQL queries.

LDAP Authentication

LDAP authentication uses Lightweight Directory Access Protocol to authenticate users from a directory server.

```
import org.springframework.security.config.annotation.authentication.builders.
    AuthenticationManagerBuilder;

@Override
protected void configure(AuthenticationManagerBuilder auth) throws Exception {
    auth.ldapAuthentication()
        .userDnPatterns("uid={0},ou=people")
        .groupSearchBase("ou=groups")
        .contextSource()
            .url("ldap://localhost:8389/dc=springframework,dc=org")
        .and()
        .passwordCompare()
            .passwordAttribute("userPassword");
}
```

The userDnPatterns sets the pattern for user DN, groupSearchBase sets the base from where group searches start, and the contextSource configures the LDAP directory source. The passwordCompare method ensures the provided password matches the stored password attribute.

Custom Authentication Providers

For more tailored authentication mechanisms, custom authentication providers can be defined by implementing the AuthenticationProvider interface.

```
import org.springframework.security.authentication.AuthenticationProvider;
import org.springframework.security.core.Authentication;
import org.springframework.security.core.AuthenticationException;

public class CustomAuthenticationProvider implements AuthenticationProvider {

    @Override
    public Authentication authenticate(Authentication authentication)
            throws AuthenticationException {
        String username = authentication.getName();
        String password = authentication.getCredentials().toString();
        // Perform custom authentication logic
        return authentication;
    }

    @Override
    public boolean supports(Class<?> authentication) {
        return true; // or specific authentication type
```

```
    }
}
```

This custom provider needs to be registered within the security configuration class.

```
import org.springframework.beans.factory.annotation.Autowired;

@Autowired
private CustomAuthenticationProvider customAuthenticationProvider;

@Override
protected void configure(AuthenticationManagerBuilder auth) throws Exception {
    auth.authenticationProvider(customAuthenticationProvider);
}
```

Implementing and configuring multiple providers and including advanced options like multi-factor authentication and integration with OAuth2 or OpenID Connect adds robustness to the authentication mechanism. However, this requires adhering to best practices and staying updated with evolving security standards.

8.5 Configuring Authorization

Authorization is a critical component in any application, responsible for determining whether a user has the necessary permissions to access a resource or perform an action. In Spring Security, authorization is configured to control access to web pages, methods, and other resources based on roles and permissions.

Spring Security provides comprehensive mechanisms to manage authorization. Most of these mechanisms revolve around the concept of "roles" which are typically designated for different levels of access within an application. Configuring authorization in Spring involves setting up these roles and closely defining the security constraints that map to these roles.

Role-Based Authorization

Spring Security uses role-based access control (RBAC) as a standard practice for managing user permissions. Defining roles and mapping them to users can be achieved through configuration files or programmatically.

```
@Configuration
```

```
@EnableWebSecurity
public class WebSecurityConfig extends WebSecurityConfigurerAdapter {

    @Override
    protected void configure(HttpSecurity http) throws Exception {
        // Define access rules
        http
            .authorizeRequests()
                .antMatchers("/admin/**").hasRole("ADMIN")
                .antMatchers("/user/**").hasRole("USER")
                .antMatchers("/", "/home").permitAll()
                .anyRequest().authenticated()
            .and()
            .formLogin()
                .loginPage("/login")
                .permitAll()
            .and()
            .logout()
                .permitAll();
    }

    @Override
    protected void configure(AuthenticationManagerBuilder auth) throws
        Exception {
        // Define in-memory users
        auth
            .inMemoryAuthentication()
                .withUser("user").password(passwordEncoder().encode("password"
                    )).roles("USER")
                .and()
                .withUser("admin").password(passwordEncoder().encode("admin")
                    ).roles("ADMIN");
    }

    @Bean
    public PasswordEncoder passwordEncoder() {
        return new BCryptPasswordEncoder();
    }
}
```

In this example, the HttpSecurity object is configured to define access rules using the antMatchers method. The roles "ADMIN" and "USER" are assigned to specific URL patterns. The AuthenticationManager-Builder is used to set up in-memory authentication for simplicity, but it can be configured to use other data sources.

Expression-Based Access Control

Spring Security also supports expression-based access control, allowing for more granular and dynamic access control rules. This feature uses SpEL (Spring Expression Language) to define complex authorization rules.

```
@Override
protected void configure(HttpSecurity http) throws Exception {
    http
        .authorizeRequests()
            .antMatchers("/admin/**").access("hasRole('ADMIN') and
                hasIpAddress('192.168.1.0/24')")
            .antMatchers("/user/**").access("hasRole('USER')")
            .antMatchers("/", "/home").permitAll()
            .anyRequest().authenticated()
        .and()
        .formLogin()
            .loginPage("/login")
            .permitAll()
        .and()
        .logout()
            .permitAll();
}
```

In this configuration, access to the "/admin/**" URL pattern is restricted not only by role but also by IP address. This provides an additional layer of security, ensuring that only users with specific roles and IP addresses can access the resource.

Method-Level Security

Method-level security provides a way to secure individual methods within your services. This powerful feature allows you to check authorization at the method level, giving you fine-grained control over access.

To use method-level security, you must enable it first:

```
@EnableGlobalMethodSecurity(prePostEnabled = true)
public class MethodSecurityConfig extends GlobalMethodSecurityConfiguration {
    // Custom configurations if needed
}
```

After enabling method-level security, you can use annotations like @PreAuthorize and @Secured to enforce security rules on methods:

```
@Service
public class UserService {

    @PreAuthorize("hasRole('ADMIN')")
    public List<User> getAllUsers() {
        // Method logic
    }

    @PreAuthorize("hasRole('USER') or hasRole('ADMIN')")
    public User getUserById(Long id) {
```

```
        // Method logic
    }
}
```

@PreAuthorize allows for highly flexible security rules using SpEL. This example ensures that only users with the "ADMIN" role can access the getAllUsers method, while both "USER" and "ADMIN" roles can access the getUserById method.

Declarative Authorization with Filters

Filters allow for declarative security policies by processing the request before it reaches the controller. Spring Security includes several built-in filters, which can be customized or extended as needed.

```
public class CustomFilter extends OncePerRequestFilter {
    @Override
    protected void doFilterInternal(HttpServletRequest request,
                                    HttpServletResponse response,
                                    FilterChain filterChain) throws
                                        ServletException, IOException {
        // Custom filter logic
        filterChain.doFilter(request, response);
    }
}

@Configuration
public class WebSecurityConfig extends WebSecurityConfigurerAdapter {
    @Override
    protected void configure(HttpSecurity http) throws Exception {
        http
            .addFilterBefore(new CustomFilter(),
                UsernamePasswordAuthenticationFilter.class)
            .authorizeRequests()
            // Other configurations
    }
}
```

In this setup, the custom filter (CustomFilter) is added to the security filter chain before UsernamePasswordAuthenticationFilter. This lets you insert custom logic to be executed at specific points in the request processing lifecycle.

Additional Strategies and Best Practices

When configuring authorization, it is important to follow best practices to ensure a secure and maintainable security configuration. Here are some key strategies:

- **Principle of Least Privilege**: Always assign the minimum necessary permissions to users.

- **Role Hierarchies**: Use role hierarchies to simplify the management of roles and permissions.
- **Centralized Configuration**: Keep your security configuration in a central place for easier management.
- **Regular Audits**: Periodically review and update your security configurations to address new security threats.

Applying these strategies helps maintain robust security measures while simplifying the management of roles and permissions.

8.6 Working with UserDetailsService

The UserDetailsService interface plays a pivotal role in Spring Security. Implementing this interface enables developers to retrieve user-specific data, instrumental in the authentication process. This interface provides a single method, loadUserByUsername, which is designed to locate a user entity based on the provided username. It then returns a UserDetails object that encapsulates core user information.

To integrate UserDetailsService into your Spring application, follow these steps:

1. Implement the UserDetailsService interface.
2. Configure an authentication provider that uses your custom UserDetailsService.
3. Integrate this authentication provider within the security configuration.

Consider the following example where we define a custom UserDetailsService that retrieves user information from a hypothetical user repository:

```
import org.springframework.security.core.userdetails.UserDetailsService;
import org.springframework.security.core.userdetails.UsernameNotFoundException
    ;
import org.springframework.security.core.userdetails.UserDetails;
import org.springframework.stereotype.Service;
```

```
@Service
public class CustomUserDetailsService implements UserDetailsService {

    private final UserRepository userRepository;

    public CustomUserDetailsService(UserRepository userRepository) {
        this.userRepository = userRepository;
    }

    @Override
    public UserDetails loadUserByUsername(String username) throws
          UsernameNotFoundException {
        User user = userRepository.findByUsername(username);
        if (user == null) {
            throw new UsernameNotFoundException("User not found with
                  username: " + username);
        }
        return new CustomUserDetails(user);
    }
}
```

In the example:

- The CustomUserDetailsService class implements the UserDetailsService interface.
- It overrides the loadUserByUsername method to fetch the user details from a UserRepository.
- If the user is found, it returns a CustomUserDetails object; otherwise, it throws a UsernameNotFoundException.

The CustomUserDetails class is a custom implementation of the UserDetails interface that wraps the User entity. Here is a possible implementation:

```
import org.springframework.security.core.GrantedAuthority;
import org.springframework.security.core.authority.SimpleGrantedAuthority;
import org.springframework.security.core.userdetails.UserDetails;

import java.util.Collection;
import java.util.stream.Collectors;

public class CustomUserDetails implements UserDetails {

    private final User user;

    public CustomUserDetails(User user) {
        this.user = user;
    }
```

```
    @Override
    public Collection<? extends GrantedAuthority> getAuthorities() {
        return user.getRoles().stream()
                .map(role -> new SimpleGrantedAuthority(role.getName()))
                .collect(Collectors.toList());
    }

    @Override
    public String getPassword() {
        return user.getPassword();
    }

    @Override
    public String getUsername() {
        return user.getUsername();
    }

    @Override
    public boolean isAccountNonExpired() {
        return true;
    }

    @Override
    public boolean isAccountNonLocked() {
        return true;
    }

    @Override
    public boolean isCredentialsNonExpired() {
        return true;
    }

    @Override
    public boolean isEnabled() {
        return user.isEnabled();
    }
}
```

This class performs the following:

- Retrieves user authorities by converting roles to GrantedAuthority objects.
- Provides implementations for getPassword, getUsername, and other account status checks.

Next, configure an authentication provider that incorporates this UserDetailsService. Use DaoAuthenticationProvider for this purpose. Below is the configuration example:

```
import org.springframework.context.annotation.Bean;
import org.springframework.context.annotation.Configuration;
import org.springframework.security.authentication.dao.
    DaoAuthenticationProvider;
import org.springframework.security.config.annotation.authentication.builders.
    AuthenticationManagerBuilder;
import org.springframework.security.config.annotation.web.configuration.
    EnableWebSecurity;
import org.springframework.security.config.annotation.web.configuration.
    WebSecurityConfigurerAdapter;
import org.springframework.security.crypto.bcrypt.BCryptPasswordEncoder;

@Configuration
@EnableWebSecurity
public class SecurityConfiguration extends WebSecurityConfigurerAdapter {

    private final CustomUserDetailsService userDetailsService;

    public SecurityConfiguration(CustomUserDetailsService userDetailsService) {
        this.userDetailsService = userDetailsService;
    }

    @Bean
    public DaoAuthenticationProvider authenticationProvider() {
        DaoAuthenticationProvider authProvider = new
            DaoAuthenticationProvider();
        authProvider.setUserDetailsService(userDetailsService);
        authProvider.setPasswordEncoder(passwordEncoder());
        return authProvider;
    }

    @Bean
    public BCryptPasswordEncoder passwordEncoder() {
        return new BCryptPasswordEncoder();
    }

    @Override
    protected void configure(AuthenticationManagerBuilder auth) throws
        Exception {
        auth.authenticationProvider(authenticationProvider());
    }
}
```

In this configuration:

- SecurityConfiguration extends WebSecurityConfigurerAdapter.
- It defines a DaoAuthenticationProvider bean.
- The DaoAuthenticationProvider is configured with the CustomUserDetailsService and a password encoder.

- AuthenticationManagerBuilder is configured to use the custom authentication provider.

Utilizing UserDetailsService as illustrated ensures that Spring Security is leveraged to handle authentication based on the application's unique user repository setup. This approach is critical for both security and flexibility, allowing for diverse authentication sources and more granular user information management.

8.7 Customizing Login and Logout

Customizing the login and logout processes in Spring Security allows developers to tailor the user authentication experience to fit the unique requirements of their applications. Spring Security provides a high degree of configurability through its form login support, enabling customization of the login page, login processing URL, and logout mechanisms. This section details the procedures for customizing these aspects within a Spring project, ensuring a secure and user-friendly authentication flow.

Configuring a custom login page in Spring Security involves specifying a URL for the login page and ensuring the appropriate form handling. Firstly, we can configure the custom login page through the HttpSecurity configuration using the formLogin() method.

```
import org.springframework.security.config.annotation.web.builders.HttpSecurity;
import org.springframework.security.config.annotation.web.configuration.
    WebSecurityConfigurerAdapter;

public class SecurityConfig extends WebSecurityConfigurerAdapter {

    @Override
    protected void configure(HttpSecurity http) throws Exception {
        http
            .authorizeRequests()
                .anyRequest().authenticated()
                .and()
            .formLogin()
                .loginPage("/custom-login")
                .loginProcessingUrl("/perform_login")
                .defaultSuccessUrl("/homepage", true)
                .failureUrl("/login?error=true")
                .and()
            .logout()
                .logoutUrl("/perform_logout")
                .deleteCookies("JSESSIONID")
```

```
            .logoutSuccessUrl("/login");
    }
}
```

In this configuration, the loginPage("/custom-login") method specifies the URL to the custom login page. The loginProcessingUrl("/perform_-login") method sets the URL to which the login form should be submitted. The defaultSuccessUrl("/homepage", true) method defines the URL to redirect to upon successful authentication, and the failureUrl("/login?error=true") method specifies the URL to redirect to if authentication fails.

To handle the custom login page, we create a corresponding HTML file that contains the login form. The form submits the credentials (i.e., username and password) to the configured loginProcessingUrl.

```
<!DOCTYPE html>
<html lang="en">
<head>
    <meta charset="UTF-8">
    <meta name="viewport" content="width=device-width, initial-scale=1.0">
    <title>Custom Login</title>
</head>
<body>
    <form action="/perform_login" method="post">
        <div>
            <label for="username">Username:</label>
            <input type="text" id="username" name="username">
        </div>
        <div>
            <label for="password">Password:</label>
            <input type="password" id="password" name="password">
        </div>
        <div>
            <button type="submit">Login</button>
        </div>
    </form>
    <div>
        \begin{FittedVerbatim}
        <c:if test="${param.error != null}">
            <span>Invalid username or password.</span>
        </c:if>
        \end{FittedVerbatim}
    </div>
</body>
</html>
```

The logout configuration in Spring Security is equally customizable. The logout() method provides various options to define the logout behavior. The logoutUrl("/perform_logout") method specifies the URL to trigger the logout action. By default, Spring Security clears the security context and invalidates the HTTP session upon logout. Additionally, the deleteCookies("JSESSIONID") method removes the specified cookies, which can be used to ensure that no session-based information is retained. The logoutSuccessUrl("/login") method specifies the URL to redirect to after a successful logout.

For finer control over the logout process, we can implement a custom logout handler by leveraging the LogoutHandler interface.

```
import org.springframework.security.core.Authentication;
import org.springframework.security.web.authentication.logout.LogoutHandler;

import javax.servlet.http.HttpServletRequest;
import javax.servlet.http.HttpServletResponse;

public class CustomLogoutHandler implements LogoutHandler {

    @Override
    public void logout(HttpServletRequest request, HttpServletResponse response,
            Authentication authentication) {
        // Custom logic to handle logout, e.g., logging or additional cleanup.
        System.out.println("User " + authentication.getName() + " has logged
            out.");
    }
}
```

To use the custom logout handler, we need to configure it in the HttpSecurity setup.

```
import org.springframework.security.config.annotation.web.builders.HttpSecurity;
import org.springframework.security.config.annotation.web.configuration.
    WebSecurityConfigurerAdapter;
import org.springframework.security.web.authentication.logout.LogoutHandler;

public class SecurityConfig extends WebSecurityConfigurerAdapter {

    @Override
    protected void configure(HttpSecurity http) throws Exception {
        http
            .authorizeRequests()
                .anyRequest().authenticated()
                .and()
            .formLogin()
                .loginPage("/custom-login")
                .loginProcessingUrl("/perform_login")
                .defaultSuccessUrl("/homepage", true)
                .failureUrl("/login?error=true")
                .and()
            .logout()
```

```
                .logoutUrl("/perform_logout")
                .addLogoutHandler(new CustomLogoutHandler())
                .deleteCookies("JSESSIONID")
                .logoutSuccessUrl("/login");
    }
}
```

This configuration ensures that upon logout, the custom logout handler's logic is executed, providing an opportunity for additional actions such as logging user activities or performing application-specific cleanup tasks.

By customizing the login and logout processes, developers can enhance the security and user experience of their applications, ensuring that authentication flows align with the application's specific requirements. The flexibility provided by Spring Security's configuration options facilitates a seamless integration of custom authentication mechanisms, reinforcing the robustness and reliability of the security infrastructure.

8.8 Securing Web Applications

In this section, we will delve into the various mechanisms provided by Spring Security to secure web applications. Securing web applications involves implementing constraints that ensure only authorized users can access certain resources while maintaining a seamless and user-friendly experience.

Spring Security uses a specific, customizable configuration to handle authentication, authorization, session management, and more. To secure a web application, it's essential to understand the core components and configurations that Spring Security provides.

1. Setting Up Security Configuration:

Spring Security configuration in a Spring Boot application is typically done via a class that extends WebSecurityConfigurerAdapter. This class allows us to define custom security rules.

```
import org.springframework.security.config.annotation.web.builders.HttpSecurity;
import org.springframework.security.config.annotation.web.configuration.
    EnableWebSecurity;
import org.springframework.security.config.annotation.web.configuration.
    WebSecurityConfigurerAdapter;

@EnableWebSecurity
```

```
public class SecurityConfig extends WebSecurityConfigurerAdapter {

    @Override
    protected void configure(HttpSecurity http) throws Exception {
        http
            .authorizeRequests()
                .antMatchers("/public/**").permitAll()
                .antMatchers("/admin/**").hasRole("ADMIN")
                .anyRequest().authenticated()
                .and()
            .formLogin()
                .loginPage("/login")
                .permitAll()
                .and()
            .logout()
                .permitAll();
    }
}
```

In this example, we configure Spring Security to:

- Allow unrestricted access to any URL that starts with /public/.
- Restrict access to URLs beginning with /admin/ to users with the role ADMIN.
- Require all other requests to be authenticated.
- Provide a custom login page located at "/login".
- Permit all users to access the logout functionality.

2. Defining User Roles and Permissions:

User roles and permissions are essential in defining the security requirements for different parts of a web application. Roles are typically defined in UserDetailsService implementations.

```
import org.springframework.context.annotation.Bean;
import org.springframework.context.annotation.Configuration;
import org.springframework.security.core.userdetails.User;
import org.springframework.security.core.userdetails.UserDetailsService;
import org.springframework.security.provisioning.InMemoryUserDetailsManager;

@Configuration
public class UserConfig {

    @Bean
    public UserDetailsService userDetailsService() {
        InMemoryUserDetailsManager manager = new
            InMemoryUserDetailsManager();
```

```
        manager.createUser(User.withDefaultPasswordEncoder()
            .username("user")
            .password("password")
            .roles("USER")
            .build());
        manager.createUser(User.withDefaultPasswordEncoder()
            .username("admin")
            .password("admin")
            .roles("ADMIN")
            .build());
        return manager;
    }
}
```

In this configuration, an in-memory user store with two users is set up. One user has the USER role, and another has the ADMIN role.

3. Customizing Login Form:

Creating a custom login form enhances the user experience. The login form can be a simple HTML form or a sophisticated front-end component.

```
<!DOCTYPE html>
<html xmlns:th="http://www.thymeleaf.org">
<head>
    <title>Login</title>
</head>
<body>
    <h1>Login</h1>
    <form th:action="@{/login}" method="post">
        <div>
            <label for="username">Username:</label>
            <input type="text" id="username" name="username"/>
        </div>
        <div>
            <label for="password">Password:</label>
            <input type="password" id="password" name="password"/>
        </div>
        <div>
            <button type="submit">Login</button>
        </div>
    </form>
</body>
</html>
```

This HTML file represents a basic custom login page that submits credentials to the /login endpoint. Spring Security handles the authentication automatically.

4. Session Management:

Proper session management ensures that the security context is maintained across multiple requests and manages issues like session fixation attacks.

```
@Override
protected void configure(HttpSecurity http) throws Exception {
    http
        .sessionManagement()
            .sessionFixation().migrateSession()
            .maximumSessions(1);
}
```

In this configuration snippet, session fixation protection is enabled, and the system is restricted to a single active session per user.

5. Exception Handling:

Handling security exceptions and providing appropriate feedback to users is critical for usability and security.

```
@Override
protected void configure(HttpSecurity http) throws Exception {
    http
        .exceptionHandling()
            .accessDeniedPage("/403");
}
```

This configuration ensures that users who try to access resources without sufficient permissions are redirected to a custom 403 error page.

```
// Complete security filter chain configuration example
@Override
protected void configure(HttpSecurity http) throws Exception {
    http
        .authorizeRequests()
            .antMatchers("/public/**").permitAll() // public accessible URLs
            .antMatchers("/admin/**").hasRole("ADMIN") // admin specific
                URLs
            .anyRequest().authenticated() // any other request must be
                authenticated
            .and()
        .formLogin()
            .loginPage("/login") // custom login page URL
            .permitAll()
            .and()
        .logout()
            .permitAll()
            .and()
        .sessionManagement()
            .sessionFixation().migrateSession()
            .maximumSessions(1)
            .and()
```

```
        .exceptionHandling()
            .accessDeniedPage("/403"); // handle access denied exception
}
```

The security filter chain comprises numerous segments that guarantee comprehensive security based on the application's requirements. Through proper configuration and customizations, Spring Security ensures that web applications remain secure without compromising usability.

With these configurations and implementations, one can significantly enhance the security of a Spring-based web application, ensuring that only authorized users access protected resources, while providing an intuitive user interface for authentication and error handling.

8.9 Securing RESTful Web Services

Securing RESTful web services is crucial in ensuring the data integrity and authenticity of the client-server interactions. The flexibility and ubiquity of RESTful services make them a common target for security threats such as unauthorized access, data interception, and modification. Spring Security plays an instrumental role in safeguarding these services through various mechanisms that encompass authentication, authorization, and protective measures against potential attacks.

Spring Security seamlessly integrates with Spring's RESTful services, enabling developers to apply security measures in a granular and configurable manner. To illustrate the process, we will cover the essential steps and mechanisms using a practical example.

```
dependencies {
    implementation 'org.springframework.boot:spring-boot-starter-security'
    implementation 'org.springframework.boot:spring-boot-starter-web'
    // Additional dependencies
}
```

To begin, add the required dependencies in your build.gradle file.

- **Configuring Authentication**

  Authentication verifies the identity of users or systems interacting with the RESTful service. We can configure various types of authentication mechanisms, such as HTTP Basic, OAuth2, JWT, etc. Here, we focus on HTTP Basic and OAuth2 authentication.

- **HTTP Basic Authentication**

  HTTP Basic authentication is a straightforward approach where the client sends the username and password encoded in the request header.

```
import org.springframework.context.annotation.Configuration;
import org.springframework.security.config.annotation.web.builders.
    HttpSecurity;
import org.springframework.security.config.annotation.web.configuration.
    EnableWebSecurity;
import org.springframework.security.config.annotation.web.configuration.
    WebSecurityConfigurerAdapter;

@Configuration
@EnableWebSecurity
public class SecurityConfig extends WebSecurityConfigurerAdapter {
    @Override
    protected void configure(HttpSecurity http) throws Exception {
        http
            .csrf().disable()
            .authorizeRequests()
                .antMatchers("/api/public/**").permitAll()
                .anyRequest().authenticated()
            .and()
            .httpBasic();
    }
}
```

  In this configuration, we disable Cross-Site Request Forgery (CSRF) protection for simplicity. We allow public access to endpoints prefixed with /api/public/. All other endpoints require authentication, achieved through HTTP Basic authentication.

- **Configuring Authorization**

  Authorization determines what authenticated users can do. We can define roles and specify access control rules to fine-tune authorization.

```
import org.springframework.security.core.userdetails.User;
import org.springframework.security.core.userdetails.UserDetailsService;
import org.springframework.security.core.userdetails.
    UsernameNotFoundException;
import org.springframework.security.core.userdetails.UserDetails;
import org.springframework.stereotype.Service;

import java.util.Collections;

@Service
public class UserDetailsServiceImpl implements UserDetailsService {
```

```
    @Override
    public UserDetails loadUserByUsername(String username) throws
            UsernameNotFoundException {
        if ("user".equals(username)) {
            return new User("user", "{noop}password", Collections.
                    emptyList());
        } else {
            throw new UsernameNotFoundException("User not found");
        }
    }
}
```

The above implementation of UserDetailsService hardcodes a single user for demonstration purposes. In a production scenario, user details would typically be retrieved from a database.

- **OAuth2 Authentication**

  OAuth2 allows third-party applications to grant limited access to a user's resources without exposing their credentials. Spring Security offers robust support for OAuth2.

```
dependencies {
    implementation 'org.springframework.boot:spring-boot-starter-oauth2-
            client'
}
```

We add the OAuth2 client dependency to our project. Then, configure the application.properties file with the necessary details for OAuth2 clients.

```
spring.security.oauth2.client.registration.my-client.client-id=client-id
spring.security.oauth2.client.registration.my-client.client-secret=client-secret
spring.security.oauth2.client.registration.my-client.scope=read,write
spring.security.oauth2.client.registration.my-client.redirect-uri=http://
        localhost:8080/login/oauth2/code/my-client
spring.security.oauth2.client.registration.my-client.authorization-grant-type
        =authorization_code
spring.security.oauth2.client.registration.my-client.client-name=My Client
spring.security.oauth2.client.provider.my-provider.authorization-uri=https
        ://provider.com/oauth2/authorize
spring.security.oauth2.client.provider.my-provider.token-uri=https://
        provider.com/oauth2/token
```

The next step involves configuring our security settings to handle OAuth2 authentication:

```
import org.springframework.context.annotation.Bean;
import org.springframework.security.config.annotation.web.builders.
        HttpSecurity;
```

```
import org.springframework.security.config.annotation.web.configuration.
    EnableWebSecurity;
import org.springframework.security.config.annotation.web.configuration.
    WebSecurityConfigurerAdapter;
import org.springframework.security.oauth2.client.oidc.userinfo.
    OidcUserService;
import org.springframework.security.oauth2.client.registration.
    ClientRegistrationRepository;
import org.springframework.security.oauth2.client.web.
    OAuth2LoginAuthenticationFilter;

@EnableWebSecurity
public class SecurityConfigOAuth2 extends WebSecurityConfigurerAdapter
    {

    @Override
    protected void configure(HttpSecurity http) throws Exception {
        http
            .authorizeRequests()
                .antMatchers("/api/public/**").permitAll()
                .anyRequest().authenticated()
            .and()
            .oauth2Login()
                .loginPage("/oauth2/authorization/my-client");
    }
}
```

- **Protecting Endpoints**

  With authentication and authorization in place, it is essential to protect specific endpoints, ensuring they cater to the security requirements.

```
import org.springframework.web.bind.annotation.GetMapping;
import org.springframework.web.bind.annotation.RequestMapping;
import org.springframework.web.bind.annotation.RestController;

@RestController
@RequestMapping("/api")
public class MyRestController {

    @GetMapping("/public/info")
    public String publicInfo() {
        return "This is a public endpoint.";
    }

    @GetMapping("/private/data")
    public String privateData() {
        return "This is a protected endpoint.";
    }
}
```

The endpoint /api/public/info is accessible without authentication, while /api/private/data requires the client to be authenticated.

- **Handling Security Exceptions**

  Handling exceptions that arise due to security violations should provide a clear and concise response to the client.

```
import org.springframework.http.HttpStatus;
import org.springframework.security.access.AccessDeniedException;
import org.springframework.web.bind.annotation.ExceptionHandler;
import org.springframework.web.bind.annotation.RestControllerAdvice;

@RestControllerAdvice
public class RestExceptionHandler {

    @ExceptionHandler(AccessDeniedException.class)
    public HttpResponse handleAccessDeniedException() {
        return new HttpResponse(HttpStatus.FORBIDDEN, "Access
             Denied");
    }
}
```

  By implementing a RestExceptionHandler, we ensure that clients receive appropriate HTTP responses when they encounter access issues.

Spring Security offers the flexibility and extensive tooling needed to secure RESTful web services effectively. The examples provided emphasize essential practices in configuring authentication and outlining authorization strategies.

8.10 Method-Level Security

Method-level security in Spring Security empowers developers to secure individual methods within their applications. This feature is essential for fine-grained access control, allowing specific security rules to be applied at the business logic level.

To enable method-level security, begin by annotating your Spring configuration class with @EnableGlobalMethodSecurity. This annotation activates pre- and post-invocation security checks, allowing the use of method-level security annotations such as @PreAuthorize, @PostAuthorize, @Secured, and @RolesAllowed. These annotations define security constraints that must be met before and after method invocation. The @EnableGlobalMethodSecurity requires specifying appropriate flags, such as securedEnabled, prePostEnabled, and jsr250Enabled, based on the annotations you plan to use.

```
@Configuration
@EnableGlobalMethodSecurity(
    securedEnabled = true,
    prePostEnabled = true,
    jsr250Enabled = true
)
public class MethodSecurityConfig extends GlobalMethodSecurityConfiguration {
    // Custom security configurations if necessary
}
```

Using @PreAuthorize and @PostAuthorize:

@PreAuthorize and @PostAuthorize utilize Spring Expression Language (SpEL) to define security expressions. @PreAuthorize specifies constraints evaluated before method execution, whereas @PostAuthorize evaluates constraints after method execution, allowing access based on the method's return value.

```
@Service
public class ProductService {

    @PreAuthorize("hasRole('ADMIN')")
    public void deleteProduct(Long productId) {
        // Method logic here
    }

    @PostAuthorize("returnObject.owner == authentication.name")
    public Product findProductById(Long productId) {
        // Method logic here
        return productRepository.findById(productId).orElse(null);
    }
}
```

In the example above, @PreAuthorize("hasRole('ADMIN')") ensures that only users with the 'ADMIN' role can invoke the deleteProduct method. The @PostAuthorize("returnObject.owner == authentication.name") checks if the returned product's owner matches the authenticated user's name, enforcing security based on the returned data.

Using @Secured:

The @Secured annotation specifies security constraints at the method level using Spring Security's role-based access control. This annotation does not use SpEL but straightforward role names.

```
@Service
public class OrderService {

    @Secured({"ROLE_USER", "ROLE_MANAGER"})
    public void placeOrder(Order order) {
        // Method logic here
    }
}
```

In this case, the placeOrder method can only be executed by users with either 'ROLE_USER' or 'ROLE_MANAGER'.

Using @RolesAllowed:

Similar to @Secured, @RolesAllowed is part of the JSR-250 annotations and provides an additional way to enforce role-based security.

```
@Service
public class CustomerService {

    @RolesAllowed("ROLE_MANAGER")
    public Customer getCustomerDetails(Long customerId) {
        // Method logic here
        return customerRepository.findById(customerId).orElse(null);
    }
}
```

Here, only users with 'ROLE_MANAGER' can invoke the getCustomerDetails method.

Aspect Oriented Programming (AOP) Interceptors:

Spring Security integrates well with AOP, allowing the implementation of security concerns independently of business logic. By default, method security operates through AOP proxies, ensuring that security checks are applied transparently.

Advanced Configurations:

For advanced scenarios, developers might need to create custom security annotations or security expression handlers. Custom annotations are created by combining meta-annotations and can encapsulate complex security logic.

```
@Target(ElementType.METHOD)
@Retention(RetentionPolicy.RUNTIME)
@PreAuthorize("hasPermission(#id, 'customPermission')")
public @interface CustomSecurity { }
```

Custom security expressions require a permission evaluator configured in your Spring Security setup.

```
@Component("customPermissionEvaluator")
public class CustomPermissionEvaluator implements PermissionEvaluator {

    @Override
    public boolean hasPermission(Authentication auth, Object
        targetDomainObject, Object permission) {
        // Custom logic here
        return true;
    }

    @Override
    public boolean hasPermission(Authentication auth, Serializable targetId,
        String targetType, Object permission) {
        // Custom logic here
        return true;
    }
}
```

Finally, register the evaluator within the global configuration.

```
@Configuration
@EnableGlobalMethodSecurity(prePostEnabled = true)
public class MethodSecurityConfig extends GlobalMethodSecurityConfiguration {

    @Override
    protected MethodSecurityExpressionHandler createExpressionHandler() {
        DefaultMethodSecurityExpressionHandler expressionHandler =
            new DefaultMethodSecurityExpressionHandler();
        expressionHandler.setPermissionEvaluator(new
                CustomPermissionEvaluator());
        return expressionHandler;
    }
}
```

These configurations make the custom permission evaluator available for interpreting security expressions.

8.11 Integrating OAuth2 with Spring Security

OAuth2 is an open standard protocol for authorization, which Spring Security supports extensively. It delegates access rights to a third party without sharing actual credentials and is essential for modern web applications requiring secure authentication and authorization across various services.

The integration process can be delineated into several steps: configuring the authorization server, setting up the resource server, and finally, creating and managing client credentials.

- **Configuring the Authorization Server**

Spring Boot with Spring Security provides built-in support to configure an OAuth2 authorization server using the spring-security-oauth2-autoconfigure dependency.

In the pom.xml, include the following dependency:

```
<dependency>
    <groupId>org.springframework.boot</groupId>
    <artifactId>spring-security-oauth2-autoconfigure</artifactId>
    <version>${spring-security-oauth2.version}</version>
</dependency>
```

Next, we need to define a configuration class to set up the authorization server by extending AuthorizationServerConfigurerAdapter:

```
import org.springframework.context.annotation.Configuration;
import org.springframework.security.oauth2.config.annotation.configurers.
    ClientDetailsServiceConfigurer;
import org.springframework.security.oauth2.config.annotation.web.configuration.
    AuthorizationServerConfigurerAdapter;
import org.springframework.security.oauth2.config.annotation.web.configuration.
    EnableAuthorizationServer;
import org.springframework.security.oauth2.config.annotation.web.configurers.
    AuthorizationServerEndpointsConfigurer;
import org.springframework.security.oauth2.config.annotation.web.configurers.
    AuthorizationServerSecurityConfigurer;

@Configuration
@EnableAuthorizationServer
public class AuthorizationServerConfig extends
    AuthorizationServerConfigurerAdapter {

    @Override
    public void configure(ClientDetailsServiceConfigurer clients) throws Exception
        {
        clients.inMemory()
            .withClient("client-id")
            .secret("{noop}client-secret")
            .authorizedGrantTypes("password", "authorization_code", "
                refresh_token")
            .scopes("read", "write")
            .accessTokenValiditySeconds(3600)
            .refreshTokenValiditySeconds(7200);
    }
```

```
    @Override
    public void configure(AuthorizationServerSecurityConfigurer security) throws
        Exception {
        security.tokenKeyAccess("permitAll()")
                .checkTokenAccess("isAuthenticated()");
    }

    @Override
    public void configure(AuthorizationServerEndpointsConfigurer endpoints)
        throws Exception {
        // Endpoint configurations if necessary
    }
}
```

This class defines client credentials, grant types, and token validity settings. Tokens can have various configurations for expiry and renewal based on the application's requirements.

- **Setting Up the Resource Server**

The resource server is where protected resources reside, enforcing the security measures by validating tokens. Extend ResourceServerConfigurerAdapter to configure the resource server.

In pom.xml, include:

```
<dependency>
    <groupId>org.springframework.boot</groupId>
    <artifactId>spring-boot-starter-oauth2-resource-server</artifactId>
</dependency>
```

Create the ResourceServerConfig class as follows:

```
import org.springframework.context.annotation.Configuration;
import org.springframework.security.config.annotation.web.builders.HttpSecurity;
import org.springframework.security.oauth2.config.annotation.web.configuration.
    EnableResourceServer;
import org.springframework.security.oauth2.config.annotation.web.configuration.
    ResourceServerConfigurerAdapter;

@Configuration
@EnableResourceServer
public class ResourceServerConfig extends ResourceServerConfigurerAdapter {

    @Override
    public void configure(HttpSecurity http) throws Exception {
        http
            .authorizeRequests()
            .antMatchers("/public/**").permitAll()
            .anyRequest().authenticated();
```

```
    }
}
```

The above configuration protects all endpoints except those under /public, ensuring that valid tokens are necessary to access secured resources.

- **Creating and Managing Client Credentials**

Client credentials represent applications authorized to obtain an authentication token on behalf of users. For example, client credentials are defined in the AuthorizationServerConfig class.

To retrieve an Access Token using client credentials, a POST request is used:

```
curl --location --request POST 'http://localhost:8080/oauth/token' \
--header 'Authorization: Basic Y2xpZW50LWlkOmNsaWVudC1zZWNyZXQ=' \
--header 'Content-Type: application/x-www-form-urlencoded' \
--data-urlencode 'grant_type=client_credentials'
```

The response will provide an access token:

```
{
    "access_token": "eyJhbGciOiJIUzI1NiIsInR5cCI6IkpXVCJ9...",
    "token_type": "bearer",
    "expires_in": 3600,
    "scope": "read write"
}
```

Combining the aforementioned steps ensures a system where tokens are regularly issued and validated, maintaining secure access to protected resources.

Proper logging and monitoring of token usage and state are integral to maintaining the system's security. Tools like Spring Boot Actuator can assist in monitoring authentication activities, thus ensuring a robust OAuth2 integrated application.

8.12 Handling Security Exceptions

Handling security exceptions effectively is a crucial part of building robust and user-friendly Spring applications. Exceptions can arise from various security-related issues such as authentication failures, access denials, and invalid session states. Spring Security provides a comprehensive mechanism to handle these exceptions, ensuring that your application can respond appropriately to security threats and user errors.

When a security exception occurs, Spring Security delegates the handling of the exception to a dedicated 'ExceptionTranslationFilter' located within the security filter chain. This filter intercepts exceptions and processes them according to the criteria defined in your security configuration. The following relevant security exceptions are commonly encountered and require specific handling:

- **AuthenticationException**: This exception is triggered when authentication fails, for example, due to invalid credentials or a disabled user account.
- **AccessDeniedException**: This exception occurs when an authenticated user attempts to access a resource for which they lack sufficient permissions.
- **SessionAuthenticationException**: This exception is thrown when there are issues related to session management, such as an expired session or invalid session state.

To handle these exceptions elegantly, Spring Security allows developers to define custom authentication failure handlers, access denied handlers, and session management configurations. Below are detailed descriptions and examples to illustrate the process.

Handling Authentication Exceptions

To handle authentication exceptions, you can implement a custom authentication failure handler. This involves creating a class that implements 'AuthenticationFailureHandler' and overriding the 'onAuthenticationFailure' method:

```
import org.springframework.security.core.AuthenticationException;
import org.springframework.security.web.authentication.
     AuthenticationFailureHandler;

import javax.servlet.ServletException;
import javax.servlet.http.HttpServletRequest;
import javax.servlet.http.HttpServletResponse;
import java.io.IOException;

public class CustomAuthenticationFailureHandler implements
     AuthenticationFailureHandler {
   @Override
```

```
    public void onAuthenticationFailure(HttpServletRequest request,
            HttpServletResponse response, AuthenticationException exception)
            throws IOException, ServletException {
        response.setStatus(HttpServletResponse.SC_UNAUTHORIZED);
        response.getWriter().write("Authentication Failed: " + exception.
            getMessage());
    }
}
```

Next, you need to register this custom handler in your security configuration class:

```
import org.springframework.context.annotation.Bean;
import org.springframework.security.config.annotation.web.builders.HttpSecurity;
import org.springframework.security.config.annotation.web.configuration.
    WebSecurityConfigurerAdapter;
import org.springframework.security.web.authentication.
    AuthenticationFailureHandler;

public class SecurityConfig extends WebSecurityConfigurerAdapter {
    @Bean
    public AuthenticationFailureHandler customAuthenticationFailureHandler() {
        return new CustomAuthenticationFailureHandler();
    }

    @Override
    protected void configure(HttpSecurity http) throws Exception {
        http
            .formLogin()
            .failureHandler(customAuthenticationFailureHandler())
            .and()
            .authorizeRequests()
            .anyRequest().authenticated();
    }
}
```

Handling Access Denied Exceptions

For handling access denied exceptions, you can create a custom access denied handler by implementing the 'AccessDeniedHandler' interface and overriding the 'handle' method:

```
import org.springframework.security.access.AccessDeniedException;
import org.springframework.security.web.access.AccessDeniedHandler;

import javax.servlet.ServletException;
import javax.servlet.http.HttpServletRequest;
import javax.servlet.http.HttpServletResponse;
import java.io.IOException;

public class CustomAccessDeniedHandler implements AccessDeniedHandler {
    @Override
```

```
    public void handle(HttpServletRequest request, HttpServletResponse response,
            AccessDeniedException exc) throws IOException, ServletException {
        response.setStatus(HttpServletResponse.SC_FORBIDDEN);
        response.getWriter().write("Access Denied: " + exc.getMessage());
    }
}
```

Then, register this handler in your security configuration:

```
@Override
protected void configure(HttpSecurity http) throws Exception {
    http
        .exceptionHandling()
        .accessDeniedHandler(new CustomAccessDeniedHandler())
        .and()
        .authorizeRequests()
        .anyRequest().authenticated();
}
```

Handling Session Authentication Exceptions

To manage session authentication exceptions, you can configure the session management in your 'HttpSecurity' configuration and add appropriate handlers. Below is an example of how to set up these configurations:

```
import org.springframework.context.annotation.Configuration;
import org.springframework.security.config.annotation.web.builders.HttpSecurity;
import org.springframework.security.config.annotation.web.configuration.
    WebSecurityConfigurerAdapter;

@Configuration
public class SessionManagementConfig extends WebSecurityConfigurerAdapter {
    @Override
    protected void configure(HttpSecurity http) throws Exception {
        http
            .sessionManagement()
                .invalidSessionUrl("/invalidSession")
                .maximumSessions(1)
                .maxSessionsPreventsLogin(true)
            .and()
            .authorizeRequests()
            .anyRequest().authenticated();
    }
}
```

In this example, when a session expires ('invalidSessionUrl') or multiple sessions are prevented ('maxSessionsPreventsLogin'), users are redirected to the specified URL '/invalidSession'.

User Notification and Logging

In addition to defining custom exception handlers, it is essential to log and notify users of security exceptions appropriately. Logging can help in auditing and troubleshooting security incidents, while notifying users enhances the user experience by providing clear feedback.

For logging, you can use a logging framework such as Logback or SLF4J:

```
import org.slf4j.Logger;
import org.slf4j.LoggerFactory;
import org.springframework.security.core.AuthenticationException;
import org.springframework.security.web.authentication.
    AuthenticationFailureHandler;

import javax.servlet.ServletException;
import javax.servlet.http.HttpServletRequest;
import javax.servlet.http.HttpServletResponse;
import java.io.IOException;

public class CustomAuthenticationFailureHandler implements
    AuthenticationFailureHandler {
    private static final Logger logger = LoggerFactory.getLogger(
        CustomAuthenticationFailureHandler.class);

    @Override
    public void onAuthenticationFailure(HttpServletRequest request,
        HttpServletResponse response, AuthenticationException exception)
        throws IOException, ServletException {
        logger.warn("Authentication failed: " + exception.getMessage());
        response.setStatus(HttpServletResponse.SC_UNAUTHORIZED);
        response.getWriter().write("Authentication Failed: " + exception.
            getMessage());
    }
}
```

Ensuring robust handling of security exceptions in your Spring application helps maintain secure, user-friendly interactions while providing clear and informative responses to security events. This, in turn, enhances the application's overall security posture and user experience.

8.13 Best Practices for Security in Spring Applications

Securing Spring applications involves employing a set of best practices that consistently strengthen the security posture of the systems. Adopting these practices not only ensures compliance with established security standards but also mitigates the risk of potential vulnerabilities. This section aims to provide a comprehensive guide on the best practices essential for safeguarding Spring applications.

- **Enforce Strong Authentication**
  Implementing strong authentication mechanisms is fundamental. Use robust hashing algorithms like bcrypt for storing passwords securely. Spring Security supports bcrypt out-of-the-box, which can be configured as shown:

```
@Bean
public PasswordEncoder passwordEncoder() {
    return new BCryptPasswordEncoder();
}
```

- **Apply Principle of Least Privilege**
  Restrict user roles and permissions to the minimum necessary for functionality. This approach is crucial in throttling privilege escalation attacks. Configuration of role-based access is demonstrated below:

```
http.authorizeRequests()
    .antMatchers("/admin/**").hasRole("ADMIN")
    .antMatchers("/user/**").hasRole("USER")
    .antMatchers("/public/**").permitAll();
```

- **Secure Sensitive Endpoints**
  Segregate sensitive endpoints from public access and ensure they are adequately protected by requiring authentication and appropriate authorization checks.

```
http.authorizeRequests()
    .antMatchers("/secure/**").authenticated()
    .anyRequest().permitAll();
```

- **Utilize HTTPS**
  HTTPS ensures the transmission of data over an encrypted channel, safeguarding against eavesdropping and man-in-the-middle (MITM) attacks. Enforce HTTPS using Spring Security configuration:

```
http.requiresChannel()
    .anyRequest().requiresSecure();
```

  Server settings must be adjusted to redirect HTTP traffic to

HTTPS, often done via server configurations or within the application itself utilizing URL mappings.

- **Implement Content Security Policy (CSP)**
  Mitigate cross-site scripting (XSS) attacks by deploying a strict Content Security Policy. Spring Security allows adding CSP headers through its configuration. Example implementation:

```
http.headers()
    .contentSecurityPolicy("script-src 'self'");
```

- **Handle Sessions Properly**
  Protect against session fixation attacks by regenerating session IDs upon authentication, and enforce session timeouts to reduce risks from abandoned sessions.

```
http.sessionManagement()
    .sessionFixation().migrateSession()
    .invalidSessionUrl("/session-timeout")
    .maximumSessions(1)
    .expiredUrl("/login?expired");
```

- **Validate Inputs Rigorously**
  Sanitize and validate all inputs from users to prevent injection attacks such as SQL injection. Utilize Spring Validator for processing form inputs:

```
@Autowired
private Validator validator;

@PostMapping("/submitForm")
public String submitForm(@ModelAttribute @Valid UserForm userForm,
                         BindingResult result) {
    if (result.hasErrors()) {
        return "errorPage";
    }
    return "successPage";
}
```

- **Sanitize Outputs**
  Encode outputs to neutralize potentially malicious data before rendering on web pages. This practice is vital for preventing XSS attacks. Use frameworks like Thymeleaf, which provide built-in support for escaping HTML.

- **Monitor and Audit**
  Set up logging and auditing mechanisms to maintain comprehen-

sive records of access and activities within the application. Spring Security supports auditing capabilities:

```
@EnableGlobalMethodSecurity(prePostEnabled = true)
@EnableJpaAuditing(auditorAwareRef = "auditorProvider")

@Bean
public AuditorAware<String> auditorProvider() {
    return new AuditorAwareImpl();
}
```

- **Implement Security Headers**
  Enforce additional security headers to mitigate various types of attacks, such as clickjacking, XSS, and content sniffing:

```
http.headers()
    .xssProtection()
        .block(true)
        .and()
    .contentTypeOptions()
        .and()
    .frameOptions()
        .sameOrigin();
```

- **Keep Dependencies Updated**
  Regularly update application dependencies, particularly those affecting security. Use tools like Maven or Gradle to check for outdated libraries:

```
mvn versions:display-dependency-updates
```

- **Enable CORS Safely**
  When enabling Cross-Origin Resource Sharing (CORS), configure it judiciously to avoid excessive exposure:

```
@Bean
public WebMvcConfigurer corsConfigurer() {
    return new WebMvcConfigurer() {
        @Override
        public void addCorsMappings(CorsRegistry registry) {
            registry.addMapping("/api/**")
                    .allowedOrigins("https://trusted-domain.com");
        }
    };
}
```

Employing these security best practices in Spring applications leads to enhanced protection against a wide range of vulnerabilities, ensuring robust and resilient software systems.

Chapter 9

Testing in Spring

This chapter addresses the testing strategies and tools available within the Spring Framework. It begins with setting up the necessary test environment and progresses through unit testing using JUnit and mocking dependencies with Mockito. The chapter covers the use of the Spring TestContext Framework and methods for integration testing. Specific focus is given to testing Spring MVC controllers, Spring Data repositories, and Spring Security configurations. Additionally, it explores advanced topics like testing with Spring Boot and employing Testcontainers for integration tests, concluding with best practices for effective test implementation in Spring applications.

9.1 Introduction to Testing in Spring

Testing is a crucial component of software development, ensuring that applications perform as expected and maintain robustness over time. Within the Spring Framework, testing is not merely an afterthought but an integral part of the development process. Spring provides a comprehensive suite of tools and methodologies to facilitate all levels of testing, from unit tests to full integration tests. This section aims to provide a detailed overview of the various testing paradigms and strategies employed in the Spring ecosystem.

The cornerstone of testing in Spring revolves around ensuring that each component or unit within the application functions correctly in isolation. This can be achieved through unit testing, typically leveraging tools such as JUnit. A unit test focuses on a single "unit" of code - generally a method or a small cluster of methods within a class. The primary objective is to verify that individual units of code work as intended, independent of external dependencies.

To illustrate a basic unit test in Spring, consider the following example using JUnit:

```
import org.junit.jupiter.api.Test;
import static org.junit.jupiter.api.Assertions.assertEquals;

public class CalculatorTest {

    @Test
    void testAddition() {
        Calculator calculator = new Calculator();
        int result = calculator.add(10, 5);
        assertEquals(15, result, "10 + 5 should equal 15");
    }
}
```

In the example above, a simple unit test verifies the functionality of an 'add' method within a 'Calculator' class. The 'assertEquals' method asserts that the result of 'calculator.add(10, 5)' is '15', ensuring the correctness of the addition operation.

Beyond unit testing, mocking plays an essential role when tests involve interactions with external systems or dependencies. Mockito is a widely-used framework for creating mock objects in Java and can be seamlessly integrated with Spring to mock dependencies and facilitate isolated testing of components.

Consider an example where a service class depends on a repository interface:

```
import org.junit.jupiter.api.Test;
import org.mockito.Mockito;
import static org.junit.jupiter.api.Assertions.assertTrue;

public class UserServiceTest {

    @Test
    void testFindUser() {
        UserRepository mockRepository = Mockito.mock(UserRepository.class);
        UserService userService = new UserService(mockRepository);
```

```
        User user = new User("testUser");
        Mockito.when(mockRepository.findByName("testUser")).thenReturn(user)
            ;

        assertTrue(userService.findUser("testUser").isPresent());
    }
}
```

In the code snippet, 'UserRepository' is mocked using Mockito. The 'when' method configures the mock to return a predefined 'User' object when 'findByName("testUser")' is called. This allows testing of 'UserService''s 'findUser' method without needing an actual database or repository implementation.

Spring's TestContext Framework (TCF) provides extensive support for integration testing. The TCF manages the Spring IoC container, provides dependency injection, and handles transactional boundaries. By utilizing the '@ContextConfiguration' annotation, one can define the configuration classes or XML files required to load the context for integration tests.

For instance:

```
import org.junit.jupiter.api.Test;
import org.springframework.beans.factory.annotation.Autowired;
import org.springframework.boot.test.context.SpringBootTest;
import org.junit.jupiter.api.extension.ExtendWith;
import org.springframework.test.context.junit.jupiter.SpringExtension;

@ExtendWith(SpringExtension.class)
@SpringBootTest
public class ApplicationIntegrationTest {

    @Autowired
    private UserService userService;

    @Test
    void testServiceLayer() {
        User user = userService.findUser("integrationTestUser");
        assertNotNull(user, "User should not be null");
    }
}
```

In this example, '@SpringBootTest' initializes the entire Spring context, making it suitable for full integration tests where the complete application context is required. The '@ExtendWith(SpringExtension.class)' annotation integrates Spring TestContext with JUnit 5. By autowiring 'UserService', the test verifies service layer functionality within the context of the application's environment.

Integration testing goes beyond isolated components, ensuring that different parts of the application work together correctly. Tools like Spring MVC Test and WebTestClient enable testing of web layer components, while databases can be tested using in-memory databases such as H2 or tools like Testcontainers for extensive integration scenarios.

The following is a REST controller test leveraging Spring MVC Test:

```
import org.junit.jupiter.api.Test;
import org.springframework.beans.factory.annotation.Autowired;
import org.springframework.boot.test.autoconfigure.web.servlet.
    AutoConfigureMockMvc;
import org.springframework.boot.test.context.SpringBootTest;
import org.springframework.test.web.servlet.MockMvc;

import static org.springframework.test.web.servlet.request.
    MockMvcRequestBuilders.get;
import static org.springframework.test.web.servlet.result.MockMvcResultMatchers.
    status;

@SpringBootTest
@AutoConfigureMockMvc
public class UserControllerTest {

    @Autowired
    private MockMvc mockMvc;

    @Test
    void testGetUser() throws Exception {
        mockMvc.perform(get("/users/testUser"))
                .andExpect(status().isOk());
    }
}
```

This example demonstrates testing a REST endpoint using Spring MVC Test. The 'MockMvc' instance performs a 'GET' request to the endpoint '/users/testUser' and asserts that the HTTP status is '200 OK'.

The breadth of testing support in Spring ensures that a range of testing needs are met, from unit testing individual components to full-blown integration testing across multiple systems. Emphasizing testing throughout the Spring application development lifecycle promotes reliability, maintainability, and quality of the software.

Understanding and utilizing Spring's extensive testing capabilities are fundamental for developers aiming to build robust, high-quality Spring applications.

9.2 Setting Up a Test Environment

Configuring a reliable and manageable test environment is a crucial first step in the software development lifecycle, particularly when employing the Spring Framework. Establishing this environment ensures consistency in test execution and helps developers pinpoint and address issues with confidence. This section outlines the essential components and configurations required to set up an effective test environment for Spring applications.

A foundational aspect of setting up a test environment is incorporating the necessary dependencies. In a typical Spring project, this process involves ensuring that the project's build configuration includes the appropriate testing libraries. For a project utilizing Maven as the build tool, the pom.xml file should be modified to include dependencies for JUnit, Spring TestContext Framework, and Mockito, among others. Below is an example configuration for these dependencies:

```
<dependencyManagement>
    <dependencies>
        <dependency>
            <groupId>org.springframework.boot</groupId>
            <artifactId>spring-boot-dependencies</artifactId>
            <version>2.6.0</version>
            <type>pom</type>
            <scope>import</scope>
        </dependency>
    </dependencies>
</dependencyManagement>

<dependencies>
    <!-- JUnit Jupiter API -->
    <dependency>
        <groupId>org.junit.jupiter</groupId>
        <artifactId>junit-jupiter-api</artifactId>
        <scope>test</scope>
    </dependency>

    <!-- JUnit Jupiter Engine -->
    <dependency>
        <groupId>org.junit.jupiter</groupId>
        <artifactId>junit-jupiter-engine</artifactId>
        <scope>test</scope>
    </dependency>

    <!-- Spring TestContext Framework -->
    <dependency>
        <groupId>org.springframework.boot</groupId>
        <artifactId>spring-boot-starter-test</artifactId>
```

```
        <scope>test</scope>
        <exclusions>
            <exclusion>
                <groupId>org.junit.vintage</groupId>
                <artifactId>junit-vintage-engine</artifactId>
            </exclusion>
        </exclusions>
    </dependency>

    <!-- Mockito -->
    <dependency>
        <groupId>org.mockito</groupId>
        <artifactId>mockito-core</artifactId>
        <version>3.12.4</version>
        <scope>test</scope>
    </dependency>
</dependencies>
```

After adding the necessary dependencies to the build configuration, you need to annotate your test classes to integrate with the Spring TestContext Framework. This allows the Spring ApplicationContext to be automatically managed across your test cases. A basic configuration to enable Spring's integration with JUnit 5 can be achieved by using the SpringExtension.

```
import org.junit.jupiter.api.Test;
import org.junit.jupiter.api.extension.ExtendWith;
import org.springframework.test.context.junit.jupiter.SpringExtension;

@ExtendWith(SpringExtension.class)
public class ExampleTest {

    @Test
    void exampleTestMethod() {
        // Test logic here
    }
}
```

Ensuring that your test environment accurately reflects the deployment environment is critical for reliable testing. This is particularly true for integration tests, which necessitate the configuration of environment-specific properties and initialization procedures. Spring Boot facilitates externalized configurations through the application.properties or application.yml files, where environment-specific settings — such as database connections, port numbers, and other resources — can be configured.

Furthermore, the directory structure of your project must be organized to segregate application code from test code. A conventional Maven project structure achieves this by placing the application code in the src/main/java directory and the test code in the src/test/java directory. This separation ensures that test resources do not interfere with the main application code.

Tying into the subject of managing configurations, the use of profiles in Spring Boot allows you to define different environment settings, aiding in the setup of isolated test environments. A sample application-test.properties file can be used to define configuration properties specific to the testing environment:

```
# Database configurations
spring.datasource.url=jdbc:h2:mem:testdb
spring.datasource.driverClassName=org.h2.Driver
spring.datasource.username=sa
spring.datasource.password=password

# Hibernate configurations
spring.jpa.hibernate.ddl-auto=update
spring.jpa.show-sql=true
```

Incorporating the @ActiveProfiles annotation in your test classes can activate the appropriate profile for the testing environment:

```
import org.junit.jupiter.api.Test;
import org.junit.jupiter.api.extension.ExtendWith;
import org.springframework.test.context.ActiveProfiles;
import org.springframework.test.context.junit.jupiter.SpringExtension;

@ExtendWith(SpringExtension.class)
@ActiveProfiles("test")
public class ProfiledTest {

    @Test
    void testWithTestProfile() {
        // Test logic utilizing configurations defined in application-test.properties
    }
}
```

Effective integration of the described components and configurations constitutes a robust foundation for a test environment within the Spring Framework. This setup ensures consistent and reliable execution of tests, facilitating the identification and resolution of issues early in the development process.

9.3 Unit Testing with JUnit

JUnit is a widely adopted framework for unit testing in Java, and its seamless integration with the Spring Framework makes it a vital tool for developers. Unit testing ensures that individual components of an application function as intended, allowing for early detection of bugs and issues. In this section, we delve into the critical aspects of leveraging JUnit for unit testing in Spring applications.

JUnit Setup

Before implementing unit tests, it is essential to set up JUnit within a Spring project. Dependencies should be added to the pom.xml file if using Maven or build.gradle for Gradle-based projects. For Maven, the following dependencies are required:

```
<dependency>
    <groupId>org.junit.jupiter</groupId>
    <artifactId>junit-jupiter-engine</artifactId>
    <version>5.7.0</version>
    <scope>test</scope>
</dependency>
<dependency>
    <groupId>org.springframework.boot</groupId>
    <artifactId>spring-boot-starter-test</artifactId>
    <version>2.5.4</version>
    <scope>test</scope>
</dependency>
```

For Gradle, include the following in the build.gradle file:

```
testImplementation 'org.junit.jupiter:junit-jupiter-engine:5.7.0'
testImplementation 'org.springframework.boot:spring-boot-starter-test:2.5.4'
```

Writing a Basic Unit Test

A basic unit test in JUnit 5 is annotated with @Test, which marks the method as a test method. The @SpringBootTest annotation is used when testing Spring Boot applications to bootstrap the entire application context. Here's an illustration with a simple service class and its corresponding test class.

```
package com.example.demo.service;

import org.springframework.stereotype.Service;

@Service
public class CalculatorService {
    public int add(int a, int b) {
```

```
        return a + b;
    }

    public int subtract(int a, int b) {
        return a - b;
    }
}
```

The corresponding test class for CalculatorService would look like this:

```
package com.example.demo.service;

import org.junit.jupiter.api.Test;
import static org.junit.jupiter.api.Assertions.assertEquals;

public class CalculatorServiceTest {

    private final CalculatorService calculatorService = new CalculatorService();

    @Test
    void testAdd() {
        int result = calculatorService.add(2, 3);
        assertEquals(5, result);
    }

    @Test
    void testSubtract() {
        int result = calculatorService.subtract(5, 3);
        assertEquals(2, result);
    }
}
```

Assertions and Assumptions

JUnit 5 provides a variety of assertions to validate the expected outcomes of test cases. The most commonly used assertions include assertEquals, assertTrue, assertFalse, and assertNotNull, among others.

```
assertEquals(expected, actual);
assertTrue(condition);
assertFalse(condition);
assertNotNull(object);
```

Assumptions are conditional checks that determine whether a test should proceed. The Assumptions class provides methods such as assumeTrue and assumeFalse.

```
import org.junit.jupiter.api.Assumptions;

@Test
void whenSystemPropertyIsSet() {
```

```
    Assumptions.assumeTrue("CI".equals(System.getenv("ENV")));
    // test case logic here
}
```

Parameterized Tests

Parameterized tests allow running the same test multiple times with different input values. This is achieved using the @ParameterizedTest annotation and relevant sources such as @ValueSource, @CsvSource, or @MethodSource.

```
import org.junit.jupiter.params.ParameterizedTest;
import org.junit.jupiter.params.provider.ValueSource;
import static org.junit.jupiter.api.Assertions.assertTrue;

public class ParameterizedTestExample {

    @ParameterizedTest
    @ValueSource(strings = { "racecar", "radar", "level" })
    void palindromes(String candidate) {
        assertTrue(isPalindrome(candidate));
    }

    boolean isPalindrome(String str) {
        return str.equals(new StringBuilder(str).reverse().toString());
    }
}
```

Testing Exceptions

JUnit 5 provides a convenient way to test if a method throws an expected exception using the assertThrows method.

```
import org.junit.jupiter.api.Test;
import static org.junit.jupiter.api.Assertions.assertThrows;

public class ExceptionTesting {

    @Test
    void throwsException() {
        Exception exception = assertThrows(IllegalArgumentException.class, () ->
                {
            throw new IllegalArgumentException("Invalid argument");
        });
        assertEquals("Invalid argument", exception.getMessage());
    }
}
```

Mocking Dependencies

In unit tests, the goal is to isolate the class under test. Dependencies can be mocked using frameworks like Mockito to ensure that tests focus solely on the logic of the class being tested. Here's an example demonstrating how to mock dependencies using Mockito.

First, add Mockito to your project's dependencies. For Maven:

```
<dependency>
    <groupId>org.mockito</groupId>
    <artifactId>mockito-core</artifactId>
    <version>3.11.2</version>
    <scope>test</scope>
</dependency>
```

For Gradle:

```
testImplementation 'org.mockito:mockito-core:3.11.2'
```

Consider a service that relies on a repository:

```
package com.example.demo.service;

import org.springframework.beans.factory.annotation.Autowired;
import org.springframework.stereotype.Service;

@Service
public class UserService {

    private final UserRepository userRepository;

    @Autowired
    public UserService(UserRepository userRepository) {
        this.userRepository = userRepository;
    }

    public User findUserById(Long id) {
        return userRepository.findById(id).orElse(null);
    }
}
```

The test class with a mocked repository:

```
package com.example.demo.service;

import static org.mockito.Mockito.*;
import static org.junit.jupiter.api.Assertions.*;

import com.example.demo.repository.UserRepository;
import com.example.demo.model.User;
import org.junit.jupiter.api.Test;
import org.mockito.InjectMocks;
import org.mockito.Mock;
import org.mockito.junit.jupiter.MockitoExtension;
```

```
import org.junit.jupiter.api.extension.ExtendWith;

@ExtendWith(MockitoExtension.class)
public class UserServiceTest {

    @Mock
    private UserRepository userRepository;

    @InjectMocks
    private UserService userService;

    @Test
    void testFindUserById() {
        User user = new User(1L, "John Doe");
        when(userRepository.findById(1L)).thenReturn(Optional.of(user));

        User result = userService.findUserById(1L);
        assertNotNull(result);
        assertEquals("John Doe", result.getName());
    }
}
```

This meticulous approach to unit testing with JUnit in Spring applications ensures robust validation of individual components, leading to more reliable and maintainable code.

9.4 Mocking Dependencies with Mockito

Mocking in unit tests allows developers to simulate the behavior of complex dependencies, isolating the unit under test. Mockito, a widely-used Java mocking framework, provides the necessary tools to mock dependencies efficiently, making unit tests both robust and straightforward.

Mockito Basics

To use Mockito, you must first include the Mockito library in your project dependencies. For a Maven project, include the following dependency in your pom.xml:

```
<dependency>
    <groupId>org.mockito</groupId>
    <artifactId>mockito-core</artifactId>
    <version>3.9.0</version>
    <scope>test</scope>
</dependency>
```

For a Gradle project, add the dependency in your build.gradle file:

```
testImplementation 'org.mockito:mockito-core:3.9.0'
```

Creating Mocks

In a typical Spring application, services and repositories are often injected into other beans using dependency injection. When writing unit tests, these injected dependencies need to be mocked to ensure the unit tests are focusing solely on the unit under test. Suppose we have a UserService class that depends on a UserRepository:

```
public class UserService {
    private final UserRepository userRepository;

    @Autowired
    public UserService(UserRepository userRepository) {
        this.userRepository = userRepository;
    }

    public User findUserById(Long id) {
        return userRepository.findById(id).orElse(null);
    }
}
```

To test the UserService class without requiring an actual UserRepository implementation or a database connection, we can use Mockito to create a mock UserRepository.

```
import static org.mockito.Mockito.*;
import static org.junit.jupiter.api.Assertions.*;

import org.junit.jupiter.api.BeforeEach;
import org.junit.jupiter.api.Test;
import org.mockito.InjectMocks;
import org.mockito.Mock;
import org.mockito.MockitoAnnotations;

class UserServiceTest {

    @Mock
    private UserRepository userRepository;

    @InjectMocks
    private UserService userService;

    @BeforeEach
    void setUp() {
        MockitoAnnotations.openMocks(this);
    }

    @Test
```

```
    void testFindUserById() {
        User user = new User(1L, "John Doe");
        when(userRepository.findById(1L)).thenReturn(Optional.of(user));

        User foundUser = userService.findUserById(1L);

        assertNotNull(foundUser);
        assertEquals("John Doe", foundUser.getName());
    }
}
```

The @Mock annotation creates a mock object for the UserRepository. The @InjectMocks annotation instructs Mockito to inject the mocks into the UserService. The MockitoAnnotations.openMocks(this) method initializes the annotated mocks.

Mocking Return Values

In the example above, the when(...).thenReturn(...) construct is used to specify the behavior of the mock UserRepository. You can mock different return values based on various input conditions. For instance:

```
@Test
void testFindUserById_NotFound() {
    when(userRepository.findById(2L)).thenReturn(Optional.empty());

    User foundUser = userService.findUserById(2L);

    assertNull(foundUser);
}
```

Here, when userRepository.findById(2L) is called, it returns Optional.empty(), simulating a scenario where the user is not found.

Verifying Interactions

Mockito also provides the capability to verify that certain methods on your mocks were called with specific arguments. This can be useful to ensure that interactions with dependencies are occurring as expected:

```
@Test
void testVerifyRepositoryInteraction() {
    userService.findUserById(1L);

    verify(userRepository).findById(1L);
    verify(userRepository, times(1)).findById(1L); // alternatively
}
```

In this example, verify(userRepository).findById(1L) checks that the findById method was invoked with the argument 1L.

Argument Matchers

Mockito allows the use of argument matchers to specify flexible verification or stub setups. Common matchers like any(), eq(), and isNull() enable you to write generalized tests:

```
@Test
void testArgumentMatchers() {
    when(userRepository.findById(anyLong())).thenReturn(Optional.of(new User
        (1L, "John Doe")));

    User foundUser = userService.findUserById(5L);

    assertNotNull(foundUser);
    assertEquals("John Doe", foundUser.getName());

    verify(userRepository).findById(anyLong());
}
```

anyLong() matches any Long argument passed to the findById method, while verify(userRepository).findById(anyLong()) ascertains that findById was called with any Long value.

Mocking complex dependencies with Mockito is crucial for writing isolated, reliable unit tests. By mastering these fundamental techniques, developers enhance the quality and maintainability of their Spring applications.

9.5 Using Spring TestContext Framework

The Spring TestContext Framework provides a robust foundation for creating and managing integration tests within the Spring ecosystem. This framework simplifies the process of loading application contexts, managing transactions, and injecting dependencies into tests. By integrating tightly with test frameworks such as JUnit and TestNG, Spring TestContext Framework ensures that tests are not only easy to configure but also maintainable over time.

The core component of the Spring TestContext Framework is the org.springframework.test.context.ContextConfiguration annotation which specifies how to load the application context for tests. It is typically used in conjunction with org.junit.runner.RunWith, which tells JUnit to run the test using a specific runner. For Spring-based tests, the SpringRunner is the preferred runner.

```
@RunWith(SpringRunner.class)
```

```
@ContextConfiguration(classes = MyAppConfig.class)
public class MyAppIntegrationTest {

    @Autowired
    private MyService myService;

    @Test
    public void testService() {
        String result = myService.performAction();
        assertEquals("Expected Result", result);
    }
}
```

In this example, MyAppIntegrationTest is an integration test that uses SpringRunner to load the Spring application context defined in MyAppConfig.class. The myService bean is injected into the test class, and the test method testService validates its behavior.

Annotations such as @Autowired for dependency injection and @Test for denoting test methods remain consistent with standard JUnit practices, ensuring seamless integration of Spring features.

Another useful annotation is @SpringBootTest, which bootstraps the entire Spring Boot application context. This annotation is particularly beneficial when the test requires a fully initialized Spring Boot context. It can be used as follows:

```
@RunWith(SpringRunner.class)
@SpringBootTest
public class ApplicationIntegrationTest {

    @Autowired
    private ApplicationContext context;

    @Test
    public void contextLoads() {
        assertNotNull(context);
    }
}
```

The @SpringBootTest annotation tells Spring Boot to look for a main configuration class and use that to start a Spring application context.

One common requirement in integration tests is transaction management. By using the @Transactional annotation, you can configure your tests to run within a database transaction that is rolled back after the test completes. This ensures that the database state remains consistent and isolated between tests.

```
@RunWith(SpringRunner.class)
@ContextConfiguration(classes = AppConfig.class)
@Transactional
public class TransactionalIntegrationTest {

    @Autowired
    private UserService userService;

    @Test
    public void testUserCreation() {
        userService.createUser("testUser");

        User user = userService.findUser("testUser");
        assertNotNull(user);

        // Transaction will be rolled back after the test
    }
}
```

The @Transactional annotation automatically rolls back any transactions started in the testUserCreation method, ensuring that the user created in the test does not persist beyond the test's scope.

For more complex scenarios, the TestPropertySource annotation allows you to define custom properties for your tests, overriding properties defined in the application configuration. This annotation is instrumental when you need to adjust certain properties to suit the test environment.

```
@RunWith(SpringRunner.class)
@SpringBootTest
@TestPropertySource(properties = {"spring.datasource.url=jdbc:h2:mem:testdb"
    })
public class CustomPropertyIntegrationTest {

    @Autowired
    private DataSource dataSource;

    @Test
    public void customPropertyTest() throws Exception {
        Connection connection = dataSource.getConnection();
        assertNotNull(connection);
        connection.close();
    }
}
```

In this example, TestPropertySource is used to override the default datasource.url property, setting it to an in-memory H2 database for the duration of the test.

Handling application context initialization and teardown efficiently is critical for test performance. Spring TestContext Framework provides lifecycle management methods, such as beforeTestClass, prepareTestInstance, beforeTestMethod, afterTestMethod, and afterTestClass. These methods enable fine-grained control over context management throughout the test lifecycle.

To reduce the overhead of repeatedly loading application contexts, Spring caches contexts by default, reusing them across different tests that request the same configuration. This caching mechanism significantly speeds up test execution.

Combining these features allows for powerful, maintainable integration tests that leverage the full capabilities of the Spring framework, ensuring your application's components work harmoniously together. The subtle application of lifecycle management, custom property settings, and transaction control forms the bedrock of effective Spring-based integration testing.

9.6 Integration Testing in Spring

Integration testing is critical for ensuring that different parts of the application work together as expected. While unit testing aims at isolating each part of the program and testing it separately, integration testing combines these parts and tests them as a whole to verify the interactions among them.

In Spring, integration testing typically involves the application context and its components such as controllers, services, and repositories. These tests verify that the Spring components correctly integrate within the application context, and the Spring environment is correctly configured.

To facilitate integration testing, Spring provides a rich set of features through the Spring TestContext Framework. This framework supports loading an application context, managing transactions, and caching contexts between tests to improve performance.

To illustrate the concepts of integration testing in Spring, consider the following steps:

- Setting up the Spring TestContext Framework
- Loading the application context

- Defining transaction management for tests
- Writing an integration test

To set up the Spring TestContext Framework, you need to include the relevant Spring Test dependencies in your pom.xml if you are using Maven:

```
<dependency>
    <groupId>org.springframework.boot</groupId>
    <artifactId>spring-boot-starter-test</artifactId>
    <scope>test</scope>
</dependency>
```

Next, annotate your test class to leverage Spring's testing support. Typically, you will use the @SpringBootTest annotation, which indicates that the test will use Spring Boot's context that includes auto-configuration. This annotation is crucial for bootstrapping the entire container and embedding the server, if applicable.

```
import org.springframework.boot.test.context.SpringBootTest;
import org.springframework.test.context.junit4.SpringRunner;
import org.junit.runner.RunWith;

@RunWith(SpringRunner.class)
@SpringBootTest
public class ApplicationContextTest {

    @Test
    public void contextLoads() {
        // Test if the context is loaded correctly.
    }
}
```

The @SpringBootTest annotation is flexible and can be customized as needed. One powerful capability includes controlling the environment properties for tests by using properties files or directly within the annotation, thereby modifying the context for testing purposes.

```
@SpringBootTest(properties = {"spring.config.name=testapplication"})
public class CustomContextTest {

    @Test
    public void contextLoads() {
        // Custom context test logic
    }
}
```

Transaction management in integration testing is handled using the

@Transactional annotation. By annotating a test method with @Transactional, Spring will start a transaction before the test method and roll it back after the test method finishes. This ensures that database state is consistent between tests.

```
import org.springframework.transaction.annotation.Transactional;

@SpringBootTest
public class TransactionalIntegrationTest {

    @Transactional
    @Test
    public void testServiceMethod() {
        // Call service method that involves database operations.
        // Assertions to check expected results.
    }
}
```

The use of @Transactional ensures each test method leaves no lasting impact on the database, making tests repeatable in a stable state.

For more complex test scenarios, you might need to set up mock components or specific configurations. Spring supports the use of @MockBean to replace certain beans within the context with mock implementations.

```
import org.springframework.boot.test.mock.mockito.MockBean;

@SpringBootTest
public class MockedBeanIntegrationTest {

    @MockBean
    private SomeService someService;

    @Test
    public void someTest() {
        // Define mock behavior
        when(someService.someMethod()).thenReturn(someValue);

        // Perform the integration test
        // Assertions to validate behavior
    }
}
```

In scenarios where the application context should be cached to enhance performance, the TestContext framework automatically caches the Spring context between test executions, eliminating the overhead of repeatedly constructing the context.

For example, testing a Spring controller in an integration test involves the following:

```
import static org.springframework.test.web.servlet.request.
    MockMvcRequestBuilders.*;
import static org.springframework.test.web.servlet.result.MockMvcResultMatchers
    .*;

import org.springframework.beans.factory.annotation.Autowired;
import org.springframework.boot.test.autoconfigure.web.servlet.
    AutoConfigureMockMvc;
import org.springframework.test.web.servlet.MockMvc;

@SpringBootTest
@AutoConfigureMockMvc
public class ControllerIntegrationTest {

    @Autowired
    private MockMvc mockMvc;

    @Test
    public void getSomeEntityTest() throws Exception {
        mockMvc.perform(get("/entities/1"))
               .andExpect(status().isOk())
               .andExpect(jsonPath("$.name").value("EntityName"));
    }
}
```

In this example, the @AutoConfigureMockMvc annotation configures the MockMvc object used to simulate HTTP requests and verify responses. This approach allows testing of the web layer without requiring a running server.

Through careful management of the Spring TestContext Framework, transaction handling, and dependency mocking, Spring facilitates comprehensive and efficient integration testing. This enables not only verification of individual units but also their interaction and integration within the application as a whole.

```
{
  "status": 200,
  "name": "EntityName"
}
```

The executed test verifies the correct endpoint behavior and the expected JSON response structure.

Continuing to build on the principles outlined, integration tests should aim for thoroughness, executing realistic scenarios to identify potential faults in the context configuration or inter-component interactions.

9.7 Testing Spring MVC Controllers

Testing Spring MVC controllers is an essential aspect of ensuring the robustness and accuracy of web applications built using the Spring Framework. Controllers are responsible for handling HTTP requests, processing data, and returning appropriate responses, typically in the form of views or RESTful outputs. Effective testing strategies for these controllers can significantly enhance the reliability of the application. This section delves into methods for unit testing and integration testing Spring MVC controllers, encompassing the use of MockMvc, Spring Boot Test, and other pertinent tools.

The MockMvc class is a powerful utility that enables testing Spring MVC controllers in a standalone setup without the necessity of deploying the entire application. This is advantageous as it allows for the simulation of HTTP requests and the verification of responses in a controlled environment.

To initiate MockMvc testing, begin by setting up the test environment, ensuring the inclusion of necessary dependencies in the pom.xml for Maven or build.gradle for Gradle.

For Maven:

```
<dependency>
    <groupId>org.springframework.boot</groupId>
    <artifactId>spring-boot-starter-test</artifactId>
    <scope>test</scope>
</dependency>
```

For Gradle:

```
testImplementation 'org.springframework.boot:spring-boot-starter-test'
```

Next, an example of a basic Spring MVC controller is necessary to illustrate the testing process.

```
@RestController
@RequestMapping("/api")
public class ExampleController {

    @GetMapping("/hello")
    public ResponseEntity<String> sayHello() {
        return new ResponseEntity<>("Hello, World!", HttpStatus.OK);
    }
}
```

For testing the ExampleController, instantiate MockMvc and set up a test class, leveraging JUnit 5 and Spring Boot Test.

```
@SpringBootTest
@AutoConfigureMockMvc
public class ExampleControllerTest {

    @Autowired
    private MockMvc mockMvc;

    @Test
    public void testSayHello() throws Exception {
        this.mockMvc.perform(get("/api/hello"))
                    .andExpect(status().isOk())
                    .andExpect(content().string("Hello, World!"));
    }
}
```

Here, the @SpringBootTest annotation initializes the full application context, and the @AutoConfigureMockMvc annotation configures MockMvc. The test method testSayHello() performs a GET request to the /api/hello endpoint and verifies that the HTTP status code is 200 OK and the response content is "Hello, World!".

For more complex scenarios, controllers interacting with services or repositories require mocking those dependencies. Utilize the Mockito framework to mock such components.

Consider an enhanced controller example with a service dependency:

```
@RestController
@RequestMapping("/api")
public class GreetingController {

    private final GreetingService greetingService;

    @Autowired
    public GreetingController(GreetingService greetingService) {
        this.greetingService = greetingService;
    }

    @GetMapping("/greet")
    public ResponseEntity<String> greet() {
        String greeting = greetingService.getGreeting();
        return new ResponseEntity<>(greeting, HttpStatus.OK);
    }
}
```

And the corresponding service interface and implementation:

```
public interface GreetingService {
```

```
    String getGreeting();
}

@Service
public class GreetingServiceImpl implements GreetingService {
    @Override
    public String getGreeting() {
        return "Greetings from Service!";
    }
}
```

Testing this setup requires the mocking of GreetingService within the test class:

```
@ExtendWith(MockitoExtension.class)
@SpringBootTest
@AutoConfigureMockMvc
public class GreetingControllerTest {

    @Autowired
    private MockMvc mockMvc;

    @MockBean
    private GreetingService greetingService;

    @Test
    public void testGreet() throws Exception {
        when(greetingService.getGreeting()).thenReturn("Mocked Greeting");

        this.mockMvc.perform(get("/api/greet"))
                    .andExpect(status().isOk())
                    .andExpect(content().string("Mocked Greeting"));
    }
}
```

The @MockBean annotation is utilized to create a mock instance of GreetingService within the Spring application context. The when method from Mockito is used to define the behavior of the mock service. This setup tests the controller's behavior when interacting with mocked services.

Additionally, integration testing can encompass the full context of the application to verify the complete flow. This includes loading a real application context and performing end-to-end tests.

```
@SpringBootTest(webEnvironment = SpringBootTest.WebEnvironment.
    RANDOM_PORT)
@AutoConfigureMockMvc
public class FullContextIntegrationTest {
```

```
    @Autowired
    private MockMvc mockMvc;

    @Test
    public void testFullContext() throws Exception {
        this.mockMvc.perform(get("/api/greet"))
                    .andExpect(status().isOk())
                    .andExpect(jsonPath("$.message").value("Greetings from
                        Service!"));
    }
}
```

Here, the @SpringBootTest annotation with webEnvironment set to SpringBootTest.WebEnvironment.RANDOM_PORT ensures that the application runs on a random port, providing a true integration testing environment. The jsonPath method from the org.springframework.test.web.servlet.result package can validate JSON responses.

For applications using Thymeleaf or other templating engines, verifying the rendered views is crucial. This is demonstrated using MockMvc with view resolvers.

```
@Controller
@RequestMapping("/view")
public class ViewController {

    @GetMapping("/home")
    public String home(Model model) {
        model.addAttribute("message", "Welcome to the Home Page");
        return "home";
    }
}
```

Testing such a controller involves verifying the view name and model attributes.

```
@WebMvcTest(ViewController.class)
public class ViewControllerTest {

    @Autowired
    private MockMvc mockMvc;

    @Test
    public void testHomeView() throws Exception {
        this.mockMvc.perform(get("/view/home"))
                    .andExpect(status().isOk())
                    .andExpect(view().name("home"))
                    .andExpect(model().attribute("message", "Welcome to the
                        Home Page"));
    }
```

```
}
```

The @WebMvcTest annotation focuses only on the web layer and does not load full application context, providing a lightweight testing environment for controller layers. Complete and thorough testing of Spring MVC controllers, comprising unit tests and integration tests, ensures the consistent and expected behavior of web applications, enhancing both reliability and maintainability.

9.8 Testing Spring Data Repositories

Testing Spring Data repositories effectively ensures the correct implementation of data access layers, promoting robustness and reliability in applications. This section delves into various approaches and best practices for testing repositories, emphasizing techniques that leverage Spring's powerful testing support.

Spring Data repositories abstract the data access code, enabling developers to focus on defining query methods rather than implementing database operations. To validate the functionality of these repositories, we primarily utilize unit tests, leveraging in-memory databases (such as H2) and integration tests, which utilize actual database engines. The former ensures rapid feedback during development, while the latter guarantees consistency with production environments.

Setting Up Testing Dependencies

Add the necessary dependencies in your pom.xml file to enable repository testing. Include JUnit, Spring Test, Spring Data JPA, and H2.

```
<dependency>
    <groupId>org.springframework.boot</groupId>
    <artifactId>spring-boot-starter-test</artifactId>
    <scope>test</scope>
</dependency>
<dependency>
    <groupId>com.h2database</groupId>
    <artifactId>h2</artifactId>
    <scope>test</scope>
</dependency>
<dependency>
    <groupId>org.springframework.boot</groupId>
    <artifactId>spring-boot-starter-data-jpa</artifactId>
</dependency>
```

Configuring the Repository Test Class

Annotation configuration enables the test class to load the application context with the necessary beans. The important annotations for this context are @RunWith and @DataJpaTest. The @DataJpaTest annotation focuses only on JPA components and configures an in-memory database by default.

```
import org.junit.jupiter.api.Test;
import org.springframework.beans.factory.annotation.Autowired;
import org.springframework.boot.test.autoconfigure.orm.jpa.DataJpaTest;
import org.springframework.test.context.junit.jupiter.SpringExtension;
import org.junit.jupiter.api.extension.ExtendWith;
import static org.assertj.core.api.Assertions.assertThat;

@ExtendWith(SpringExtension.class)
@DataJpaTest
public class UserRepositoryTest {

    @Autowired
    private UserRepository userRepository;

    // Test cases will be added here
}
```

Writing Repository Test Cases

Asserting repository behavior involves creating test cases for standard CRUD operations as well as custom query methods. The following demonstrates testing for a simple entity class User with properties id, name, and email.

```
import javax.persistence.Entity;
import javax.persistence.GeneratedValue;
import javax.persistence.GenerationType;
import javax.persistence.Id;

@Entity
public class User {
    @Id
    @GeneratedValue(strategy = GenerationType.IDENTITY)
    private Long id;

    private String name;
    private String email;

    // constructors, getters, setters
}
```

Next, assume a repository interface with custom query methods defined:

```
import org.springframework.data.jpa.repository.JpaRepository;

public interface UserRepository extends JpaRepository<User, Long> {
    User findByEmail(String email);
}
```

To test the repository, create the following methods in the UserRepositoryTest class:

```
@Test
public void testSaveUser() {
    User user = new User();
    user.setName("John Doe");
    user.setEmail("john.doe@example.com");

    User savedUser = userRepository.save(user);

    assertThat(savedUser).isNotNull();
    assertThat(savedUser.getId()).isNotNull();
    assertThat(savedUser.getName()).isEqualTo("John Doe");
    assertThat(savedUser.getEmail()).isEqualTo("john.doe@example.com");
}

@Test
public void testFindById() {
    User user = new User();
    user.setName("Jane Doe");
    user.setEmail("jane.doe@example.com");
    userRepository.save(user);

    User foundUser = userRepository.findById(user.getId()).orElse(null);

    assertThat(foundUser).isNotNull();
    assertThat(foundUser.getName()).isEqualTo("Jane Doe");
}

@Test
public void testFindByEmail() {
    User user = new User();
    user.setName("Jim Beam");
    user.setEmail("jim.beam@example.com");
    userRepository.save(user);

    User foundUser = userRepository.findByEmail("jim.beam@example.com");

    assertThat(foundUser).isNotNull();
    assertThat(foundUser.getName()).isEqualTo("Jim Beam");
}
```

Testing with a Real Database

While in-memory databases like H2 are time-efficient for rapid testing, they do not always replicate the exact behavior of production databases. Testing against a real database, such as PostgreSQL or MySQL, mitigates discrepancies and ensures that SQL queries and configurations work as expected.

To configure the test to use a real database, update the application properties under src/test/resources:

```
spring.datasource.url=jdbc:postgresql://localhost:5432/testdb
spring.datasource.username=testuser
spring.datasource.password=testpass
spring.jpa.hibernate.ddl-auto=create-drop
```

Ensure that the database service is running, and its schema is correctly set up for the tests to execute seamlessly. Modify the @DataJpaTest to include the properties file:

```
@DataJpaTest(properties = {
    "spring.datasource.url=jdbc:postgresql://localhost:5432/testdb",
    "spring.datasource.username=testuser",
    "spring.datasource.password=testpass"
})
```

Executing the test cases in this configuration validates that the repository interacts correctly with the actual database system.

Conclusions and Best Practices

In repository testing, focus on simplicity and avoid over-reliance on mocks, as it could lead to overlooking configuration and query issues. Use in-memory databases during development and real databases for integration testing stages to ensure comprehensive coverage. Maintain a clear separation of unit tests and integration tests, automating both to streamline the continuous integration and delivery pipeline. By adhering to these practices, repository testing will be both effective and maintainable, facilitating the reliable development of data access layers in Spring applications.

9.9 Testing Spring Security

When testing Spring Security configurations, it is essential to ensure that the security mechanisms implemented in the application are robust and behave as expected under various conditions. Spring Security provides comprehensive tools to facilitate testing security policies, roles, and access controls.

Spring Security testing primarily involves:

- Verifying authentication mechanisms.
- Testing authorization policies.
- Ensuring secure endpoints.
- Handling security contexts appropriately.

Authentication testing ensures that the system correctly identifies users. Typically, testing involves creating mock authentication tokens and validating successful and failed login attempts. Spring Security provides the SecurityMockMvcRequestPostProcessors class, which allows for simulating security contexts within MVC tests.

```
import static org.springframework.test.web.servlet.request.
    MockMvcRequestBuilders.get;
import static org.springframework.test.web.servlet.result.MockMvcResultMatchers.
    status;
import static org.springframework.security.test.web.servlet.request.
    SecurityMockMvcRequestPostProcessors.user;
import static org.springframework.security.test.web.servlet.request.
    SecurityMockMvcRequestPostProcessors.httpBasic;

@Test
public void givenUser_whenGetSecuredEndpoint_thenOk() throws Exception {
   mockMvc.perform(get("/secured-endpoint").with(user("user").password("
        password")))
          .andExpect(status().isOk());
}

@Test
public void givenWrongUser_whenGetSecuredEndpoint_thenUnauthorized()
    throws Exception {
   mockMvc.perform(get("/secured-endpoint").with(httpBasic("wrongUser", "
        wrongPassword")))
          .andExpect(status().isUnauthorized());
}
```

In the above tests, we simulate a user trying to access a secured endpoint, verifying both successful authorization and rejection scenarios.

Authorization testing focuses on ensuring that users with different roles and permissions can access or are denied specific resources appropriately. This can be done by configuring MockMvc to simulate various roles.

```
@Test
```

```
public void givenAdminRole_whenGetAdminEndpoint_thenOk() throws
        Exception {
    mockMvc.perform(get("/admin").with(user("admin").roles("ADMIN")))
            .andExpect(status().isOk());
}

@Test
public void givenUserRole_whenGetAdminEndpoint_thenForbidden() throws
        Exception {
    mockMvc.perform(get("/admin").with(user("user").roles("USER")))
            .andExpect(status().isForbidden());
}
```

In these tests, an admin user is granted access to the "/admin" endpoint, while a regular user attempting the same access is forbidden.

When writing unit tests that involve secured methods, it is often necessary to mock the security context. This ensures that the security aspect can be tested independently of the actual user authentication process.

```
import org.springframework.security.test.context.support.WithMockUser;
import static org.junit.jupiter.api.Assertions.assertEquals;

@Test
@WithMockUser(username = "testUser", roles = {"USER"})
public void givenMockUser_whenCallSecuredMethod_thenSuccess() {
    String result = securedService.securedMethod();
    assertEquals("Expected Result", result);
}
```

Using the @WithMockUser annotation, we can define a mock user with specified roles, allowing the test to focus on the business logic within the security context.

Method-level security is tested to ensure that method invocations are properly guarded by security constraints such as @PreAuthorize and @Secured annotations. Spring Security provides the @TestConfiguration annotation to simplify this process.

```
import org.springframework.security.access.prepost.PreAuthorize;

public class SecuredService {

    @PreAuthorize("hasRole('ADMIN')")
    public String adminOnlyMethod() {
        return "Admin Content";
    }
}

@TestConfiguration
```

```
public static class MethodSecurityConfig extends
    GlobalMethodSecurityConfiguration {
    // Configuration details
}

@Test
@WithMockUser(roles = "ADMIN")
public void givenAdminRole_whenCallAdminMethod_thenSuccess() {
    assertEquals("Admin Content", securedService.adminOnlyMethod());
}

@Test
@WithMockUser(roles = "USER")
public void givenUserRole_whenCallAdminMethod_thenAccessDenied() {
    assertThrows(AccessDeniedException.class, () -> {
        securedService.adminOnlyMethod();
    });
}
```

The MethodSecurityConfig class and GlobalMethodSecurityConfiguration help set up method security configurations for tests, allowing for effective validation of @PreAuthorize functionality.

For applications developed with Spring WebFlux, the WebTestClient can be used to test security configurations. WebTestClient is naturally asynchronous and is suited for non-blocking web applications.

```
@WebFluxTest
public class SecurityWebFluxTests {

    @Autowired
    private WebTestClient webTestClient;

    @Test
    public void whenNoCredentials_thenUnauthorized() {
        webTestClient.get().uri("/secured-endpoint")
                .exchange()
                .expectStatus().isUnauthorized();
    }

    @Test
    public void whenValidCredentials_thenAuthorized() {
        webTestClient.get().uri("/secured-endpoint")
                .headers(headers -> headers.setBasicAuth("user", "password"))
                .exchange()
                .expectStatus().isOk();
    }
}
```

Using WebTestClient, we can effectively test authorization for endpoints in a reactive application, thereby covering authentication and authorization mechanisms seamlessly.

OK

Given these methods and tools, rigorous testing of Spring Security guarantees that the application's security configuration remains robust across various scenarios and user interactions, ensuring protection and reliability in real-world deployments.

9.10 Testing with Spring Boot

Spring Boot provides a comprehensive testing framework that simplifies the process of writing and running tests in Spring applications. Spring Boot's testing features include support for various testing libraries and frameworks, auto-configuration of tests, and utilities for managing test data.

To start testing with Spring Boot, it is essential to understand the structure and components involved. Here we explore the main features and strategies for effective testing using Spring Boot.

Setting Up Test Dependencies

To enable testing in a Spring Boot application, include the necessary dependencies in the pom.xml file for Maven or build.gradle for Gradle. The typical dependencies required are Spring Boot Starter Test and JUnit.

For Maven:

```
<dependency>
    <groupId>org.springframework.boot</groupId>
    <artifactId>spring-boot-starter-test</artifactId>
    <scope>test</scope>
</dependency>
```

For Gradle:

```
testImplementation 'org.springframework.boot:spring-boot-starter-test'
```

These dependencies include JUnit, Spring Test, AssertJ, Hamcrest, Mockito, and other useful libraries for testing purposes.

Writing Unit Tests

Unit tests in Spring Boot are similar to standard Spring applications. A basic unit test for a service class can be written using JUnit and Mockito for mocking dependencies.

Consider the following service class:

```
@Service
public class UserService {

    @Autowired
    private UserRepository userRepository;

    public User findUserById(Long id) {
        return userRepository.findById(id).orElse(null);
    }
}
```

The corresponding unit test can be written as follows:

```
@RunWith(SpringRunner.class)
@SpringBootTest
public class UserServiceTest {

    @MockBean
    private UserRepository userRepository;

    @Autowired
    private UserService userService;

    @Test
    public void testFindUserById() {
        User user = new User();
        user.setId(1L);
        Mockito.when(userRepository.findById(1L)).thenReturn(Optional.of(user))
            ;

        User result = userService.findUserById(1L);
        assertEquals(1L, result.getId().longValue());
    }
}
```

In the test class, the @SpringBootTest annotation is used to enable Spring Boot features. The @MockBean annotation is utilized to mock UserRepository, and the @Autowired annotation injects the UserService to be tested.

Writing Integration Tests

Integration tests in Spring Boot verify that different components of the application work together as expected. Spring Boot provides the necessary tools to load the application context and perform tests within it.

Consider an integration test for a controller class:

```
@RestController
@RequestMapping("/api/users")
public class UserController {

    @Autowired
    private UserService userService;

    @GetMapping("/{id}")
    public ResponseEntity<User> getUserById(@PathVariable Long id) {
        User user = userService.findUserById(id);
        if (user == null) {
            return ResponseEntity.notFound().build();
        }
        return ResponseEntity.ok(user);
    }
}
```

The integration test for the UserController can be written as follows:

```
@RunWith(SpringRunner.class)
@SpringBootTest(webEnvironment = SpringBootTest.WebEnvironment.
    RANDOM_PORT)
public class UserControllerIT {

    @Autowired
    private TestRestTemplate testRestTemplate;

    @MockBean
    private UserService userService;
    @Test
    public void testGetUserById() {
        User user = new User();
        user.setId(1L);
        Mockito.when(userService.findUserById(1L)).thenReturn(user);

        ResponseEntity<User> response = testRestTemplate.getForEntity("/api/
            users/1", User.class);
        assertEquals(HttpStatus.OK, response.getStatusCode());
        assertEquals(1L, response.getBody().getId().longValue());
    }
}
```

In this integration test, @SpringBootTest is used to load the application context, and TestRestTemplate is used to make HTTP requests to the UserController. The @MockBean annotation is employed to mock UserService.

Testing with Slices

Spring Boot includes specialized test annotations called *Test annotations that facilitate testing a particular layer of the application in isolation. For example, @WebMvcTest focuses on web layer testing and @DataJpaTest for testing JPA repositories.

Using @WebMvcTest:

```
@RunWith(SpringRunner.class)
@WebMvcTest(UserController.class)
public class UserControllerSliceTest {

    @Autowired
    private MockMvc mockMvc;

    @MockBean
    private UserService userService;

    @Test
    public void testGetUserById() throws Exception {
        User user = new User();
        user.setId(1L);
        Mockito.when(userService.findUserById(1L)).thenReturn(user);

        mockMvc.perform(MockMvcRequestBuilders.get("/api/users/1"))
                .andExpect(status().isOk())
                .andExpect(jsonPath("$.id").value(1L));
    }
}
```

This test leverages @WebMvcTest to focus on the web layer without loading the entire application context. The MockMvc utility is used for simulating HTTP requests.

Using @DataJpaTest:

```
@RunWith(SpringRunner.class)
@DataJpaTest
public class UserRepositoryTest {

    @Autowired
    private TestEntityManager entityManager;

    @Autowired
    private UserRepository userRepository;

    @Test
    public void testFindById() {
        User user = new User();
        user.setId(1L);
        entityManager.persistAndFlush(user);

        Optional<User> foundUser = userRepository.findById(1L);
```

```
        assertTrue(foundUser.isPresent());
        assertEquals(1L, foundUser.get().getId().longValue());
    }
}
```

@DataJpaTest is used to configure the application context with JPA components, focusing on testing the repository layer. The TestEntityManager is used to interact with the entity manager to manage test data.

Testing with Spring Boot is designed to be straightforward and systematic. By understanding and utilizing the provided annotations and utilities, you can write effective and comprehensive tests that ensure the reliability and stability of your Spring Boot applications.

9.11 Using Testcontainers for Integration Tests

In traditional integration testing within the Spring framework, one might encounter limitations when dealing with external resources like databases, message queues, or REST APIs. Testcontainers provide a robust and flexible solution to these challenges by enabling the automatic creation of disposable Docker containers for testing purposes. This approach ensures that tests are run in an environment that closely mirrors the production setting without the manual setup overhead or the persistence of changes across tests.

To begin using Testcontainers in a Spring application, it is crucial to add the necessary dependencies to the build configuration. For a Maven-based project, this involves including the following dependencies in the pom.xml file:

```
<dependency>
    <groupId>org.testcontainers</groupId>
    <artifactId>testcontainers</artifactId>
    <version>1.15.3</version>
    <scope>test</scope>
</dependency>
<dependency>
    <groupId>org.testcontainers</groupId>
    <artifactId>junit-jupiter</artifactId>
    <version>1.15.3</version>
    <scope>test</scope>
</dependency>
<dependency>
```

```
    <groupId>org.testcontainers</groupId>
    <artifactId>mysql</artifactId>
    <version>1.15.3</version>
    <scope>test</scope>
</dependency>
```

For a Gradle-based project, these dependencies should be added to the build.gradle file:

```
testImplementation 'org.testcontainers:testcontainers:1.15.3'
testImplementation 'org.testcontainers:junit-jupiter:1.15.3'
testImplementation 'org.testcontainers:mysql:1.15.3'
```

Once the dependencies are configured, you can proceed to define and manage Docker containers directly within your test classes. Here, we provide a detailed example of leveraging Testcontainers to start a MySQL container for integration testing.

```
import org.junit.jupiter.api.Test;
import org.junit.jupiter.api.extension.ExtendWith;
import org.springframework.beans.factory.annotation.Autowired;
import org.springframework.boot.test.context.SpringBootTest;
import org.springframework.test.context.junit.jupiter.SpringExtension;
import org.springframework.test.context.DynamicPropertyRegistry;
import org.springframework.test.context.DynamicPropertySource;
import org.testcontainers.containers.MySQLContainer;
import org.testcontainers.junit.jupiter.Container;
import org.testcontainers.junit.jupiter.Testcontainers;

import javax.sql.DataSource;

import static org.assertj.core.api.Assertions.assertThat;

@Testcontainers
@SpringBootTest
@ExtendWith(SpringExtension.class)
public class MySQLContainerTest {

    @Container
    public static MySQLContainer<?> mysqlContainer = new MySQLContainer
        <>("mysql:8.0.26")
            .withDatabaseName("testdb")
            .withUsername("testuser")
            .withPassword("testpass");

    @DynamicPropertySource
    static void mysqlProperties(DynamicPropertyRegistry registry) {
        registry.add("spring.datasource.url", mysqlContainer::getJdbcUrl);
        registry.add("spring.datasource.username", mysqlContainer::getUsername);
        registry.add("spring.datasource.password", mysqlContainer::getPassword);
    }
```

```
    @Autowired
    DataSource dataSource;

    @Test
    void testDatabaseConnection() throws Exception {
        assertThat(dataSource.getConnection().isValid(1)).isTrue();
    }
}
```

Let us break down the key aspects of this code:

- MySQLContainer: This class is used to create and configure a MySQL Docker container. The builder pattern is employed to set the database name, username, and password.
- @Container: This annotation manages the lifecycle of the test container. The container is started before tests are run and stopped afterward.
- @DynamicPropertySource: Spring dynamically sets the properties for the datasource URL, username, and password, managing the necessary integration with the running container.
- DataSource: The Spring DataSource bean is autowired, allowing for interaction with the configured database in test methods.
- @Testcontainers: This annotation ensures that Testcontainers-based tests are properly initialized.
- @SpringBootTest and @ExtendWith: These annotations boot up the Spring context and integrate with JUnit 5.

To enhance functionality, Testcontainers offer modules for various technologies such as PostgreSQL, Redis, Kafka, and more. Employing these specialized containers follows the same pattern shown in the MySQL example, enabling developers to easily swap out components for different external systems.

Integration testing with Testcontainers allows the verification of interactions with external services in an isolated, repeatable environment. This alignment with real-world conditions strengthens the reliability and robustness of Spring applications. The usage of dynamically managed Docker containers ensures that tests remain independent and clean, accurately reflecting dependencies defined in production configurations.

9.12 Best Practices for Testing in Spring

Effective testing is critical to maintaining the quality and robustness of Spring applications. Adhering to best practices ensures not only that the test suite is thorough and reliable but also that it remains maintainable and performant as the application evolves. This section outlines key principles and techniques to achieve these objectives in the context of the Spring Framework.

1. Write Tests Early and Often

Testing should not be an afterthought. Begin writing tests during the early stages of development. Creating tests in tandem with the application code leads to better-designed, more testable code. Employ Test-Driven Development (TDD) where feasible, which emphasizes writing a test before the actual implementation code. This approach helps to clarify requirements and drives the development process in small, manageable increments.

2. Keep Tests Isolated

Ensure that each test is isolated and independent. An individual test should not depend on the outcome of other tests. Spring's dependency injection makes it easier to configure and manage the necessary state without relying on the global application state. Use embedded or in-memory databases like H2 for tests that interact with the database, which allows the database state to be easily reset between tests.

3. Mock External Dependencies

External dependencies such as databases, file systems, or web services should be mocked to speed up tests and avoid flaky test behavior due to network issues or other external factors. Mockito can be extensively used for creating mock objects and defining their behavior. The @Mock and @InjectMocks annotations facilitate clear and maintainable mock configurations.

```
@RunWith(MockitoJUnitRunner.class)
public class UserServiceTest {

    @Mock
    private UserRepository userRepository;

    @InjectMocks
    private UserService userService;

    @Test
```

```
    public void testFindUserById() {
        User user = new User(1L, "John Doe");
        Mockito.when(userRepository.findById(1L)).thenReturn(Optional.of(user))
            ;

        User result = userService.findUserById(1L);
        Assert.assertEquals("John Doe", result.getName());
    }
}
```

4. Use the Spring TestContext Framework Correctly

The Spring TestContext Framework simplifies testing by providing consistent support for loading and configuring Spring IoC containers. When using @SpringBootTest or other test annotations, take care to load application contexts only as necessary to avoid impacting test performance. Tests that do not require full application context can use @WebMvcTest or @DataJpaTest to load only the specific slices relevant to the test.

5. Write Integration Tests for Critical Paths

While unit tests are important for individual components, integration tests are essential for validating system-wide behavior. Focus integration tests on critical paths and core business logic. Use Spring's @SpringBootTest annotation to bootstrap the entire application context for such tests, ensuring that all layers from controllers to repositories are appropriately wired and tested together.

6. Validate Security Configurations

Testing security configurations is crucial for ensuring that access controls and permissions are correctly enforced. Spring Security test support provides mock authentication and HTTP requests to validate security settings. Use annotations such as @WithMockUser to simulate various user roles and permissions during tests.

```
@WebMvcTest(MyController.class)
public class MyControllerTest {

    @Autowired
    private MockMvc mockMvc;

    @Test
    @WithMockUser(username = "admin", roles = {"ADMIN"})
    public void testAdminAccess() throws Exception {
        mockMvc.perform(get("/admin"))
                .andExpect(status().isOk());
    }
```

```
    @Test
    @WithMockUser(username = "user", roles = {"USER"})
    public void testUserAccessDenied() throws Exception {
        mockMvc.perform(get("/admin"))
                .andExpect(status().isForbidden());
    }
}
```

7. Leverage Testcontainers for Realistic Integration Testing

For more realistic integration tests, consider using Testcontainers to run Docker containers during tests. This approach allows you to test against a variety of environments such as different database versions or cloud services, enhancing the authenticity of the tests.

```
@Testcontainers
public class MyRepositoryTest {

    @Container
    public static PostgreSQLContainer<?> postgreSQLContainer = new
         PostgreSQLContainer<>("postgres:latest")
        .withDatabaseName("mydb")
        .withUsername("user")
        .withPassword("password");

    @Autowired
    private MyRepository myRepository;

    @Test
    public void testSave() {
        MyEntity entity = new MyEntity();
        entity.setName("test");
        myRepository.save(entity);

        List<MyEntity> entities = myRepository.findAll();
        Assert.assertFalse(entities.isEmpty());
    }
}
```

8. Pay Attention to Performance

Keep an eye on the performance of your test suite. Long-running tests can slow down the development process and deter developers from running the full suite often. Profile and identify slow tests. Where possible, optimize tests by reducing unnecessary context loads and eliminating redundant setup tasks.

9. Maintain a Clean Codebase for Tests

Just like production code, test code should be clean, readable, and maintainable. Follow standard coding conventions, use meaningful names for test methods, and keep tests small and focused. Ensure that test data setup is clear and concise, and leverage reusable methods or fixtures to avoid duplication.

10. Continuously Review and Refactor Tests

Testing is an ongoing process. Regularly review and refactor your tests to ensure they remain relevant and efficient as the application changes. Add new tests for new features and functionalities, and remove outdated tests that no longer provide value. Foster a culture of accountability where all team members are responsible for the health of the test suite.

Implementing these practices consistently will lead to a robust, reliable, and maintainable test suite that not only verifies your application's correctness but also serves as a valuable tool for continuous integration and deployment.

Chapter 10

Microservices with Spring Cloud

This chapter explores the implementation of microservices architecture using Spring Cloud. It starts with setting up a Spring Cloud project and covers building microservices with Spring Boot. Key components such as Eureka for service discovery, Ribbon for client-side load balancing, and Feign for inter-service communication are discussed. The chapter also addresses Spring Cloud Config for centralized configuration management, circuit breakers with Hystrix, and API Gateway with Zuul. It includes tracing and monitoring with Spring Cloud Sleuth, deployment strategies, and concludes with best practices for developing and managing microservices using Spring Cloud.

10.1 Introduction to Microservices Architecture

Microservices architecture represents an evolution in software design that aims to tackle the limitations of monolithic architectures. This paradigm involves breaking down applications into smaller, independently deployable services that communicate over well-defined APIs. Each microservice is designed to fulfill a specific business capability and operates as a separate deployable unit.

The microservices approach has several distinct properties:

- **Decentralized Data Management**: Each microservice manages its database, which allows for a decoupled data model, increasing flexibility and scalability. For example, an e-commerce system may have different databases for orders, products, and customers.
- **Independent Deployment**: Microservices can be developed, deployed, and scaled independently, which reduces the risks associated with deploying changes. This is particularly beneficial in a continuous delivery environment.
- **Fault Isolation**: Because microservices are isolated, a fault in one service does not propagate across the system, thus enhancing robustness. Failure in the payment service would not affect the inventory service.
- **Technology Diversity**: Different microservices can be built with different programming languages and technologies best suited for their specific tasks. This polyglot environment allows teams to leverage the latest advancements in technology.

To gain deeper insights, let's consider how these properties manifest in a typical microservices-based application.

Example: An Online Retailer

Imagine an online retailer application. In a monolithic architecture, this application might involve a single, large codebase handling user authentication, product catalog, order processing, payment, and shipping.

In contrast, with a microservices architecture, this application is split into clearly defined services:

- **User Service**: Manages user accounts, profiles, and authentication.
- **Product Service**: Handles the product catalog, including product details and inventory status.
- **Order Service**: Manages order creation, updates, and history.
- **Payment Service**: Processes payments and handles payment gateways.

- **Shipping Service**: Manages shipping logistics, tracking, and notifications.

Service Communication

Inter-service communication in microservices is generally achieved via lightweight mechanisms such as HTTP/REST or messaging queues. For instance, when a user places an order, the Order Service may communicate with the Product Service to check inventory availability and the Payment Service to process the payment.

Consider a simple inter-service communication using RESTful APIs:

```
@RestController
public class OrderController {

    @Autowired
    private RestTemplate restTemplate;

    @PostMapping("/createOrder")
    public ResponseEntity<Order> createOrder(@RequestBody OrderRequest
        orderRequest) {
        // Check product availability
        String productServiceUrl = "http://product-service/products/" +
            orderRequest.getProductId();
        ResponseEntity<Product> response = restTemplate.getForEntity(
            productServiceUrl, Product.class);

        if (response.getStatusCode() == HttpStatus.OK && response.getBody().
            isAvailable()) {
            // Process Order
            Order order = orderService.createOrder(orderRequest);
            return new ResponseEntity<>(order, HttpStatus.CREATED);
        } else {
            return new ResponseEntity<>(HttpStatus.BAD_REQUEST);
        }
    }
}
```

In this code snippet, the Order Service uses a RestTemplate to call the Product Service and check the availability of a product before creating an order.

Microservices Challenges

Despite its advantages, microservices architecture also introduces several complexities:

- **Service Management**: The increased number of deployable units requires effective service discovery and management solutions.

- **Data Consistency**: Maintaining consistent data across distributed services can be challenging, often requiring eventual consistency and distributed transactions.
- **Monitoring and Debugging**: Observability tools are essential to monitor, trace, and debug an inherently more complex system.
- **Security**: Each service needs to be secured individually, demanding robust security practices such as authentication, authorization, and encryption.

Understanding microservices architecture provides a foundation for leveraging the Spring Cloud ecosystem effectively. By decomposing applications into smaller services, we can create systems that are scalable, resilient, and easier to manage. Subsequent sections will delve into specific tools and techniques within the Spring Cloud framework that facilitate the development and management of microservices, including service discovery, load balancing, and inter-service communication.

10.2 Overview of Spring Cloud

Spring Cloud is an extensive suite designed to simplify the development of distributed systems. The primary focus of Spring Cloud is on providing tools for managing the inherent complexity that arises when building microservices architectures. Spring Cloud offers a comprehensive framework for developing microservices in Java while integrating seamlessly with the Spring Boot ecosystem.

Spring Cloud components are structured to support the varied architectural needs of microservices, including service registration and discovery, load balancing, configuration management, and circuit breaking. By leveraging existing libraries and best practices, Spring Cloud streamlines microservices development, enabling scalable and resilient applications.

A key element of Spring Cloud is its modular structure, where each module addresses a specific concern of microservices architecture. This modularity enables developers to apply only what is necessary for their particular use case.

- **Service Discovery and Registration:** Spring Cloud facilitates the detection and registration of services through Eureka, a service registry maintained by Netflix. Eureka server acts as a service registry, while Eureka clients register themselves and periodically send heartbeats to indicate their availability. This dynamic nature of service discovery simplifies the interaction between microservices and ensures robustness in case of service instance failures.

```
// Application class with Eureka Client
@SpringBootApplication
@EnableEurekaClient
public class Application {
    public static void main(String[] args) {
        SpringApplication.run(Application.class, args);
    }
}
```

- **Client-Side Load Balancing:** Spring Cloud integrates Ribbon, another Netflix library, for client-side load balancing. Ribbon allows various client-side routing strategies, including round-robin, weighted, and zone-based load balancing. This approach distributes client requests across available service instances, optimizing resource utilization and improving response times.

```
// RestTemplate bean with load-balanced configuration
@Configuration
public class RibbonConfig {
    @LoadBalanced
    @Bean
    public RestTemplate restTemplate() {
        return new RestTemplate();
    }
}
```

- **Inter-Service Communication:** Feign, a declarative web service client, simplifies making HTTP calls to other microservices. Feign abstracts complexities by allowing developers to define service interfaces and ensuring type safety. Combined with Ribbon and Eureka, Feign handles load balancing and service discovery automatically.

```
// Feign client interface for communication
```

```
@FeignClient(name = "service-name")
public interface ServiceClient {
    @RequestMapping(method = RequestMethod.GET, value = "/endpoint")
    String getResponseFromService();
}
```

- **Centralized Configuration Management:** Spring Cloud Config provides server and client-side support for externalized configuration in a distributed system. Using a central configuration server, configurations can be stored in a version-controlled repository such as Git. This approach ensures consistent configuration across all microservices and simplifies management.

```
// Spring Cloud Config server configuration
server:
  port: 8888
spring:
  cloud:
    config:
      server:
        git:
          uri: https://github.com/user/config-repo
          cloneOnStart: true
```

- **Fault Tolerance and Circuit Breakers:** Hystrix, another Netflix OSS component, is integrated into Spring Cloud to provide fault tolerance and resilience. By acting as a circuit breaker, Hystrix prevents cascading failures across microservices by isolating failures and providing fallback mechanisms.

```
// Service method with Hystrix command
@Service
public class MyService {
    @HystrixCommand(fallbackMethod = "fallback")
    public String callService() {
        // Call remote service
    }

    public String fallback() {
        return "Fallback response";
    }
}
```

- **API Gateway:** Zuul, yet another Netflix OSS component, functions as an edge service in Spring Cloud, acting as an API Gateway. Zuul handles routing, monitoring, resiliency, and security.

It serves as a single entry point for all client requests, simplifying the interaction with backend services and providing a unified interface.

```
// Zuul configuration
zuul:
  routes:
    service1:
      path: /service1/**
      url: http://localhost:8081
    service2:
      path: /service2/**
      url: http://localhost:8082
```

- **Tracing and Monitoring:** Spring Cloud Sleuth enables distributed tracing for Spring applications. By adding tracing headers to HTTP requests, Sleuth allows tracking the flow of requests across microservices, aiding in monitoring and debugging.

```
// Sample configuration of Sleuth
spring:
  sleuth:
    sampler:
      probability: 0.1
```

The integration of these components within Spring Cloud provides a robust platform for developing microservices-based applications. Each module's functionality ensures scalability, robustness, and maintainability of distributed systems, allowing developers to focus on implementing business logic while relying on Spring Cloud to handle infrastructural complexities.

10.3 Setting Up a Spring Cloud Project

Spring Cloud offers a suite of tools for building and managing microservices architectures. Setting up a Spring Cloud project involves creating a foundational architecture that supports microservices development and integration. This section outlines the detailed steps for initializing and configuring a Spring Cloud project with a focus on establishing a base for subsequent development.

1. Initializing a Spring Cloud Project

First, create a new Spring Boot application using Spring Initializr, which can be accessed via start.spring.io. Choose project metadata as follows:

- Project: Maven Project
- Language: Java
- Spring Boot: Choose the latest stable version
- Group: com.example
- Artifact: spring-cloud-project
- Name: spring-cloud-project
- Dependencies: Eureka Server, Spring Web, Config Server

Download the generated project and unzip it to a convenient location on your development environment.

2. Configuring the Maven pom.xml

Open the pom.xml file in your preferred Integrated Development Environment (IDE). Add the Spring Cloud dependencies and specify the Spring Cloud version using the dependency management tag as shown below:

```
<dependencyManagement>
    <dependencies>
        <dependency>
            <groupId>org.springframework.cloud</groupId>
            <artifactId>spring-cloud-dependencies</artifactId>
            <version>Hoxton.SR8</version>
            <type>pom</type>
            <scope>import</scope>
        </dependency>
    </dependencies>
</dependencyManagement>

<dependencies>
    <dependency>
        <groupId>org.springframework.cloud</groupId>
        <artifactId>spring-cloud-starter-netflix-eureka-server</artifactId>
    </dependency>
    <dependency>
        <groupId>org.springframework.cloud</groupId>
        <artifactId>spring-cloud-starter-config</artifactId>
    </dependency>
    <dependency>
```

```
        <groupId>org.springframework.boot</groupId>
        <artifactId>spring-boot-starter-web</artifactId>
    </dependency>
</dependencies>
```

3. Setting Up the Eureka Server

In the Spring Cloud project, configure the Eureka Server, which will act as the service registry. Open the application.properties file (or application.yml if you prefer YAML format) and add the following configuration:

```
server.port=8761
eureka.client.register-with-eureka=false
eureka.client.fetch-registry=false
```

Next, enable the Eureka Server in your main Spring Boot application class using the @EnableEurekaServer annotation. Update the main application class as follows:

```
package com.example.springcloudproject;

import org.springframework.boot.SpringApplication;
import org.springframework.boot.autoconfigure.SpringBootApplication;
import org.springframework.cloud.netflix.eureka.server.EnableEurekaServer;

@SpringBootApplication
@EnableEurekaServer
public class SpringCloudProjectApplication {
    public static void main(String[] args) {
        SpringApplication.run(SpringCloudProjectApplication.class, args);
    }
}
```

4. Configuring Spring Cloud Config Server

Add the necessary configuration to set up the Config Server, which provides centralized configuration management. Open the application.properties file again and add:

```
server.port=8888
spring.cloud.config.server.git.uri=https://github.com/example/config-repo
```

Create a new class to enable the Config Server by using the @EnableConfigServer annotation:

```
package com.example.springcloudproject;

import org.springframework.boot.SpringApplication;
import org.springframework.boot.autoconfigure.SpringBootApplication;
```

```
import org.springframework.cloud.config.server.EnableConfigServer;

@SpringBootApplication
@EnableConfigServer
public class SpringCloudConfigServer {
    public static void main(String[] args) {
        SpringApplication.run(SpringCloudConfigServer.class, args);
    }
}
```

5. Creating a Simple Microservice

With the Eureka Server and Config Server up and running, the next step involves creating a simple microservice that registers with Eureka. Use Spring Initializr again to generate a new Spring Boot application with the following dependencies:

- Eureka Discovery Client
- Spring Web

In the pom.xml of the newly created microservice, add the same dependency management block for Spring Cloud:

```
<dependencies>
    <dependency>
        <groupId>org.springframework.cloud</groupId>
        <artifactId>spring-cloud-starter-netflix-eureka-client</artifactId>
    </dependency>
    <dependency>
        <groupId>org.springframework.boot</groupId>
        <artifactId>spring-boot-starter-web</artifactId>
    </dependency>
</dependencies>
```

Configure Eureka client properties in the microservice's application.properties:

```
spring.application.name=simple-microservice
eureka.client.serviceUrl.defaultZone=http://localhost:8761/eureka/
```

To enable Eureka client functionality, annotate the main application class with @EnableEurekaClient:

```
package com.example.simplemicroservice;

import org.springframework.boot.SpringApplication;
import org.springframework.boot.autoconfigure.SpringBootApplication;
import org.springframework.cloud.netflix.eureka.EnableEurekaClient;
```

```
@SpringBootApplication
@EnableEurekaClient
public class SimpleMicroserviceApplication {
    public static void main(String[] args) {
        SpringApplication.run(SimpleMicroserviceApplication.class, args);
    }
}
```

Finally, verify the integration by running the Eureka Server, Config Server, and the simple microservice. Access the Eureka dashboard at http://localhost:8761 to confirm that the simple microservice has registered successfully. Use the Spring Boot logs to ensure all services start correctly and interact as expected.

Through these steps, you establish a foundational Spring Cloud project that supports Eureka-based service discovery and management, enabling further microservices development.

10.4 Building Microservices with Spring Boot

Java Spring Boot facilitates building production-ready microservices swiftly by providing a suite of pre-configured, opinionated setups. It abstracts much of the boilerplate code, allowing developers to focus on implementing business logic. This section delves into practical aspects of creating microservices using Spring Boot, from initializing a project to writing and testing microservices.

When starting a new microservice, the first step is to set up a Spring Boot project. Spring Initializr (available at https://start.spring.io) is a useful tool for generating boilerplate code. It allows you to select dependencies specific to your microservice. For the purposes of this discussion, we'll include the following starter dependencies: web, actuator, and devtools. Each dependency plays a critical role:

- web: Integrates Spring MVC and other useful libraries to build RESTful services.
- actuator: Adds production-ready features such as metrics, health checks, and monitoring.
- devtools: Simplifies development by enabling live reload and other developer-friendly features.

After generating the project and importing it into an IDE (such as IntelliJ IDEA or Eclipse), the project structure will look as follows:

```
src
├── main
│   ├── java
│   │   └── com.example.microservice
│   │       └── MicroserviceApplication.java
│   └── resources
│       └── application.properties
└── test
    └── java
        └── com.example.microservice
            └── MicroserviceApplicationTests.java
```

The MicroserviceApplication.java class serves as the entry point of the Spring Boot application. It is annotated with @SpringBootApplication, which is a composite annotation encompassing @Configuration, @EnableAutoConfiguration, and @ComponentScan. Review the class below:

```
package com.example.microservice;

import org.springframework.boot.SpringApplication;
import org.springframework.boot.autoconfigure.SpringBootApplication;

@SpringBootApplication
public class MicroserviceApplication {
    public static void main(String[] args) {
        SpringApplication.run(MicroserviceApplication.class, args);
    }
}
```

A key element in microservices is the RESTful API. To create a REST controller, define a class annotated with @RestController and map endpoints using @RequestMapping or shorthand annotations like @GetMapping, @PostMapping, etc. Below is an example demonstrating a basic controller:

```
package com.example.microservice.controller;

import org.springframework.web.bind.annotation.GetMapping;
import org.springframework.web.bind.annotation.RequestMapping;
import org.springframework.web.bind.annotation.RestController;

@RestController
@RequestMapping("/api")
public class HelloController {

    @GetMapping("/hello")
    public String sayHello() {
        return "Hello, World!";
    }
}
```

Here, a simple endpoint /api/hello is created that returns a "Hello, World!" message. You can run the application and access this endpoint via a web browser or a tool like curl or Postman to observe the output.

Adding more complexity often involves interacting with databases. Spring Boot simplifies this with Spring Data JPA. Include spring-boot-starter-data-jpa as a dependency in your pom.xml. Set up the database configuration in application.properties:

```
spring.datasource.url=jdbc:mysql://localhost:3306/microservice
spring.datasource.username=root
spring.datasource.password=yourpassword
spring.jpa.hibernate.ddl-auto=update
```

Define an entity class and a corresponding repository. For instance, consider a simple User entity and a UserRepository:

```
package com.example.microservice.entity;

import javax.persistence.Entity;
import javax.persistence.GeneratedValue;
import javax.persistence.GenerationType;
import javax.persistence.Id;

@Entity
public class User {

    @Id
    @GeneratedValue(strategy = GenerationType.IDENTITY)
    private Long id;
    private String name;
    private String email;
```

```
    // getters and setters
}
```

```
package com.example.microservice.repository;

import org.springframework.data.jpa.repository.JpaRepository;
import com.example.microservice.entity.User;

public interface UserRepository extends JpaRepository<User, Long> {
}
```

With these classes in place, you can integrate repository methods within your controller to perform CRUD operations. Below is an enhanced version of HelloController to handle users:

```
package com.example.microservice.controller;

import com.example.microservice.entity.User;
import com.example.microservice.repository.UserRepository;
import org.springframework.beans.factory.annotation.Autowired;
import org.springframework.http.ResponseEntity;
import org.springframework.web.bind.annotation.*;

import java.util.List;

@RestController
@RequestMapping("/api/users")
public class UserController {

    @Autowired
    private UserRepository userRepository;

    @GetMapping
    public List<User> getAllUsers() {
        return userRepository.findAll();
    }

    @PostMapping
    public User createUser(@RequestBody User user) {
        return userRepository.save(user);
    }

    @GetMapping("/{id}")
    public User getUserById(@PathVariable Long id) {
        return userRepository.findById(id).orElseThrow(() -> new
                ResourceNotFoundException("User not found"));
    }

    @PutMapping("/{id}")
    public User updateUser(@PathVariable Long id, @RequestBody User
        userDetails) {
```

```
        User user = userRepository.findById(id).orElseThrow(() -> new
                ResourceNotFoundException("User not found"));
        user.setName(userDetails.getName());
        user.setEmail(userDetails.getEmail());
        return userRepository.save(user);
    }

    @DeleteMapping("/{id}")
    public ResponseEntity<Void> deleteUser(@PathVariable Long id) {
        User user = userRepository.findById(id).orElseThrow(() -> new
                ResourceNotFoundException("User not found"));
        userRepository.delete(user);
        return ResponseEntity.noContent().build();
    }
}
```

Microservices should be independently deployable and scalable. Implement application-specific logic, configure necessary dependencies, and test meticulously. The endpoints provided should be thoroughly validated using unit tests and integration tests. Here is an example of a unit test for the HelloController:

```
package com.example.microservice;

import com.example.microservice.controller.HelloController;
import org.junit.jupiter.api.Test;
import org.springframework.beans.factory.annotation.Autowired;
import org.springframework.boot.test.autoconfigure.web.servlet.WebMvcTest;
import org.springframework.test.web.servlet.MockMvc;

import static org.springframework.test.web.servlet.request.
    MockMvcRequestBuilders.get;
import static org.springframework.test.web.servlet.result.MockMvcResultMatchers.
    content;
import static org.springframework.test.web.servlet.result.MockMvcResultMatchers.
    status;

@WebMvcTest(HelloController.class)
public class HelloControllerTest {

    @Autowired
    private MockMvc mockMvc;

    @Test
    public void testSayHello() throws Exception {
        this.mockMvc.perform(get("/api/hello"))
                .andExpect(status().isOk())
                .andExpect(content().string("Hello, World!"));
    }
}
```

Spring Boot assists in creating robust microservices with minimal configuration. By leveraging its range of starter projects and powerful dependency management, developers can quickly implement, test, and deploy microservices.

10.5 Service Discovery with Eureka

Service discovery is a fundamental concept in microservices architecture. It allows services to dynamically discover and communicate with each other without hardcoding the network locations. Spring Cloud Eureka, a part of the Netflix OSS suite, provides a robust service registry and discovery mechanism. In this section, we will delve into the details of setting up and using Eureka for service discovery.

Eureka consists of two main components: the Eureka Server, which acts as the service registry, and the Eureka Client, which registers itself with the server and queries the registry to discover other services.

Setting Up Eureka Server
To implement a Eureka Server, we need to create a Spring Boot application and include the necessary dependencies. The following code snippet in the pom.xml file includes the Eureka Server dependency:

```
<dependencies>
    <dependency>
        <groupId>org.springframework.cloud</groupId>
        <artifactId>spring-cloud-starter-netflix-eureka-server</artifactId>
    </dependency>
</dependencies>
```

Next, we need to annotate the main application class with @EnableEurekaServer:

```
import org.springframework.boot.SpringApplication;
import org.springframework.boot.autoconfigure.SpringBootApplication;
import org.springframework.cloud.netflix.eureka.server.EnableEurekaServer;

@SpringBootApplication
@EnableEurekaServer
public class EurekaServerApplication {
    public static void main(String[] args) {
        SpringApplication.run(EurekaServerApplication.class, args);
    }
}
```

The final step in setting up the Eureka Server is to configure it in the application.yml file. Typically placed in the resources directory, this configuration file includes server-specific properties. Below is an example configuration:

```
server:
  port: 8761

eureka:
  instance:
    hostname: localhost
  client:
    registerWithEureka: false
    fetchRegistry: false
  server:
    waitTimeInMsWhenSyncEmpty: 0
```

Setting Up Eureka Client

Once the Eureka Server is up and running, we can set up Eureka Clients. Each microservice that needs to register with the Eureka Server will be a Eureka Client. First, include the Eureka Client dependency in the pom.xml file:

```
<dependencies>
    <dependency>
        <groupId>org.springframework.cloud</groupId>
        <artifactId>spring-cloud-starter-netflix-eureka-client</artifactId>
    </dependency>
</dependencies>
```

Next, annotate the main application class with @EnableEurekaClient:

```
import org.springframework.boot.SpringApplication;
import org.springframework.boot.autoconfigure.SpringBootApplication;
import org.springframework.cloud.netflix.eureka.EnableEurekaClient;

@SpringBootApplication
@EnableEurekaClient
public class EurekaClientApplication {
    public static void main(String[] args) {
        SpringApplication.run(EurekaClientApplication.class, args);
    }
}
```

Finally, configure the client in the application.yml file:

```
server:
  port: 8080

spring:
  application:
    name: service-name
```

```
eureka:
  client:
    serviceUrl:
      defaultZone: http://localhost:8761/eureka/
  instance:
    preferIpAddress: true
```

Discovering Services

Eureka Clients can discover other services registered with the Eureka Server. We use Spring Cloud's built-in client-side service discovery mechanism to achieve this. For example, to call one service from another, we use the DiscoveryClient interface provided by Spring Cloud.

First, autowire the DiscoveryClient in a Spring-managed bean:

```
import org.springframework.beans.factory.annotation.Autowired;
import org.springframework.cloud.client.discovery.DiscoveryClient;
import org.springframework.web.bind.annotation.GetMapping;
import org.springframework.web.bind.annotation.RestController;

import java.util.List;

@RestController
public class ServiceDiscoveryController {

    @Autowired
    private DiscoveryClient discoveryClient;

    @GetMapping("/discover")
    public List<String> discoverServices() {
        return this.discoveryClient.getServices();
    }
}
```

The getServices() method retrieves a list of service IDs for all registered services. We can also retrieve instances of a particular service by using the getInstances(String serviceId) method:

```
import org.springframework.beans.factory.annotation.Autowired;
import org.springframework.cloud.client.discovery.DiscoveryClient;
import org.springframework.cloud.client.ServiceInstance;
import org.springframework.web.bind.annotation.GetMapping;
import org.springframework.web.bind.annotation.PathVariable;
import org.springframework.web.bind.annotation.RestController;

import java.util.List;

@RestController
public class ServiceDiscoveryController {
```

```
    @Autowired
    private DiscoveryClient discoveryClient;

    @GetMapping("/discover/{serviceId}")
    public List<ServiceInstance> discoverServiceInstances(@PathVariable String
        serviceId) {
        return this.discoveryClient.getInstances(serviceId);
    }
}
```

The ServiceInstance class provides methods to get the metadata of each instance, such as hostname, port, and URI.

Eureka Dashboard

Eureka provides a web-based dashboard for monitoring registered services, available at http://<eureka-server-host>:<port>. This dashboard displays all the services and their instances, along with their status. This feature is useful for visualizing the health and availability of the services in the system.

Handling Failures

Eureka is designed to handle dynamic microservice environments. It has built-in mechanisms for handling service failures and network partitions. Clients periodically send heartbeat signals to the server. If the server misses several consecutive heartbeats, it considers the service instance as unavailable and removes it from the registry.

These heartbeat intervals and the number of missed heartbeats allowed before an instance is considered down can be configured in the application.yml:

```
eureka:
  instance:
    leaseRenewalIntervalInSeconds: 10
    leaseExpirationDurationInSeconds: 30
```

Maintaining a robust, dynamic service discovery mechanism is crucial for the effective functioning of microservices architecture. Eureka, with its server and client components, offers such a mechanism, ensuring seamless service discovery and fault tolerance.

10.6 Client-Side Load Balancing with Ribbon

Client-side load balancing, implemented through Ribbon, is a key feature in a microservices architecture that ensures even distribution of traffic across multiple service instances. Ribbon is a client-side load balancer created by Netflix, and it is integrated with Spring Cloud to enhance scalability and reliability.

When a service calls another service, it often needs to distribute requests across a set of instances. Ribbon plays a crucial role in optimizing this distribution to prevent any single instance from becoming a bottleneck.

Firstly, to integrate Ribbon into a Spring Cloud project, you need to add the necessary dependencies to your pom.xml file. Include the following Maven dependency to enable Ribbon:

```
<dependency>
    <groupId>org.springframework.cloud</groupId>
    <artifactId>spring-cloud-starter-netflix-ribbon</artifactId>
</dependency>
```

Ribbon can automatically leverage service discovery mechanisms provided by Eureka. Once Ribbon knows how to locate services via Eureka, it can distribute requests among available instances.

Assume you have a Eureka server running and registered some services. Let's illustrate how a service can use Ribbon for load balancing. Consider a service OrderService consuming the InventoryService. In the OrderService application configuration file (application.properties or application.yml), define the Ribbon client as follows:

```
# application.properties
inventory-service.ribbon.listOfServers=http://localhost:8081,http://localhost:8082
```

Alternatively, if you are using YAML:

```
# application.yml
inventory-service:
  ribbon:
    listOfServers: http://localhost:8081,http://localhost:8082
```

This manual list can be replaced when utilizing a service registry like Eureka, where Ribbon automatically retrieves the list of available instances. Next, configure RestTemplate to use Ribbon for load balancing by annotating a configuration class with @LoadBalanced:

```
@Configuration
public class RibbonConfiguration {

    @Bean
    @LoadBalanced
    RestTemplate restTemplate() {
        return new RestTemplate();
    }
}
```

The @LoadBalanced annotation tells Spring Cloud to use Ribbon to handle service-to-service calls. Now, all calls made using this RestTemplate instance will be load-balanced. For instance, in the OrderService, make a call to the InventoryService as follows:

```
@Autowired
private RestTemplate restTemplate;

public InventoryResponse getInventoryForProduct(String productId) {
    return restTemplate.getForObject("http://inventory-service/inventory/" +
            productId, InventoryResponse.class);
}
```

By default, Ribbon uses a round-robin strategy for load balancing, but you can customize this behavior with custom rules. Implementing custom rules is done by configuring the IRule interface. Spring Cloud Ribbon provides several built-in rules such as:

- RoundRobinRule: Distributes requests across each instance in round-robin fashion.
- AvailabilityFilteringRule: Filters out instances that are deemed "circuit tripped" or have high concurrent connections and then uses round-robin for the rest.
- WeightedResponseTimeRule: Assigns a weight based on the response time and uses it to distribute requests.
- RetryRule: Retries a failed request on different instances.

To apply a custom rule, override the default configuration within your application configuration class:

```
@Configuration
public class CustomRibbonConfiguration {
```

```
    @Bean
    public IRule ribbonRule() {
        return new AvailabilityFilteringRule();
    }
}
```

If your microservices ecosystem already employs a configuration service such as Spring Cloud Config, Ribbon configurations can also be externalized.

```
# application.yml in Spring Cloud Config
inventory-service:
  ribbon:
    NFLoadBalancerRuleClassName: com.netflix.loadbalancer.
        AvailabilityFilteringRule
```

This integration ensures that Ribbon uses the AvailabilityFilteringRule to determine which instances should receive the incoming traffic.

Testing load-balanced requests in local development environments requires simulating multiple instances. One approach is to run multiple instances of a service on different ports and list them under the Ribbon configuration.

When properly configured, Ribbon significantly increases the resilience and scalability of your application. By distributing requests evenly across multiple instances and implementing fault tolerance mechanisms, microservices handle higher loads and provide seamless user experiences even under varying traffic conditions.

Finally, monitoring the performance of Ribbon and the effectiveness of your load balancing strategies is vital. Tools like Spring Cloud Sleuth and Zipkin offer valuable telemetry data, tracing requests across services to ensure optimal load distribution.

10.7 Inter-Service Communication with Feign

Inter-service communication is a foundational aspect of microservices architecture, enabling different services to interact seamlessly. In Spring Cloud, Feign is a declarative web service client that simplifies the process of making HTTP calls between services. It integrates tightly with other Spring Cloud components, such as Eureka for service discovery and Ribbon for load balancing.

Feign reduces the boilerplate code required to communicate with other services and supports powerful features like request compression, pluggable encoders and decoders, and integration with Ribbon for load balancing. This section delves into how Feign works, its configuration, and practical implementation in a Spring Cloud application.

To start using Feign, include the necessary dependencies in your project. The 'spring-cloud-starter-openfeign' dependency enables Feign in a Spring Boot application.

```
<dependency>
    <groupId>org.springframework.cloud</groupId>
    <artifactId>spring-cloud-starter-openfeign</artifactId>
</dependency>
```

After adding the dependency, enable Feign clients in your application by using the '@EnableFeignClients' annotation. This annotation scans for interfaces that declare they are Feign clients using the '@FeignClient' annotation.

```
@SpringBootApplication
@EnableFeignClients
public class Application {
    public static void main(String[] args) {
        SpringApplication.run(Application.class, args);
    }
}
```

Declare a Feign client interface that specifies how to call the external service. Use the '@FeignClient' annotation to define the service interface and its configurations.

```
@FeignClient(name = "user-service", url = "http://localhost:8081")
public interface UserServiceClient {

    @RequestMapping(method = RequestMethod.GET, value = "/users/{id}",
        consumes = "application/json")
    User getUserById(@PathVariable("id") Long id);
}
```

In this example, 'UserServiceClient' is a Feign client interface that communicates with the 'user-service'. The '@FeignClient' annotation specifies the name of the service and its URL. The 'getUserById' method is mapped to an HTTP GET request to the '/users/id' endpoint, consuming a JSON response.

To use the Feign client in your service, inject it using '@Autowired' and call its methods like a regular Java service.

```
@Service
public class OrderService {

    @Autowired
    private UserServiceClient userServiceClient;

    public OrderDetail getOrderDetail(Long orderId) {
        User user = userServiceClient.getUserById(orderId);
        // Additional code to fetch and assemble OrderDetail
        return new OrderDetail(orderId, user);
    }
}
```

Feign clients communicate with services registered in the Eureka server, removing the need to hardcode service URLs. Use the '@FeignClient(name = "user-service")' annotation without specifying the URL, allowing Feign to fetch the service's location from Eureka.

Enable Eureka service discovery by including the 'spring-cloud-starter-netflix-eureka-client' dependency:

```
<dependency>
    <groupId>org.springframework.cloud</groupId>
    <artifactId>spring-cloud-starter-netflix-eureka-client</artifactId>
</dependency>
```

Then, configure your application to register with Eureka by adding the 'eureka.client' properties to your 'application.yml' or 'application.properties' file:

```
eureka:
  client:
    serviceUrl:
      defaultZone: http://localhost:8761/eureka/
```

With these configurations, Feign can discover services dynamically from Eureka, facilitating robust and scalable inter-service communication.

Feign also supports advanced features like request interceptors, custom error decoders, and Hystrix integration for circuit breaking.

Use request interceptors to add headers, such as authentication tokens, to every request. Implement the 'RequestInterceptor' interface and define custom logic in the 'apply' method:

```
public class AuthRequestInterceptor implements RequestInterceptor {
    @Override
    public void apply(RequestTemplate template) {
```

```
        template.header("Authorization", "Bearer " + getToken());
    }

    private String getToken() {
        // Logic to fetch or generate token
        return "some-auth-token";
    }
}
```

Register the interceptor as a bean in your configuration class:

```
@Configuration
public class FeignConfig {

    @Bean
    public AuthRequestInterceptor authRequestInterceptor() {
        return new AuthRequestInterceptor();
    }
}
```

Custom error decoders handle errors more effectively, providing detailed error messages or custom exceptions. Implement the 'ErrorDecoder' interface to define custom error-handling logic:

```
public class CustomErrorDecoder implements ErrorDecoder {

    private final ErrorDecoder defaultDecoder = new Default();

    @Override
    public Exception decode(String methodKey, Response response) {
        if (response.status() == 404) {
            return new NotFoundException("Resource not found");
        }
        return defaultDecoder.decode(methodKey, response);
    }
}
```

Register the custom error decoder as a bean in your configuration class:

```
@Configuration
public class FeignConfig {

    @Bean
    public CustomErrorDecoder customErrorDecoder() {
        return new CustomErrorDecoder();
    }
}
```

Integrate Feign with Hystrix for circuit breaking by enabling Hystrix in your application with the '@EnableCircuitBreaker' annotation and configure Hystrix properties in your 'application.yml' or 'application.properties' file. Annotate Feign client methods with '@HystrixCommand' to define fallback methods for handling failure scenarios.

```
@FeignClient(name = "user-service", fallback = UserServiceFallback.class)
public interface UserServiceClient {

    @RequestMapping(method = RequestMethod.GET, value = "/users/{id}",
        consumes = "application/json")
    User getUserById(@PathVariable("id") Long id);
}
```

Define the fallback class to handle failures gracefully:

```
@Component
public class UserServiceFallback implements UserServiceClient {

    @Override
    public User getUserById(Long id) {
        return new User(id, "Unknown", "User"); // Default fallback user
    }
}
```

These approaches make Feign a powerful tool for inter-service communication in microservices, providing simplicity, flexibility, and resilience.

10.8 Configuring Microservices with Spring Cloud Config

Spring Cloud Config provides server-side and client-side support for externalized configuration in a distributed system. By offering a centralized configuration service, it allows the uniform management of environment-specific properties, resulting in consistent configurations across microservices. In this section, we will explore the key aspects of using Spring Cloud Config to configure microservices.

To start, one must set up a Spring Cloud Config Server. The Config Server supplies configuration properties to client applications in a Spring Boot microservices architecture.

```
@SpringBootApplication
@EnableConfigServer
```

```
public class ConfigServerApplication {
    public static void main(String[] args) {
        SpringApplication.run(ConfigServerApplication.class, args);
    }
}
```

The @EnableConfigServer annotation is crucial as it activates the Spring Cloud Config Server.

Next, we configure the server application. In the bootstrap.yml or application.yml file of the Config Server, it is imperative to specify the location of the configuration files. This can be a local file system, Git, SVN, or a database. Below is an example using a Git-based configuration repository:

```
spring:
  cloud:
    config:
      server:
        git:
          uri: https://github.com/your-repo/config-repo
```

The directory config-repo in the specified Git repository holds the configuration files. Each microservice reads its properties from a file named after its application name, typically in the format application-{profile}.yml or application-{profile}.properties.

A sample application-dev.yml in the repository could look like:

```
server:
  port: 8081

spring:
  datasource:
    url: jdbc:mysql://localhost:3306/dev_db
    username: dev_user
    password: dev_pass
```

The microservice accessing this configuration must know the location of the Config Server. This is configured in the microservice's bootstrap.yml:

```
spring:
  application:
    name: service-name

  cloud:
    config:
      uri: http://localhost:8888
```

The spring.application.name field should match with the configuration file name prefix in the Git repository. The property spring.cloud.config.uri is the URL of the Config Server.

Once configured, services can access these properties in a typical Spring Boot fashion:

```
@Value("${server.port}")
private String serverPort;

@Value("${spring.datasource.url}")
private String datasourceUrl;
```

For refreshing configurations without restarting the microservice, Spring Cloud Config supports the /actuator/refresh endpoint. This endpoint is enabled by including the spring-boot-starter-actuator dependency and configuring it as follows:

```
management:
  endpoints:
    web:
      exposure:
        include: refresh
```

POST requests to /actuator/refresh will reload the configuration properties dynamically.

```
$ curl -X POST http://localhost:8081/actuator/refresh
```

For enhanced security, ensure the configuration files do not contain sensitive information directly. Instead, use secure locations or encrypted properties. Spring Cloud Config supports property encryption. To encrypt a property, use the Spring Cloud CLI or any tool supporting JCE.

First, generate encryption keys:

```
$ keytool -genkeypair -alias config-server-key -keyalg RSA
  -dname "CN=Config Server, OU=Config, O=Spring Cloud, L=City, S=State, C=Country"
  -keypass mypassword -keystore config-server.jks -storepass mypassword
```

Then, encrypt properties:

```
$ echo "my_password" | ./spring-cloud-cli encrypt mysecret
```

In the configuration file, use the {cipher} prefix for encrypted properties:

```
spring:
  datasource:
    password: '{cipher}FRj92ndlk9vQ=='
```

Decrypt via the Config Server's private key.

By leveraging Spring Cloud Config, microservices configuration becomes centralized and more manageable, ensuring consistency and simplifying updates across distributed environments.

10.9 Circuit Breakers with Hystrix

Circuit breakers are a critical pattern for building robust microservices. They prevent an application from repeatedly trying to execute an operation likely to fail, allowing it to recover more quickly and gracefully. In Spring Cloud, Hystrix serves as such an implementation of this pattern. It is designed to isolate points of access to remote systems, services, or third-party libraries, stopping cascading failures and providing fallback options.

Why Circuit Breakers?

In a microservices architecture, services may fail for several reasons, including network issues, server downtimes, or resource unavailability. Without circuit breakers, a failed service can propagate failures throughout the architecture, creating a cascading effect that may overload the system. By employing circuit breakers, we can detect failures and provide alternative responses or logic to maintain system stability.

Integrating Hystrix with Spring Boot

To integrate Hystrix into your Spring Boot application, follow these steps:

- **Add Hystrix dependency:** Ensure you include the necessary dependencies in your pom.xml.

```
<dependency>
    <groupId>org.springframework.cloud</groupId>
    <artifactId>spring-cloud-starter-netflix-hystrix</artifactId>
</dependency>
```

- **Enable Hystrix:** Use the @EnableHystrix annotation to enable Hystrix in your Spring Boot application.

```
import org.springframework.boot.SpringApplication;
import org.springframework.boot.autoconfigure.SpringBootApplication;
```

```
import org.springframework.cloud.netflix.hystrix.EnableHystrix;

@SpringBootApplication
@EnableHystrix
public class Application {
    public static void main(String[] args) {
        SpringApplication.run(Application.class, args);
    }
}
```

- **Create a service with Hystrix commands:** Use the @HystrixCommand annotation to wrap methods in Hystrix commands.

```
import com.netflix.hystrix.contrib.javanica.annotation.HystrixCommand;
import org.springframework.stereotype.Service;

@Service
public class MyService {

    @HystrixCommand(fallbackMethod = "fallbackMethod")
    public String performOperation() {
        if (someCondition) {
            throw new RuntimeException("Failure occurred!");
        }
        return "Operation Successful";
    }

    public String fallbackMethod() {
        return "Fallback response";
    }
}
```

Configuring Hystrix

Hystrix provides several configuration options which can be specified in your application.properties or application.yml file. Here are some commonly used properties:

- hystrix.command.default.execution.isolation.thread.timeoutInMillisecond Defines the timeout duration in milliseconds for the execution of a Hystrix command.

- hystrix.command.default.circuitBreaker.requestVolumeThreshold: Specifies the minimum number of requests within a defined period before the circuit breaker will consider tripping.

- hystrix.command.default.circuitBreaker.sleepWindowInMilliseconds:

Sets the duration to wait after a circuit breaker event before allowing further attempts to execute the command.

- hystrix.command.default.circuitBreaker.errorThresholdPercentage: Determines the error percentage at which the circuit breaker will trip.

```
hystrix.command.default.execution.isolation.thread.timeoutInMilliseconds=2000
hystrix.command.default.circuitBreaker.requestVolumeThreshold=10
hystrix.command.default.circuitBreaker.sleepWindowInMilliseconds=5000
hystrix.command.default.circuitBreaker.errorThresholdPercentage=50
```

Monitoring Hystrix with Hystrix Dashboard and Turbine

Hystrix provides real-time monitoring of metrics in a visually appealing dashboard. To enable the Hystrix dashboard, include the following dependency in your pom.xml:

```
<dependency>
    <groupId>org.springframework.cloud</groupId>
    <artifactId>spring-cloud-starter-netflix-hystrix-dashboard</artifactId>
</dependency>
```

Then, create a simple Spring Boot application annotated with @EnableHystrixDashboard:

```
import org.springframework.boot.SpringApplication;
import org.springframework.boot.autoconfigure.SpringBootApplication;
import org.springframework.cloud.netflix.hystrix.dashboard.
     EnableHystrixDashboard;

@SpringBootApplication
@EnableHystrixDashboard
public class HystrixDashboardApplication {
    public static void main(String[] args) {
        SpringApplication.run(HystrixDashboardApplication.class, args);
    }
}
```

To aggregate Hystrix metrics from multiple services, use Turbine. Include the following dependency:

```
<dependency>
    <groupId>org.springframework.cloud</groupId>
    <artifactId>spring-cloud-starter-netflix-turbine</artifactId>
</dependency>
```

Enable Turbine in your application with @EnableTurbine:

```
import org.springframework.boot.SpringApplication;
import org.springframework.boot.autoconfigure.SpringBootApplication;
import org.springframework.cloud.netflix.turbine.EnableTurbine;

@SpringBootApplication
@EnableTurbine
public class TurbineApplication {
    public static void main(String[] args) {
        SpringApplication.run(TurbineApplication.class, args);
    }
}
```

Configurations for Turbine can be added in application.properties:

```
turbine.aggregator.clusterConfig=default
turbine.clusterNameExpression=new String("default")
turbine.instanceUrlSuffix=:8080/actuator/hystrix.stream
```

These configurations allow Hystrix Dashboard and Turbine to monitor and aggregate metrics from your microservices, providing insights into their health and performance.

Circuit breakers, backed by Hystrix in Spring Cloud, are indispensable for building resilient microservices architectures. Configuring them properly and monitoring their state ensures operational stability and helps maintain service reliability.

10.10 API Gateway with Zuul

The API Gateway pattern is fundamental in microservices architecture, acting as an entry point for all client interactions with the back-end services. Zuul, a component of Spring Cloud, provides a gateway service built by Netflix. Zuul serves several essential functions, including dynamic routing, monitoring, resiliency, security, and more.

Zuul simplifies the complexity of managing and routing client requests to various microservices through a single endpoint. This configuration ensures that back-end services do not need to handle client-specific logic, thus enabling a cleaner separation of concerns. In this section, we will explore the implementation of Zuul in a Spring Cloud environment, routing configurations, and the benefits it offers.

Setting Up Zuul in a Spring Cloud Project

To integrate Zuul in a Spring Cloud project, follow these steps:

1. Include the necessary dependencies in your build file.
2. Create a Spring Boot application to serve as the API Gateway.
3. Configure routing and filters as needed.

Add the following dependencies to your pom.xml file:

```
<dependency>
    <groupId>org.springframework.cloud</groupId>
    <artifactId>spring-cloud-starter-netflix-zuul</artifactId>
</dependency>
<dependency>
    <groupId>org.springframework.cloud</groupId>
    <artifactId>spring-cloud-starter-netflix-eureka-client</artifactId>
</dependency>
```

Create a new Spring Boot application annotated with @EnableZuulProxy in your main class:

```
package com.example.zuulgateway;

import org.springframework.boot.SpringApplication;
import org.springframework.boot.autoconfigure.SpringBootApplication;
import org.springframework.cloud.netflix.zuul.EnableZuulProxy;

@SpringBootApplication
@EnableZuulProxy
public class ZuulGatewayApplication {

    public static void main(String[] args) {
        SpringApplication.run(ZuulGatewayApplication.class, args);
    }
}
```

The @EnableZuulProxy annotation activates Zuul, enabling it to act as a gateway.

Configuring Zuul Routes

Zuul routes determine how client requests are proxied to backend services. By default, Zuul uses service discovery (e.g., Eureka) to route requests to the appropriate services. Zuul routes can be configured in the application.yml file of your Zuul Gateway application.

An example configuration might look like this:

```
zuul:
  routes:
    users-service:
      path: /users/**
```

```
    serviceId: USERS-SERVICE
  orders-service:
    path: /orders/**
    serviceId: ORDERS-SERVICE
```

In this configuration:

- Requests starting with /users/ are routed to the USERS-SERVICE.
- Requests starting with /orders/ are routed to the ORDERS-SERVICE.

Zuul can also proxy to services not registered in Eureka by specifying the URL directly:

```
zuul:
  routes:
    external-service:
      path: /external/**
      url: http://example.com
```

This directs requests to http://example.com when the path starts with /external/.

Implementing Zuul Filters

Zuul filters provide a mechanism for intercepting and processing HTTP requests and responses. Filters can be of different types, such as pre-filters, post-filters, and route-filters, each serving unique purposes, like authentication, logging, or modifying requests.

Define a Zuul filter by extending the ZuulFilter class and overriding its methods:

```
package com.example.zuulgateway.filters;

import com.netflix.zuul.ZuulFilter;
import com.netflix.zuul.context.RequestContext;
import javax.servlet.http.HttpServletRequest;

public class PreFilter extends ZuulFilter {

    @Override
    public String filterType() {
        return "pre";
    }

    @Override
    public int filterOrder() {
```

```
        return 1;
    }

    @Override
    public boolean shouldFilter() {
        return true;
    }

    @Override
    public Object run() {
        RequestContext ctx = RequestContext.getCurrentContext();
        HttpServletRequest request = ctx.getRequest();
        System.out.println("Request Method : " + request.getMethod()
                + " Request URL : " + request.getRequestURL().toString
                    ());
        return null;
    }
}
```

Register the filter as a Spring @Bean in your main application class:

```
import org.springframework.context.annotation.Bean;

@SpringBootApplication
@EnableZuulProxy
public class ZuulGatewayApplication {

    public static void main(String[] args) {
        SpringApplication.run(ZuulGatewayApplication.class, args);
    }

    @Bean
    public PreFilter preFilter() {
        return new PreFilter();
    }
}
```

Advantages of Using Zuul

Zuul provides several advantages in a microservices architecture:

- **Simplified Client Interactions:** By serving as an API gateway, Zuul reduces the complexity that clients need to manage when interacting with multiple back-end services.
- **Centralized Security and Authentication:** Zuul enables centralized security policies and authentication mechanisms, providing a single point of entry for enforcing security controls.
- **Load Balancing and Resiliency:** Through integration with Ribbon, Zuul can provide client-side load balancing and failover

mechanisms, enhancing service resiliency.

- **API Versioning and Migration:** Zuul facilitates API versioning, allowing services to evolve independently and clients to migrate to new versions gradually.
- **Monitoring and Metrics:** Zuul can be integrated with monitoring tools, offering insights into traffic patterns, request metrics, and aiding in performance optimization.

Zuul significantly enhances the capability to manage and route client requests in a microservices architecture, ensuring efficient and secure communication between clients and services. Through proper configuration and implementation of filters, Zuul becomes a powerful tool in the hands of a developer, enabling seamless integration and management of microservices.

10.11 Tracing and Monitoring with Spring Cloud Sleuth

Spring Cloud Sleuth provides distributed tracing capabilities for Spring Cloud applications by integrating with various tracing systems like Zipkin, OpenTelemetry, and others. Distributed tracing is crucial in microservices architecture to track and analyze the lifecycle of requests as they propagate through different services. This section details how to integrate Sleuth into a Spring Boot application, how it works, and the benefits it brings for monitoring and debugging microservices.

Firstly, to include Spring Cloud Sleuth in your application, you need to add the necessary dependencies in your pom.xml or build.gradle file, depending on the build tool used. For Maven, append the following dependencies:

```
<dependency>
    <groupId>org.springframework.cloud</groupId>
    <artifactId>spring-cloud-starter-sleuth</artifactId>
</dependency>
<dependency>
    <groupId>org.springframework.cloud</groupId>
    <artifactId>spring-cloud-starter-zipkin</artifactId>
</dependency>
```

For Gradle users, include the following in your build.gradle file:

```
dependencies {
    implementation 'org.springframework.cloud:spring-cloud-starter-sleuth'
    implementation 'org.springframework.cloud:spring-cloud-starter-zipkin'
}
```

Spring Cloud Sleuth automatically generates unique trace IDs and span IDs that represent specific elements of a trace, and it propagates these IDs across service boundaries. This propagation mechanism ensures that you can trace requests across many services seamlessly.

Once the dependencies are in place, Sleuth without any extra configuration will start tracing and reporting details to the console. For instance, a basic controller in your application might look like:

```
@RestController
public class MyController {

    @GetMapping("/hello")
    public String hello() {
        return "Hello, Spring Cloud Sleuth!";
    }
}
```

Upon calling this endpoint, you will observe the following output in logs:

```
2019-08-06 12:08:38.476 INFO [application,traceId=b1d937be236ccd47,spanId=b1d937be236ccd47] 1 --- [nio-8080-exec-1] ...
```

The log entry contains trace information with traceId and spanId. The traceId signifies the ID of the entire request, ensuring that all services handling that specific request share the same traceId. The spanId identifies the unit of work within the trace, allowing you to distinguish between different segments of the request lifecycle.

To visualize tracing data more effectively, Sleuth can be integrated with Zipkin, an open-source distributed tracing system. Configure Zipkin by setting the following properties in your application.properties or application.yml file:

```
spring.zipkin.base-url=http://localhost:9411/
spring.sleuth.sampler.probability=1.0
```

The spring.zipkin.base-url property points to the URL where your Zipkin server is running. The spring.sleuth.sampler.probability parameter, set to 1.0 for maximum sampling, ensures that all requests are sent to the Zipkin server. Adjust this value to limit the sampling rate in production environments.

Deploying a Zipkin server can be achieved using Docker. Use the following command to run Zipkin in a Docker container:

```
docker run -d -p 9411:9411 openzipkin/zipkin
```

With Zipkin running, all traced data from Sleuth-enabled microservices will be collected and can be visualized via the Zipkin UI. This UI helps in understanding the flow of requests, identifying latencies, and diagnosing issues across microservices.

By implementing Sleuth's tracing capabilities, developers can pinpoint the source of performance bottlenecks and understand the interaction between microservices. This insight is particularly valuable during debugging and optimization, providing a comprehensive view of the application's behavior in real-time distributed systems.

Integrating monitoring and alerting systems alongside tracing can further enhance observability. Sleuth, combined with tools like Prometheus and Grafana, can offer powerful dashboards and alert mechanisms.

Tracing and monitoring are key to maintaining robust and reliable microservices. The combination of Spring Cloud Sleuth and Zipkin offers a potent suite of tools for these purposes, ensuring applications operate smoothly in the complex distributed environments typical of modern microservices architectures.

10.12 Deploying Microservices

The deployment of microservices involves the orchestration of multiple independently deployable components, each running in its own process. Spring Cloud provides a comprehensive suite of tools to manage the lifecycle of microservices, ensuring their seamless integration in production environments.

Containerization with Docker

Containerization encapsulates a microservice and all its dependencies into a standardized unit. Docker has become the de facto standard for containerization due to its efficiency and compatibility with various platforms. Here's an example Dockerfile for a Spring Boot microservice:

```
# Using an official OpenJDK runtime as a parent image
FROM openjdk:11-jre-slim

# Set the working directory to /app
```

```
WORKDIR /app

# Copy the current directory contents into the container at /app
COPY target/my-microservice.jar /app/my-microservice.jar

# Make port 8080 available to the world outside this container
EXPOSE 8080

# Run the microservice
ENTRYPOINT ["java", "-jar", "/app/my-microservice.jar"]
```

To build and run the Docker image:

```
# Building the Docker image
docker build -t my-microservice:latest .

# Running the Docker container
docker run -p 8080:8080 my-microservice:latest
```

Container Orchestration with Kubernetes

Kubernetes, an open-source orchestration system, automates container deployment, scaling, and management. A Kubernetes deployment configuration for a Spring Boot microservice might be specified in a YAML file:

```
apiVersion: apps/v1
kind: Deployment
metadata:
  name: my-microservice-deployment
spec:
  replicas: 3
  selector:
    matchLabels:
      app: my-microservice
  template:
    metadata:
      labels:
        app: my-microservice
    spec:
      containers:
      - name: my-microservice
        image: my-microservice:latest
        ports:
        - containerPort: 8080
```

To deploy and manage the microservice:

```
# Creating the deployment
kubectl apply -f my-microservice-deployment.yaml
```

```
# Listing all deployments to verify
kubectl get deployments

# Accessing the logs of a specific pod
kubectl logs -f my-microservice-deployment-<pod-id>
```

Service Mesh with Istio

Istio enhances Kubernetes by providing a service mesh, enabling the management of microservice communication with features like traffic management, security policies, and observability. Applying Istio to a microservice involves configuring sidecar proxies for each service and defining routing rules, mutual TLS, etc.

Install Istio on a Kubernetes cluster:

```
# Installing Istio
istioctl install --set profile=demo

# Label the namespace to automatically inject Istio sidecars
kubectl label namespace default istio-injection=enabled
```

After deploying the services, Istio allows managing traffic between services using VirtualService and DestinationRule custom resources. An example configuration might include:

```
apiVersion: networking.istio.io/v1alpha3
kind: VirtualService
metadata:
  name: my-microservice
spec:
  hosts:
  - my-microservice
  http:
  - route:
    - destination:
        host: my-microservice
        subset: v1
```

Continuous Integration and Continuous Deployment (CI/CD)

For robust deployment pipelines, integrating CI/CD practices is essential. This ensures automated testing, building, and deployment. Tools like Jenkins, CircleCI, and GitHub Actions facilitate this process. An example Jenkins pipeline for deploying a microservice to Kubernetes might look like:

```
pipeline {
    agent any
    stages {
```

```
        stage('Build') {
            steps {
                script {
                    sh 'mvn clean package'
                    sh 'docker build -t my-microservice:latest .'
                }
            }
        }
        stage('Deploy') {
            steps {
                script {
                    sh 'kubectl apply -f my-microservice-deployment.yaml'
                }
            }
        }
    }
    post {
        always {
            script {
                sh 'kubectl get pods'
            }
        }
    }
}
```

Monitoring and Logging

Post-deployment, monitoring and logging are crucial for maintaining service health and debugging. Prometheus and Grafana are widely used for monitoring, while ELK (Elasticsearch, Logstash, Kibana) stack is common for logging.

The Prometheus configuration for scraping metrics from a Spring Boot application might include:

```
global:
  scrape_interval: 15s

scrape_configs:
- job_name: 'spring-microservice'
  static_configs:
  - targets: ['<microservice-ip>:8080']
```

Visualization of these metrics in Grafana aids in proactive monitoring and performance optimization.

Resilience and Scalability

Ensuring resilience and scalability within microservices architecture involves employing techniques like automatic scaling and load balancing. Kubernetes handles horizontal scaling through the HorizontalPodAutoscaler resource, configured to scale based on CPU usage:

```
apiVersion: autoscaling/v1
kind: HorizontalPodAutoscaler
metadata:
  name: my-microservice-hpa
spec:
  scaleTargetRef:
    apiVersion: apps/v1
    kind: Deployment
    name: my-microservice-deployment
  minReplicas: 2
  maxReplicas: 10
  targetCPUUtilizationPercentage: 80
```

Deploying microservices with efficient use of tools and practices ensures their reliability, scalability, and maintainability, crucial for complex systems.

10.13 Best Practices for Microservices with Spring Cloud

Designing and managing microservices requires adhering to best practices to ensure system robustness, scalability, and maintainability. This section provides detailed insights into the best practices for microservices architecture implemented using Spring Cloud.

One fundamental principle is the principle of **Single Responsibility**. Each microservice should encapsulate a single business capability. This separation allows each microservice to be developed, deployed, and scaled independently. The boundaries of microservices should align with the business domains they represent, promoting better organization and coherence.

Decentralized Governance is another crucial practice. Each microservice team should be empowered to choose the technologies and methodologies that best fit their needs. While Spring Cloud offers a standard framework, teams should maintain flexibility in their implementation choices to accommodate specific requirements and innovations.

Service Discovery, implemented using Spring Cloud's Eureka, is vital for efficient communication between microservices. It's essential to ensure that all services consistently register with the Eureka server and that clients are configured to discover these services dynamically. For instance, the configuration for a service registering with Eureka might look like this:

```
@SpringBootApplication
@EnableEurekaClient
public class ServiceApplication {
    public static void main(String[] args) {
        SpringApplication.run(ServiceApplication.class, args);
    }
}
```

Load Balancing ensures optimal distribution of traffic across multiple instances of a service. Client-side load balancing using Ribbon is a powerful feature in Spring Cloud. A sample configuration for Ribbon might involve specifying multiple service endpoints in the properties file:

```
service.ribbon.listOfServers=http://localhost:8081,http://localhost:8082
```

Centralized Configuration with Spring Cloud Config is essential for consistent environment-specific configurations across microservices. A common practice is to store configuration files in a version-controlled repository, ensuring traceability and ease of management. Below is how a microservice might utilize Spring Cloud Config server:

```
@EnableConfigServer
@SpringBootApplication
public class ConfigServerApplication {
    public static void main(String[] args) {
        SpringApplication.run(ConfigServerApplication.class, args);
    }
}
```

Resilience and Fault Tolerance are critical in a microservices ecosystem where failures are inevitable. Hystrix provides circuit breaker functionality which helps in preventing cascading failures. For instance, a Hystrix command can be used as follows:

```
@HystrixCommand(fallbackMethod = "fallbackMethod")
public String someMethod() {
    // logic
}

public String fallbackMethod() {
    return "Fallback response";
}
```

```
Fallback response
```

API Gateway functionality, usually implemented with Zuul or Spring Cloud Gateway, serves as a unified entry point, handling concerns such as authentication, routing, and rate limiting. A typical Zuul proxy setup might include:

```
@EnableZuulProxy
@SpringBootApplication
public class ApiGatewayApplication {
    public static void main(String[] args) {
        SpringApplication.run(ApiGatewayApplication.class, args);
    }
}
```

Distributed Tracing using Spring Cloud Sleuth provides insight into system performance and helps identify bottlenecks. It's crucial to ensure that tracing information is correctly propagated across service calls. A sample configuration for Sleuth might involve:

```
spring.sleuth.sampler.probability=1.0
```

Monitoring the health and performance of microservices is essential for maintaining reliability. Integrating tools like Spring Boot Actuator along with external monitoring systems such as Prometheus and Grafana ensures comprehensive observability.

Security is of paramount importance in microservices. Each service should be independently secured, often using OAuth2 for authentication and authorization. Spring Security can be configured to enforce security rules consistently across services:

```
@EnableResourceServer
@SpringBootApplication
public class SecurityApplication {
    public static void main(String[] args) {
        SpringApplication.run(SecurityApplication.class, args);
    }
}

@Configuration
@EnableWebSecurity
public class SecurityConfig extends WebSecurityConfigurerAdapter {
    @Override
    protected void configure(HttpSecurity http) throws Exception {
        http.authorizeRequests()
            .anyRequest().authenticated()
            .and()
            .oauth2Login();
    }
}
```

Logging and **Monitoring** should be standardized across services to facilitate easier troubleshooting and audits. Employing a structured logging approach using tools such as ELK Stack (Elasticsearch, Logstash, Kibana) ensures meaningful log aggregation and analysis.

Adhering to these best practices not only enhances the robustness and agility of microservices applications but also aligns with the principles of the Spring Cloud ecosystem, promoting efficient and maintainable service-oriented architectures.

Made in the USA
Monee, IL
05 November 2026

67814358R00213